D1298867

# Mutual Fund
## *Handbook*

**Written by Amy B. Crane**
*for the National Association of Investors Corporation*

Published by National Association of Investors Corporation (NAIC)
Madison Heights, Michigan
Copyright © 2003

© 2000, 2003 by National Association of Investors Corporation
All Rights Reserved

First published in the United States of America by
National Association of Investors Corporation (NAIC)
711 West 13 Mile Road, Madison Heights, Michigan  48071
1-877-275-6242 • www.better-investing.org

Manufactured in the United States of America
Edition #2
ISBN # 0-9678130-0-X

Crane, Amy B., 1961–
    NAIC Mutual Fund Handbook / written by Amy B. Crane
for the National Association of Investors Corporation.
    p. cm. -- (NAIC Better Investing Educational Series)
    Includes bibliographical references and index.
    ISBN 0-9678130-0-X

    1. Mutual Funds. 2. Investments. 3. Finance, Personal.
I. National Association of Investors Corporation.
II. Title.

HG4530.C72 2003          332.63'27
                         QBI03-200324

**NAIC Registered Trademark Rights**

NAIC Better Investing Book Series – policy statement:

# NAIC Better Investing Book Series

The Better Investing book series is designed to provide information and tools to help individuals and investment clubs become successful long-term investors. By using the series, investors will follow a self-learning pathway, gaining knowledge and building experience to make informed investment decisions. The series provides information and resources for beginners, intermediate and experienced investors.

For more information contact NAIC: 1-877-275-6242, or visit the NAIC Web site: www.better-investing.org

## Acknowledgements

### NAIC Mutual Fund *Handbook*

| | |
|---|---|
| Author/Writer: | Amy B. Crane |
| Executive Editor: | Dennis M. Genord, Manager Mutual Fund Education Program, NAIC |
| Editor: | Barrie Borich |
| Index Consultant: | Kathleen Paparchontis |
| Educational Content Consultants: | Thomas O'Hara, Chairman Emeritus, NAIC |
| | Kenneth Janke, Chairman, NAIC |
| | Richard Holthaus, President & CEO, NAIC |
| | Robert O'Hara, Vice President, Business Development, NAIC |
| | Lisa Cacovic, Order Entry, NAIC |
| | Betty Sinnock, Director, NIA |
| | Brian Lewis, Director, NIA |
| | Thomas S. Dugan, Fixed Income Strategy Committee, Dodge & Cox Income Fund |
| | Gary Simms, Director, NAIC Heart of Illinois Chapter |
| | Lynn Ostrem, NAIC Member |
| Creative Direction & Design: | Michael Bell |
| Design Consultants: | Mary Treppa, Online Editor, NAIC |
| | Ellada Azariah, Graphic Designer, NAIC |
| | Pamela Forton, Graphic Designer, NAIC |
| Production Coordinators | Renee Ross, Childers Printing & Graphics, Inc. |
| | Jonathan Strong, Manager, Member Development, NAIC |
| Technical Support: | Bradley Christensen, Information Technology, NAIC |
| | Christopher Ditri, Information Technology, NAIC |
| | Kenneth Smith, Information Technology, NAIC |
| Printing/Production: | Childers Printing & Graphics, Inc. |
| | Printwell Acquisitions, Inc. |
| | CSW Designs |

# Table of Contents

# Mutual Fund Handbook Foreword

Successful investing requires understanding. With millions of Americans investing in mutual funds, it is sad to note that many have no idea who the portfolio manager of the fund is, the names of stocks held by the fund, or how often those stocks are traded. As with any investment, knowledge is all important.

More and more individuals are asked to make decisions as to which funds to hold in their retirement accounts. In fact, the majority of Americans put their retirement money into mutual funds rather than individual stocks. Yet, their selections are made not with an analysis of those funds, but come from suggestions made by fellow employees, friends and relatives.

Instead of relying on stories, or selecting popular names, individuals should try to shed the mystery that seems to surround mutual funds. What this book attempts to do is help you make informed decisions that will lead you to become a successful mutual fund investor. While there are thousands of funds available to individuals, there are many differences from one to another. Consideration has to be given to your objectives and those of the fund

manager, past and future performance, as well as risks.

The success that NAIC has demonstrated for more than fifty years in guiding individuals to make sound decisions when purchasing common stocks also makes sense for mutual fund investing. Selecting the proper mutual funds takes time and patience, but it is vital to successful investing to have a disciplined approach. Whether you are selecting funds for your retirement account, or your personal investment portfolio, this book provides you with the educational foundation and analysis tools you need to make sound investment decisions.


Kenneth S. Janke

CHAIRMAN
NATIONAL ASSOCIATION OF INVESTORS CORPORATION

# *Investing the NAIC Way*

For more than 50 years, NAIC's four basic principles have helped millions of people successfully accumulate wealth through investing in common stocks. NAIC mutual fund investing principles empower novice investors to take control of their financial futures.

This book lays out a detailed plan for finding, comparing and following mutual funds. We introduce easy-to-understand fund analysis tools that aid investors in selecting superior mutual funds.

## Mutual Funds

For millions of investors, mutual funds are the investing vehicles of choice. Through retirement plans, college savings plans and other mutual fund accounts, Americans have accumulated billions of dollars in wealth. Because of the sheer number of funds available, sorting through them is increasingly difficult.

Fund companies don't make this easy. Ads tout performance numbers on television, radio, newspapers, magazines and on the Internet. Investment companies create new funds, tapping into the latest investment craze. Many of these funds vanish, replaced by new funds capitalizing on the next hot trend. Compounding the confusion, financial advisers, bankers, brokers and insurance agents vie against each other for your business.

Amid the buzz, it's tempting to believe that understanding investing and the workings of mutual funds is beyond you, and any person without a background in accounting or finance. It may seem easier to wash your hands of such seemingly complicated matters, leaving them to the professionals. That's exactly what many in the fund industry and investment community want you to believe.

Fortunately, you don't need a degree in accounting to understand mutual fund investing. This book demonstrates NAIC's simple methodology that will help you take control of your financial future and make your own investing decisions. Investing may seem daunting, but its ultimate reward is a secure financial future. By following NAIC principles, instead of operating through greed and fear as do many uniformed investors, you will:

- Understand the role mutual funds can play in a financial plan

- Be better positioned to reap the rewards that investing in the stock market can offer you

- Learn how to select, compare and follow mutual funds

## What the Stock Market Can Do for You

Why does NAIC focus on investing in stock and stock mutual funds? Because, over many years, stock investing provides superior returns. While there are other investing vehicles—including bonds, cash and real estate—historical results prove that investing in stocks for the long term has produced a higher return.

Historic annual returns for stocks have been about 10 percent. Historical returns for bonds have been around 6 percent. Lastly, cash or money market accounts have returned approximately 4 percent. While the 4 percent difference between stock and bond returns may not seem like much, multiply that by 20 or 30 years, and you'll see a real difference.

While NAIC promotes stock and stock mutual fund ownership, it doesn't recommend buying shares of just any company or fund. Instead, the philosophy focuses on investing in growth companies.

By selecting companies with a strong history of sales and earnings growth, and purchasing shares in those companies at a reasonable price, you can benefit from the growth these companies offer.

Taking this one step further, NAIC's mutual fund program focuses on selecting funds with managers that invest in growth companies for the long term. Not many funds meet these exacting criteria, but they do exist and our program can help you find them.

We'll also discuss diversification. Virtually all investors benefit from a portfolio diversified among various types of assets, including other types of stocks, stock funds, bonds and bond funds.

## Beginning the Journey

Take the first step on an exciting journey into your financial future. Read our book and learn what NAIC's simple, time-tested methodology can do for you. Millions of investors before you have successfully navigated their way to financial success.

In the coming chapters, you'll learn about:

- NAIC's four basic investing principles
- The basics of fund investing
- The benefits of investing in stock funds
- A fund's key elements
- NAIC fund analysis tools

We'll take you step-by-step through each tool. This process begins with the evaluation of a single fund. Using information from a mutual fund data provider, you'll discover how easy it is to evaluate a fund's key elements and compare a fund to other funds. Finally, we'll demonstrate how to keep tabs on your fund to ensure that it is still the same superior product you originally purchased.

# The Basics

## Building Blocks

*The first step along the road to mutual fund investing is to learn the basics. There are many sources of information about mutual funds, but only one with the unique long-term perspective of NAIC. Our four basic principles outline a sound basis for stock and fund investing.*

In the next seven chapters, we'll lay a foundation for your investing journey. This starts with some information about NAIC, its principles and background and why it's philosophy has worked for investors for more than 50 years.

From there, we'll move on to learn about the pros and cons of fund investing and where to find basic information about funds. Annual reports and fund prospectuses provide vitally important information about a fund's objectives, risks and costs.

Before you can even begin to select a fund for purchase, you must make critical decisions about your financial goals and decide how to allocate your assets among different types of investments. Consider your short and long-term goals when making these decisions.

There are many different types of stock funds and many ways to categorize funds. Some fund managers focus on growth, while others seek undervalued opportunities. NAIC's perspective is that investing in growth companies or growth funds provides the more dependable vehicle for appreciation in your portfolio.

Lastly, we'll spend some time becoming familiar with Morningstar, a comprehensive stock and bond fund data source. We'll look at alternatives beyond Morningstar and discuss ways to find candidates for the fund analysis we'll discuss in Section II.

# *Wealth Building The NAIC Way*

## *The Approach that Works*

*NAIC's investing philosophy works. Before computers and the Internet, the organization's founders created an easy-to-understand stock selection system. Through war and recession, through boom and bust, this basic investing approach has proven its merits.*

*It boils down to this: pick quality companies at the right price and watch them grow. Followers of NAIC's philosophy reap many financial rewards. Likewise, the mutual fund education program helps investors select superior mutual funds.*

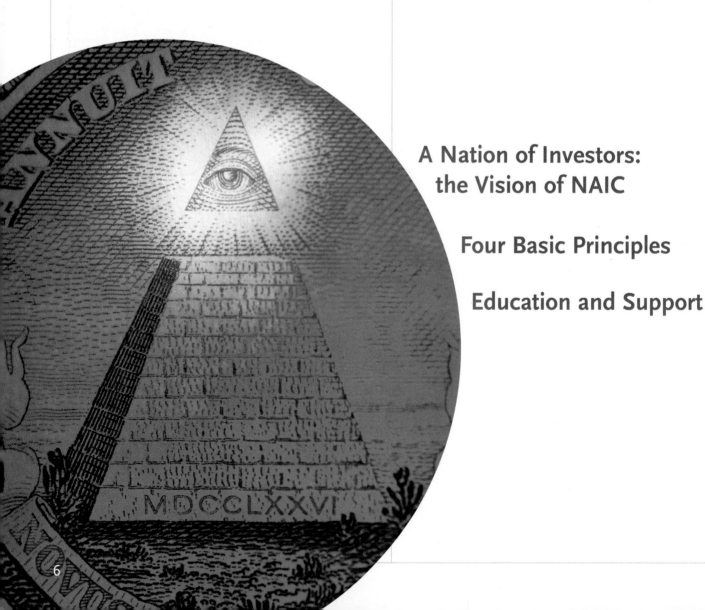

**A Nation of Investors: the Vision of NAIC**

**Four Basic Principles**

**Education and Support**

## A Nation of Investors

NAIC's vision is to create a nation of investors. Armed with a proven philosophy and the tools to put those concepts into action, NAIC investors have formed thousands of investment clubs. By harnessing the power of an investing community, a number of clubs boast results that outstrip market benchmarks. Outside of clubs, thousands of individual investors achieve personal financial success with NAIC stock and mutual fund tools.

Founded in 1951 by four Michigan investment clubs, the non-profit NAIC makes its home in Madison Heights, Michigan. One of those clubs, the Mutual Investment Club of Detroit, still exists today. Partners in this founding club built a portfolio of more than $6 million with small, regular contributions.

NAIC members live in every state and in many countries around the world. In 2002, NAIC boasted a membership of 400,000, many belonging to the more than 32,000 member clubs. Through its staff at headquarters, and dedicated volunteers across America, NAIC educates investors on the value of a long-term investing strategy. This strategy is expressed through four basic principles.

## Four Basic Principles

### 1. Invest Regularly

By focusing on the quality of individual growth companies —and the quality of mutual funds that invest in those companies—rather than on the state of the overall market, NAIC investors avoid the trap of trying to predict the direction of the market. In the short-term, stock markets are affected by many factors including the economy, politics and interest rates as well as greed, panic and fear. In the long-term, markets reward companies that have rising sales and earnings with higher stock prices.

Studies validate NAIC's long-term focus. Professors P.R. Chandy of the University of North Texas and William Riechenstein of Baylor University analyzed 62 years of stock market returns. They found that the cumulative return over the entire 62 years occurred in just 6.7 percent of the days.

Miss just one of those key days or weeks of substantial appreciation and you miss out on most of the market's returns. To achieve financial security, you must invest on a continual basis, and remain invested.

NAIC investors focus on the long term. Historically, stocks return close to 11 percent annually. Investors who purchase shares of high-quality stocks and mutual funds and hold them for the long term are usually amply rewarded.

7

| Periodic Investment | Share Price | Shares Purchased |
|---|---|---|
| $100 | $10.00 | 10.00 |
| $100 | $10.50 | 9.52 |
| $100 | $10.90 | 9.17 |
| $100 | $11.20 | 8.93 |
| $100 | $7.50 | 13.33 |
| $100 | $6.75 | 14.81 |
| $100 | $9.75 | 10.26 |
| $100 | $13.15 | 7.60 |
| $100 | $13.60 | 7.35 |
| $100 | $13.95 | 7.17 |
| $100 | $14.10 | 7.09 |
| $100 | $14.65 | 6.83 |
| **Total Amount Invested:** | | **$1,200** |
| **Number of Shares Owned:** | | **112.06** |
| **Average Cost/Share:** | | **$11.34** |
| **Current Share Price:** | | **$14.65** |

Figure 1.1: Dollar Cost Averaging.

*So, it makes sense to invest regularly in the stock market regardless of its short-term direction or outlook. Figure 1.1 shows the wealth-building potential of investing small amounts on a regular basis. Mutual funds are particularly well suited for regular, long-term investing. There are many mutual funds with low minimum investments and automatic investment plans.*

Through an automatic investment plan, you can invest a certain amount of money per month to purchase shares in a mutual fund. The fund company automatically debits your checking or savings account at a set time each month.

Investing small amounts regularly cushions you from the fluctuations of the market. Invest in a fund or funds every month and you will buy more shares when the price per share is low, and fewer shares when the price per share is higher.

### 2. Reinvest All Earnings

Many stocks pay dividends. Dividends provide a return on your investment, similar to the interest you earn on a savings account or money market fund.

Many mutual funds invest in companies that pay dividends and pass these dividends along to fund shareholders. When fund managers sell securities at a profit, those profits are passed along to fund investors in the form of capital gains distributions.

Dividends and capital gains distributions present you with two choices; you can either receive them in cash or reinvest them in fund shares. Choose reinvestment, and you will continually purchase more fund shares. Not only will you increase the number of shares

*For even more magic, let's combine principles 1 & 2 — investing regularly over the long haul*

| Annual Investment of $1,000 | | | | | |
|---|---|---|---|---|---|
| Years Invested | 4% | 6% | 8% | 10% | 12% |
| 1 | $1,040 | $1,060 | $1,080 | $1,100 | $1,120 |
| 5 | 5,600 | 6,000 | 6,300 | 6,700 | 7,100 |
| 10 | 12,500 | 14,000 | 15,600 | 17,500 | 19,700 |
| 15 | 20,800 | 24,700 | 29,300 | 35,000 | 41,800 |
| 20 | 31,000 | 39,000 | 49,400 | 63,000 | 80,700 |
| 25 | 43,300 | 58,200 | 79,000 | 108,200 | 149,300 |

Figure 1.2 Dividend Reinvestment

you own, but the new shares you acquire will also generate more returns in the form of dividends and capital gains.

Like generations of rabbits reproducing, your shares will multiply, bringing you wealth far beyond your original investment. Reinvesting dividends and capital gains in fund shares is easy, because you never actually see the money that you are reinvesting, since it is used to purchase more fund shares.

Instead, by reinvesting, your fund statements will show you how this practice supercharges your fund's returns. By taking advantage of the magic of compounding, you can reach your financial goals that much faster. When an investment compounds, reinvested dividends and capital gains distributions earn their own dividends, which continue to multiply during a long period of time.

## 3. Invest in Good Quality Growth Companies

When you buy shares in a mutual fund, you hire a fund manager to invest your money. Therefore, you have no direct control over which companies the manager buys stock in or what price he pays for those stocks. However, by using NAIC tools to analyze a fund, you can decide if the manager's strategies will help

you meet your investing goals. The best growth fund managers invest in a similar fashion to NAIC investors, who seek to buy stock in high-quality growth companies at a reasonable price.

NAIC was founded to help investors find growth companies. Stock investors using NAIC criteria select companies with rising sales and earnings. Sales are the money a company gets from what it sells, whether it is computer software, hamburgers or insurance. Earnings are a company's net income divided by the number of outstanding shares of stock.

By using NAIC's mutual fund study tools to examine a fund's portfolio, management and costs, you can see if a particular fund meets your wealth-building needs.

## 4. Diversify

The truism "don't put all of your eggs in one basket" applies to any type of investing, and is the fourth of NAIC's principles. When investors diversify, they purchase shares of stock in a number of

different types of companies and/or funds. Diversification protects investors from a devastating decline in one particular company or fund.

Diversification is a smart investing practice for a number of reasons. Different types of companies grow at different rates. Small companies tend to grow quickly via a number of methods, such as launching new products or providing top-notch service. Mid-sized companies slow down a bit compared to the torrid growth pace of a small company, but many still continue to grow rapidly.

Large companies will, on average, experience the slowest growth. Some of this is due to the sheer size of these companies. While it isn't too hard for a company with $10 million in sales to double that to $20 million in sales, it is very difficult for a company with $1 billion in sales to double that to $2 billion in sales.

Some large companies do defy those odds for a time. IBM, for example, has the distinction of being the only large company to grow its sales at a rate of more than 15 percent for 10 consecutive years. Microsoft is another large company that grew at an incredibly fast rate for years.

Beyond diversification by company size, NAIC recommends you diversify by industry. Companies in different industries possess varying growth characteristics, and economic cycles ensure that particular industries do well at particular times. For example, technology's most recent heyday was in the late 1990s. Owners of technology companies and funds couldn't go wrong. But by early 2000, technology fell out of favor, and other companies, including those in the health care and defense industries, rotated into favor. By diversifying your investments among a number of companies or a number of funds that invest in different types of companies, you'll benefit from all types of growth the market offers.

For stock investors, NAIC recommends investing 25 percent of your assets in large companies, 50 percent in mid-sized companies, and 25 percent in small companies. Fund investors could follow this same allocation strategy by investing 25 percent of their assets in funds that purchase the stock of large companies, 50 percent in funds that purchase the stock of mid-cap companies and 25 percent in funds that purchase the stock of small-cap companies.

While there are many different categories of funds, the same basic principles of fund investing apply to all. Whether a fund invests in companies around the world, or in small companies in the United States alone, NAIC tools will help you find a fund that fits your investment portfolio. You'll learn more about diversification in Chapter 4.

## MEET THE EXPERT: TOM O'HARA

*Tom O'Hara, a founder of NAIC, is its chairman emeritus and serves as co-manager of the NAIC Growth Fund, a closed-end fund.*

**Q. What is the major difference between NAIC's investing practices and other investing practices?**

Ours is a simple philosophy that has been tested for more than 50 years. Without question, it has produced above-average results for people who use it. It is simple, really: if you are going to make money, invest in growth companies and your results will be assured.

**Q: What advice would you give to a new fund investor?**

Have patience – we start with so little it is easy to get impatient. Keep up with an investing strategy based on NAIC principles for five or 10 years and then it will be obvious to you that it works. Many people get discouraged if their results aren't great right at the beginning, but you won't get good results unless you stick with it.

As one of the managers of the NAIC Growth Fund along with Ken Janke, we know to watch out for a major break or downturn in the market when people start writing to us and telling us that NAIC methods are old-fashioned and need to be updated. When P/E ratios were very high a few years ago many people were badly misled into thinking that it was normal, which it wasn't.

**Q: How can the NAIC Mutual Fund Program help investors select superior funds?**

Using our tools, NAIC investors should look for funds with long-term management. If management has changed, results will be different in the future. The NAIC fund tools help you analyze the important aspects of a fund, including how management has performed. Look for low turnover and low costs.

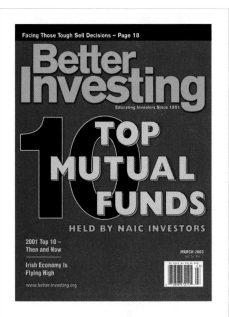

## Education and Support

As you continue your investment education journey, NAIC offers its support. On the national level, NAIC's many resources are available to help you become a better investor.

By joining NAIC, you reap many benefits. Each year, members receive 12 issues of *Better Investing* magazine, its flagship publication. It features monthly columns on mutual fund investing, investment club dynamics, stock investing and online investing. Members also enjoy access to other NAIC books and publications.

The NAIC Mutual Fund Handbook is one of a series of recently published books. Others include the NAIC Stock Selection Handbook, the NAIC Computerized Investing and the Internet Handbook and the NAIC Club Operations Handbook.

NAIC has more than 100 regional chapters across the country that offer regular classes dealing with all aspects of investing, including stocks and mutual funds. Chapter classes are taught by volunteers dedicated to carrying out NAIC's vision of creating a nation of investors.

Nationally, NAIC sponsors annual conferences that bring investors from across the nation together for investment education classes and provides opportunities for these investors to speak with representatives of various publicly traded companies as well as other investors like themselves.

Online, NAIC makes its home at www.better-investing.org. Through the Web site, members can access informative articles and data for stock and mutual fund studies.

## Your Investing Future

By implementing NAIC's principles, you can construct a portfolio of mutual funds that should, on average, double your money every five years. Begin investing early in life, and you can potentially accumulate sufficient wealth to fund your retirement, a child's college education or any other investing goal you choose.

If you've found NAIC later in life, don't fret. A disciplined, focused investing strategy can increase your financial security at any stage of life. Whether you invest on your own, or form an investment club, NAIC principles are the key to a sound wealth-building strategy.

---

### VISIT NAIC'S MUTUAL FUND EDUCATION AND RESOURCE CENTER

**MUTUAL FUND EDUCATION AND RESOURCE CENTER**

NAIC
ABOUT
MEMBERSHIP
CHAPTERS
CORPORATE MEMBERS
NAIC STORE
SITE SEARCH

MEMBER RESOURCES
MEMBER SERVICE
PUBLICATIONS
COMMUNITY
EDUCATION
CLUBS
YOUTH
SOFTWARE
GREEN SHEETS

PREMIUM SERVICES (OPS)
BITS ONLINE
COMPANY REPORTS

PREMIUM SUBSCRIPTIONS
IAS ONLINE

VOLUNTEER RESOURCES

Get a new report:
Ticker: [ ] Go  Find Ticker

**Bond Fund Comparison Guide**

| Fremont Mutual Fds:Bond Fund | TIAA-CREF Bond Plus Fund | Vanguard Total Bond Market Index | Print View |

| Fund Name | | | Fremont Mutual Fds:Bond Fund (FBDFX) remove | RANK | TIAA-CREF Bond Plus Fund (TIPBX) remove | RANK | Vanguard Total Bond Market Index (VBMFX) remove | RANK |
|---|---|---|---|---|---|---|---|---|
| Style Name | | | Fixed Income General Intermediate | | Fixed Income General Intermediate | | Fixed Income General Intermediate | |
| Portfolio Composition | Cash | | 12.45% | | 20.20% | | 1.21% | |
| | Bonds | | 75.96% | | 79.24% | | 98.79% | |
| | Stocks | | 0.74% | | 0.00% | | 0.00% | |
| | Other | | 10.85% | - ▼ | 0.56% | - ▼ | 0.00% | - ▼ |
| Average Effective Duration | | | 3.9 | - ▼ | 4.5 | - ▼ | 4.0 | - ▼ |
| Average Credit Quality | | | AAA | - ▼ | AA | - ▼ | A | - ▼ |
| P O R T F O L I O | US Govt | | 35.6% | - ▼ | 49.7% | - ▼ | 63.3% | - ▼ |
| | AAA | | 0.0% | | 0.8% | | 5.8% | |

# The ABCs of Mutual Funds

## *Know What You Own*

*With corporate pensions on the wane, people have more responsibility for both their retirement plans and their all-around financial health. Ready or not, your future prosperity is in your hands.*

*To work toward a goal of securing your financial future you need a basic knowledge of how mutual funds work, along with an understanding of the risks and rewards of fund investing. When you know what you own it's easier to make objective decisions that help you reach your investing goals.*

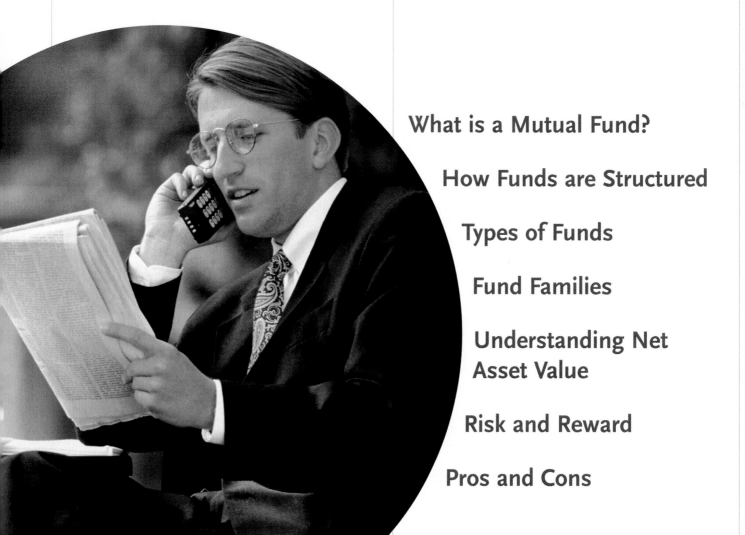

**What is a Mutual Fund?**

**How Funds are Structured**

**Types of Funds**

**Fund Families**

**Understanding Net Asset Value**

**Risk and Reward**

**Pros and Cons**

## What is a Mutual Fund?

When you invest in mutual funds, you pool your money with other investors, allowing a professional portfolio manager to select and manage the investments in the fund.

These other investors are people like you, who either invest directly in a fund, or invest through a retirement, college savings or annuity plan. Most mutual funds have thousands of shareholders.

Mutual funds invest in a variety of securities such as stocks, bonds or other instruments that investors can own and trade on financial markets.

A stock fund is a type of mutual fund that purchases shares of stock in a number of companies. A stock is a share in a business, issued by a company that trades on the public stock markets

A bond fund is another kind of mutual fund that purchases a number of different bonds. Bonds are debt issued by corporations, governments or other entities.

There are also mutual funds that invest in both stocks and bonds, and other types of funds that invest in a variety of other instruments.

Regardless of the type of securities held by a mutual fund, the people who own shares of the fund are owners of all of the fund's holdings in proportion to the amount of money contributed. If your stock fund owns 30 companies, you own part of those 30 companies. The value of your shares rises or falls depending on the success or failure of those companies in the stock market.

### Open-end and Closed-end Funds

There are two types of mutual funds: open-end and closed-end. Most funds are open-end, which means that the fund continually issues new shares to anyone willing to purchase them.

Open-end funds readily redeem shares for cash from any shareholder. Shares of open-end funds have a value that reflects what the securities in the portfolio are worth at a given time.

A closed-end fund issues a fixed number of shares and trades like a common stock on the open market. Consequently, the shares of a closed-end fund can trade at a greater or lesser price than the actual value of the fund's holdings.

The mutual fund listings in most newspapers only include open-end funds. Closed-end funds are sometimes included in the stock listings or in a separate section of their own.

While the number of mutual funds has increased immensely in the last 10 years, mutual funds aren't a new investing phenomenon. Mutual funds were created in 1924. Throughout the years, they have undergone many changes.

The federal government has enacted a number of laws that have contributed to the growth of mutual funds. These include the creation of individual retirement, 401(k) retirement plans and Section 529 college savings plans.

### How Funds are Structured

Most mutual funds are structured quite different from the set-up of traditional companies. Funds are shell companies that have no employees—just a board of directors. The board contracts with companies specializing in different areas of fund operations to handle different functions of the fund.

The board employs a management company or an investment adviser to manage the fund's portfolio. The distributor oversees the sale of fund shares, while the custodian maintains possession of the fund's assets. The transfer agent processes buy and sell orders of fund shares. Brokers execute portfolio buy and sell orders. An independent firm of public accountants audits a fund's financial statements.

When you buy shares in a mutual fund, a fund manager invests your money, but the fund's board of directors is ultimately responsible for safeguarding your interests.

Because the board of directors is the only entity that is directly affiliated with the fund, how the board conducts itself is vitally important to fund shareholders.

The board oversees how your money is invested and what fees you pay. There are two types of directors on a board. Inside directors are involved with fund management or may even be on a fund's management team. The other board members are independent directors who aren't affiliated with fund management, but who look out for shareholders' interests.

Shareholders have little voice when it comes to fund policies, so they must depend on independent directors to speak on their behalf. Generally, shareholders only vote on a major change in a fund, such as a shift in the fund's investment objective or an increase in fund fees.

Fund companies send shareholders regular

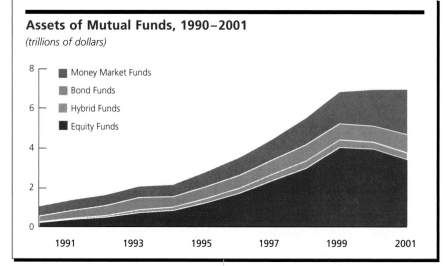

**Assets of Mutual Funds, 1990–2001**
*(trillions of dollars)*

■ Money Market Funds
■ Bond Funds
■ Hybrid Funds
■ Equity Funds

*Figure 2.1 Fund Asset Growth Explodes*
Source: 2002 Mutual Fund Fact Book, Copyright ©2002 Investment Company Institute (www.ici.org). Reprinted with permission.

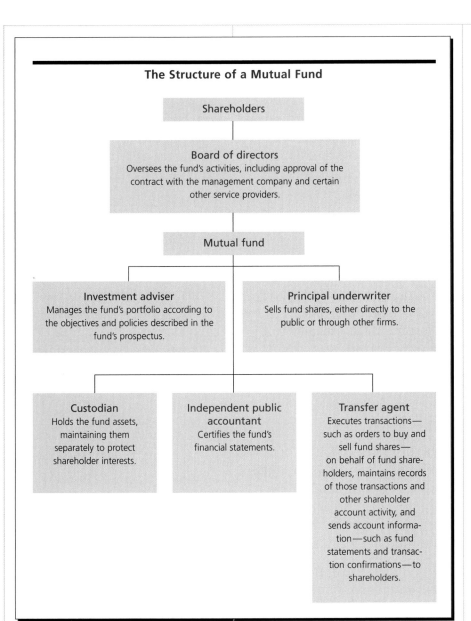

**The Structure of a Mutual Fund**

Shareholders

Board of directors
Oversees the fund's activities, including approval of the contract with the management company and certain other service providers.

Mutual fund

Investment adviser
Manages the fund's portfolio according to the objectives and policies described in the fund's prospectus.

Principal underwriter
Sells fund shares, either directly to the public or through other firms.

Custodian
Holds the fund assets, maintaining them separately to protect shareholder interests.

Independent public accountant
Certifies the fund's financial statements.

Transfer agent
Executes transactions—such as orders to buy and sell fund shares—on behalf of fund shareholders, maintains records of those transactions and other shareholder account activity, and sends account information—such as fund statements and transaction confirmations—to shareholders.

*Figure 2.2 Typical Fund Structure*
Source: 2002 Mutual Fund Fact Book, Copyright ©2002 Investment Company Institute (www.ici.org). Reprinted with permission.

statements and reports. Statements include the number of shares you own, the fund's net asset value as of a certain date, the total value of your holdings, and any dividends, interest or capital gains distributions.

## Types of Funds

The largest fund families offer many different types of funds that make it possible to construct a portfolio of funds having virtually any investing objective. As we have seen, the two basic types of mutual funds are stock and bond.

Within these broad categories are many different types of stock and bond funds. While some place money market funds in a separate category they really fall into the broad category of bond funds because money market funds invest in fixed-income securities.

## Stock Funds

Each stock fund has an investment style. The investment style is a broad philosophical umbrella under which the fund manager invests.

*There are three investment styles: growth, value and blend. Figure 2.3 shows the percentage of these three types of funds in the Morningstar fund universe. Morningstar is a company that collects, analyzes and distributes fund data.*

Managers of growth funds seek to invest in companies with rising sales and earnings. On the other hand, managers of value funds look for companies that are trading in the market at a discount. Managers of blend funds invest in both growth and value companies.

Funds can be further categorized based on their market capitalization. Morningstar, which calculates a company's market capitalization by multiplying its number

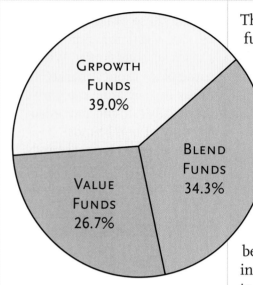

*Figure 2.3: Stock Funds by Investment Style*
Source: Morningstar, Inc.

of shares outstanding by its share price, divides funds into the large-, mid- and small-cap categories.

To determine this, Morningstar designates the top 70 percent of its stock universe as large cap; the next 20 percent as mid cap and the final 10 percent as small cap. Morningstar's stock universe, while fluid in nature to take natural market movements into consideration, covers 99 percent of the total stock market.

Beyond style and size issues, funds can be further broken down based on their investment objective. While many funds fit into the categories that we've already laid out—such as a large-cap value fund or a small-cap growth fund—many don't.

These include international funds, sector funds, index funds and socially responsible funds. There are also many balanced funds, which invest in both stocks and bonds. Look for more in Chapter 5.

### Bond Funds

A bond is a promissory note between two parties. An investor agrees to loan money to a corporation or government. In exchange for the use of these funds, the investor expects interest payments and the eventual return of the original investment.

When you buy a bond, you lend money to a governmental body or corporation. This is different than owning shares of stock, where you are in effect part owner in a company.

Bond funds invest in many different bonds. Bond funds might purchase United States government or corporate bonds or even bonds from foreign governments or companies.

There are two main types of bonds and bond funds: taxable and non-taxable. Taxable bond funds purchase bonds issued by the federal government and/or companies. The interest and any capital gain generated by these bonds are subject to federal, state and local taxes.

State and local governments issue tax-exempt bonds, which are also known as municipal bonds. The interest and any principal gain generated by these bonds is not subject to federal tax and in some cases is exempt from state taxes.

While bond funds are considered less risky than stock funds, in some cases they are more risky. This is because the value of the individual bonds in the fund portfolio can fluctuate due to outside factors such as rising and falling interest rates. Look for more detail on bond funds in chapters 16 to 20.

### Fund Families

Many fund companies are organized as fund families, offering a wide variety of funds and accounts to investors. When you invest within a fund family, you can easily move your money from one fund to another and may also receive consolidated statements, cutting down on paperwork.

If you are interested in purchasing shares in a number of funds, investigate the offerings of a particular family. While some large families such as Fidelity and Vanguard offer many different funds, other smaller families might manage only a few funds. Also, while some fund families impose strict controls on their fund managers, others allow considerable latitude.

Check into the services that a fund family offers. Common services include automatic investing and reinvesting, telephone or Internet redemption of shares and the ability to easily check net asset values and account balances. Before investing, make sure that the fund family has a strong reputation for customer service.

If your investment objectives change and you think you might want to switch from one fund to another, make sure that you can change without cost. Moving your assets into a new fund from another is a sale of shares and you may have to pay taxes on any gain you made in the original fund.

While a fund company may offer hundreds of funds, a number of these funds may have similar investment objectives and portfolios with many of the same companies. Before investing in two funds in the same family, make sure that the funds are different enough to diversify your portfolio.

### Understanding Net Asset Value

While stock prices are strongly influenced by supply and demand, mutual fund share prices are calculated by a strict formula. This calculation takes into account the value of the securities in the fund's portfolio, the number of fund shares outstanding, fund expenses charged to shareholders and any outstanding fund liabilities.

*The example in Figure 2.4 shows the formula that fund companies use to calculate your fund's net asset value (NAV).*

Unlike stock prices, which change during trading hours, traditional open-end mutual funds calculate their net asset value once a day, at the close of regular hours of trading. So, if you call to sell your fund shares in the morning, you will get the net asset value figured at the end of that trading day.

However, the actual price at which you purchase or sell fund shares may differ from the actual net asset value if you purchased fund shares with certain sales charges. You pay sales charges when you buy a fund through a broker, financial adviser or insurance agent.

The varying types of loads and sales charges are fully detailed in Chapter 11. If you sell a no-load fund—a fund without any sales charges—you will get the fund's exact net asset value.

### Fund Distributions & NAV

Any assessment of a fund's long-term track record is complicated by dividends,

---

### FIGURE 2.4 NET ASSET VALUE IN ACTION

*The net asset value is the current total market value of the portfolio holdings plus any cash...minus fund expenses charged to shareholders and any liabilities...divided by the number of shares outstanding. Shown as an equation, it looks like this:*

$$\frac{\text{Portfolio assets – expenses \& liabilities}}{\text{Total number of fund shares}} = \text{NAV}$$

*Here's an example: if the total of the XYZ Growth Fund's holdings are worth $10,000,000 at the close of trading today and the fund's expenses and liabilities are $100,000 (1 percent) and there are 1 million shares outstanding:*

$$\frac{\$10,000,000 - \$100,000}{1,000,000} = \$9.90$$

*Therefore, the net asset value on this fund is $9.90 per share.*

interest and capital gains distributions.

For example, if a fund's net asset value was $10 a share on January 1, 1997, and $20 a share on January 1, 2002, you might think your fund shares had doubled in value. You'd be wrong.

Fund managers must distribute any income gained from dividends, interest and any profit gained from selling shares of fund securities to fund shareholders. The amount of the distribution is subtracted from fund shares, but investor holdings are worth the same because investors have the fund shares plus the distribution, which they can take in cash or reinvest in additional fund shares.

Here's an example: if a fund with a net asset value of $20 a share distributes $2 per share in dividends and capital gains to shareholders, the fund's net asset value would drop to $18. This drop occurs because after distributing fund profits to shareholders, the fund has fewer assets, lowering its net asset value.

While the fund's net asset value falls under such a scenario, fund shareholders haven't lost anything, outside of the tax they may owe on the distribution. They still hold fund shares worth $18 per share and $2 per share in distributions.

Funds offer shareholders the option to either reinvest their distributions in fund shares or receive the distribution as a cash payment. In either case, shareholders face a tax liability if they own fund shares in a taxable account. Shareholders owning shares in tax-deferred vehicles such as IRAs or 401(k) plans don't owe taxes immediately on distributions.

## Risk and Reward

Virtually every type of investing entails some potential risks as well as potential rewards. Mutual funds are no different. In investing, risk involves the possibility that you will lose part or all of your investment. Reward is the potential for profit on your investment.

While it's frightening to think that you could lose some or

part of your money by investing in mutual funds, the fact is that without risk, there is no potential for reward. And the potential reward far outweighs the potential risk.

For example, say you invest $2,000 and plan to keep that amount in a stock mutual fund for 20 years to help meet your retirement savings goals. If the worst happens, and the fund you invest in loses every dime of your money—a very remote possibility given the diversification funds practice—the most you will lose is $2,000.

But, if you pick a quality mutual fund using the approach described in this handbook, it's very unlikely that your fund will lose money over the long term. Many funds do experience bad years from time to time, but a solid well-managed fund will get back on track.

No one can predict the stock market's future movements. Past returns indicate that an investment in U.S. stock gains about 11 percent annually over a period of many years. NAIC aims a bit higher, believing that investors employing solid stock and fund selection techniques can double their money in five years (an average annual compound return of about 15 percent).

With this in mind, examine the potential rewards of a $2,000 investment in a stock mutual fund. If your fund meets the goal of doubling your money every five years, you could end up with $32,000 after 20 years before taxes, which is 16 times your original investment. Even when you add inflation to this mix, you still have a very desirable return.

Keep in mind this is just an example, not the returns that you will necessarily reap. Markets can be very volatile and can rise or fall in the short term. But even if you end up with a gain averaging closer to 10 percent a year over that 20-year period of time, your potential gain will still far exceed your potential loss.

To have a better chance of meeting your financial goals, you must invest. And if you have an employee-sponsored retirement plan such as a 401(k), 403(b) or 457 plan you probably will invest in mutual funds, which are included in the menu of investments offered in your plan.

You can either invest wisely or rashly. The goal of the NAIC mutual fund program is to help you invest intelligently so that you can select superior funds with solid portfolios, experienced management and low costs.

## The Risks of Inflation

Potential for loss is only one of the risks investors encounter. Inflation is another risk that all investors face. Inflation is the general bias in the economy towards rising prices for goods and services.

While burying your money in a coffee can in the back yard will eliminate the risk that you will lose any of your money in a bad investment, these savings remain exposed to the ravages of inflation.

Every year, inflation of even 1, 2 or 3 percent will chip away at the value of that money in the coffee can. This means that over a long period of time that money will buy much less than it did when you buried it. $2,000 buried in 1980 will not purchase the same $2,000 worth of goods or services in 2010.

*Figure 2.5 illustrates how inflation erodes monetary value.*

How do you avoid the risk posed by inflation? Again, by investing your money. Because of inflation, a low potential rate of return—while posing less risk of loss—will reap far less in the long term than other higher-yielding investments that carry more risk.

Let's look at money market funds, which have little potential risk. These funds historically have maintained a net asset value of $1 a share and strive to offer a competitive interest rate.

When inflation is low, interest rates are usually low too, meaning that a money market fund will pay only a small percentage above the prevailing interest rates. When interest rates are high, money market

| FIGURE 2.5 THE EFFECT OF INFLATION | |
|---|---|

*In 1996, the inflation rate was 3.1 percent. Even if inflation remained at that historically low rate over the next 10 years, the value of $1,000 would be eroded by more than one quarter in 10 years:*

| # of years | $1,000 will be worth |
|---|---|
| 5 | $854 |
| 10 | $730 |
| 15 | $624 |
| 20 | $533 |
| 25 | $455 |
| 30 | $389 |
| 35 | $333 |
| 40 | $284 |

funds will pay more interest, but since inflation is high too, you won't actually realize much of that gain.

A money market fund is a fairly safe investment, but not one to use for long-term growth when saving for your retirement or other big-ticket items. On the other hand, money market funds are a preferable alternative to stock funds if you need access to your money in the next few years.

Like money market funds, bond funds are subject to risks from swings in interest rates. Generally speaking, bonds return far less than stocks over the long term. The value of bonds fluctuates depending upon which direction interest rates are headed.

Without realizing it, investors assume quite a bit of risk by investing in bonds or bond funds. This risk can be equal to or more than the risks of investing in stock or stock funds.

A portfolio with a sizeable percentage of stocks and stock funds is more likely to meet your long-term investing goals than a portfolio with that same percentage invested in money market and bonds or bond funds. The volatility of stock prices is a short-term risk.

Before you invest, think about how much risk you can accept on the way to your financial goals. The further away those objectives are, the more risk you can assume. If, for example, you are saving for retirement and have 20 or 30 years to go, you can comfortably select more aggressive investments with potential high returns over the long term. Investors with long-term goals who stick to their investing plans will benefit from the market bias towards growth over time.

## Pros and Cons of Mutual Fund Investing

Mutual funds offer many advantages to investors. But for every advantage, there is a disadvantage.

### Advantages

For either the novice or experienced investor, mutual funds offer many advantages.

Even an investor with $50 in mutual fund shares benefits from diversification. Any fund, whether it invests in 30 companies or 3000 companies, offers instant diversification.

You gain from diversification in several ways. It protects you against fluctuations in one area of the market. Also, you get the power of instant diversification for the fraction of the sum you'd pay for investing individually in a large number of companies.

Highly trained managers are in charge of your money when you purchase mutual fund shares. These managers can devote many more hours a week to investing than you could on your own. Funds employ analysts and researchers who assist fund managers in researching and selecting stocks for purchase.

Investing in funds is very convenient. You can purchase fund shares by mail, by phone and even over the Internet. Fund companies offer many benefits to shareholders, including automatic payment and withdrawal plans as well as free reinvestment of dividends and distributions.

Many fund families not only allow investors to move their money from one fund to another without fees, but also offer many different types of funds. Funds are a highly liquid investment. Shares can be purchased or sold on any day that the market is open.

Reports, prospectuses and other information on a particular fund are widely available. To obtain information about a fund, call or write the fund company. You can download many fund reports from the Internet.

The SEC regulates mutual funds and fund transactions stringently. The commission requires that funds meet certain standards of operation, monitors them for fraudulent representation in advertising and other communications and enforces strict disclosure rules.

### Disadvantages

The savvy investor realizes that no investment is perfect. Investing in funds has a downside. Keep the following disadvantages in mind.

Diversification is both a disadvantage and an advantage in fund investing. While investing in a large number of stocks insulates you from taking a huge loss, it also limits the potential upside you might experience with a smaller, more concentrated portfolio of individual stocks.

The government doesn't guarantee your investment in mutual funds shares. As noted earlier, investments in mutual funds are risky. You could lose some or indeed all of your money. You also stand to gain if you pick superior funds and stick with a diversified investment strategy.

Professional management is another aspect of fund investing that is both an advantage and a disadvantage. Not only does the quality and experience of fund managers vary, it also comes at a cost. You pay for fund management, and costs can eat up more than 2 percent of your fund's profits. And despite their education and experience, many fund managers fail to outperform the market indexes that track portions of the stock and bond markets.

Sales charges, ongoing expenses, brokerage fees and distribution fees can dramatically impact your returns. Every dollar you pay in fund fees is one dollar less you can invest.

If you hold fund shares in taxable accounts you may owe considerable amounts in state and federal taxes. Because fund managers are required to pass on all gains, you may receive taxable distributions.

Fund investors have no control over their fund's tax distributions, and on some occasions will receive large distributions with little or no warning, wreaking havoc on their tax planning. Unless your money is invested in an account that is sheltered from taxes such as an IRA or 401(k) plan, your fund will likely increase your tax bill.

Despite the disadvantages involved in investing in mutual funds, they are widely popular. With careful fund selection, you can avoid some of the problems involved in fund ownership and use funds to build a secure financial future.

| FIGURE 2.6: FUND PROS AND CONS: A QUICK OVERVIEW | |
|---|---|
| **Pros:** | **Cons:** |
| • Diversification | • Over-diversification |
| • Professional Management | • Fees |
| • Convenience | • Capital Gains Taxes |
| • Choice | • Sales Charges |
| • Liquidity | • Under performance |
| • Information | • No government guarantee |
| • SEC Protection | |

# The Fine Print

## Delve into the Details

Specific information about a particular fund is easy to find. Fund companies provide prospectuses and annual reports. Morningstar and other data providers analyze funds. If you know where to look, there is much valuable information amid the fine print.

We'll examine fund listings, and look at the best ways to purchase funds. Fund record keeping is another important task that no well-informed investor should ignore.

Fund Prospectus

Annual and
    Semi-Annual Reports

Buying Funds

Reading Fund Listings

Fund Record Keeping

## Overview of Important Fund Documents

All mutual funds publish documents for fund investors. These include the fund's offering prospectus and the annual and semi-annual reports.

Many fund companies post articles, fund manager interviews and other information on their Web sites. Mutual fund education Web sites offer general information about fund investing and particulars about specific funds.

There's no shortage of information about mutual funds. Your search for data about a specific fund begins with the fund's prospectus. This document is crammed with details about a fund's objectives and operations.

While the prospectus provides a general overview of the fund, the annual and semi-annual report gives a time-specific snapshot of its performance and holdings. The fund manager comments in the annual and semi-annual report about both the economy in general and the fund. A list of the fund's holdings rounds out this report.

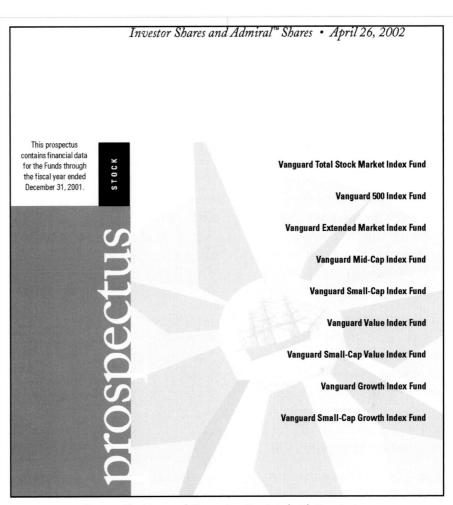

Source: The Vanguard Group, Inc. Reprinted with Permission

### The Fund Prospectus

The prospectus must fully inform investors about a fund's objectives, strategies, risks, fees and expenses. In addition, there is information about buying, redeeming, reinvesting and exchanging fund shares.

Fund companies provide a prospectus to every investor who requests an investor's kit. You can download a fund prospectus or fund annual and semi-annual reports from a fund company's Web site or the Securities Exchange Commission (SEC) Web site (www.sec.gov).

At the beginning of the prospectus, the fund lists its investment goals and strategies, as well as the risks investors assume by investing in fund shares. The document

23

| Average Annual Total Returns | | | |
| --- | --- | --- | --- |
| | Periods Ended December 31, 2001 | | |
| | 1 Year | 5 Years | 10 Years |
| **Vanguard 500 Index Fund Investor Shares** | | | |
| Return Before Taxes | –12.02% | 10.66% | 12.84% |
| Return After Taxes on Distributions | –12.45 | 10.02 | 11.95 |
| Return After Taxes on Distributions and Sale of Fund Shares | –7.33 | 8.54 | 10.56 |
| **Vanguard 500 Index Fund Admiral Shares** | | | |
| Return Before Taxes* | –11.98% | — | — |
| **S&P 500 Index** (reflects no deduction for fees, expenses, or taxes) | –11.89% | 10.70% | 12.94% |

*Average annual total return of Admiral Shares since inception (November 13, 2000) was –12.33%.

*Figure 3.1: Example of the effect of taxes on fund total returns.*
Source: The Vanguard Group, Inc. Reprinted with Permission

provides a performance overview for the past 10 years, showing the fund's performance and comparing that performance to a widely followed industry benchmark.

The prospectus also features information about a fund's returns before and after taxes. For investors who hold fund shares in taxable accounts, taxes can shave as much as 2 to 3 percent off a fund's total return, according to the SEC.

The fund's before-tax return is relevant for investors who hold their fund shares in a tax-deferred account, such as an IRA or 401(k). Funds indicate after-tax returns for three-, five- and 10-year periods. After-tax returns don't include the impact of state and local taxes and are figured using the historical highest individual federal tax rates. Your taxes may vary.

This table—as mandated by the SEC—shows after-tax

returns in two ways: including distributions and including distributions and sale of fund shares. Fund managers distribute capital gains when they sell securities at a profit.

*Investors pay taxes on distributions and when they sell fund shares at a profit. Figure 3.1 shows an example of the effect of taxes on the fund total return table that funds must provide.*

The prospectus describes the manager's experience with the fund. It also discloses whether the manager is directly employed by the fund or works for another company (known as a sub-advisor) employed by the fund.

While managers may have considerable latitude in terms of purchasing and selling securities, they must operate under the fund's investment objectives and operating strategies as laid out by the board of directors. The prospectus gives some details

about the fund's objectives and strategies.

A mutual fund's objective generally limits the types of securities the fund manager can purchase. For example, a fund with the objective of investing in large-cap growth companies may restrict the percentage of fund assets that the manager can invest in mid-cap and small-cap companies. Many funds restrict investment in foreign companies as well.

*One of the most important parts of the prospectus is the list of fund fees and expenses. Each fund presents a standardized table listing shareholder transaction expenses and fund operating expenses, shown in Figure 3.2.*

Transaction expenses include loads or sales charges imposed when you purchase, continually invest in, or sell fund shares. They also list any redemption or exchange fees.

Sales charges compensate brokers and financial advisers for advice they provide on fund investing. Many experienced fund investors eliminate load funds from consideration during their initial screening phase since there are so many no-load funds available.

Funds may charge redemption fees to discourage fund investors from selling their fund shares before a certain period of time, and impose exchange fees on investors who switch from one fund to another in the same fund family.

Operating expenses that cover the regular day-to-day costs of running the fund are deducted from fund assets. Look for more detail on fund expenses in Chapter 11.

### The Statement of Additional Information

The Statement of Additional Information, which is an addendum to the prospectus, includes data about how a fund spends the fees that you pay and detailed information about the fund's board of

directors. It lists each director by name, age and number of shares held, and whether the director is employed by the fund or is independent from fund management.

The members of the fund management team are listed along with their ages and positions with the fund. In this document the fund provides details about its brokerage transaction process, including how much in brokerage commissions the fund paid in the most recent fiscal year.

The fund discloses which brokers it uses to execute trades, and how much in commissions each received. A fund must also disclose if it received information and services in return for brokerage commission business.

### Annual and Semi-Annual Reports

At least twice a year, fund managers reveal their thoughts on the economy and their funds, giving investors an insider's look at how the fund operates. The fund manager— or the chairman of the fund company—provides this commentary.

Fund managers set the stage by discussing the economy at large and the performance of the market. Then they give details about how the economy and market trends affected the fund. Some funds go a step farther, revealing why specific stocks were bought and sold, and how the fund manager's selections further the fund's operating objectives.

*In a similar fashion to the prospectus, fund reports show performance numbers and compare these numbers to a broad-based market index. These figures are provided so you can compare the fund's performance to market indexes. The graph in Figure 3.3 contrasts the fiscal year total returns between a fund and its benchmark index.*

| EXPENSE EXAMPLE | | | |
|---|---|---|---|
| 1 Year | 3 Years | 5 Years | 10 Years |
| $93 | $290 | $504 | $1,120 |

*This example shows what you could pay in expenses over time. It uses the same hypothetical conditions other funds use in their prospectuses: $10,000 initial investment, 5% total return each year and no changes in expenses. The figures shown would be the same whether you sold your shares at the end of a period or kept them. Because actual return and expenses will be different, the example is for comparison only.*

| FEE TABLE | |
|---|---|
| **Annual fund operating expenses** | **% of average daily net assets** |
| Management fees | .0.55% |
| Shareholder services fee | .0.25% |
| Other expenses | .0.11% |
| Total | .0.91% |

*Figure 3.2: Table of Fund Fees and Expenses from a Prospectus*
Source: Dreyfus, 2003. Used with Permission.

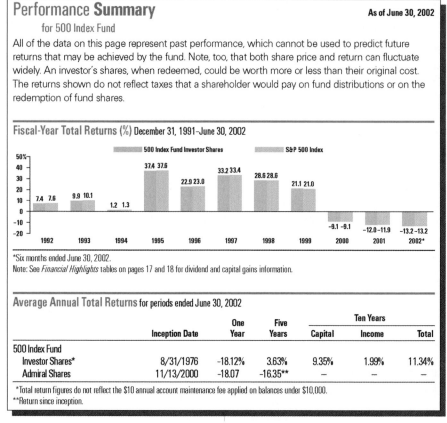

Figure 3.3: Fund Total Returns

*Source: The Vanguard Group, Inc. Reprinted with Permission*

Shareholder reports contain a complete list of the fund's portfolio holdings, usually called the Statement of Investments or the Statement of Net Assets. Stocks held are listed by market sector, and the fund's sector holdings are listed by percentage. In this section of the report, the fund names each company held in the portfolio, the total number of shares and the value of each position as of a certain date.

The fund's financial statements are part of the annual and semi-annual report. By examining the statement of operations, you can calculate how much money the fund has earned. A mutual fund company's earnings come from fees paid by investors for fund services, minus the cost of those services to the fund.

The fund's footnotes to the financial statements are at the very back of the report. While in many cases the notes to the financial statements explain or clarify mundane financial reporting matters, in other cases important information is included. The fund may reveal information about how the manager is compensated, fund director fees and other useful information.

## Proxies

Occasionally, you may receive a proxy statement asking you to vote on a major issue affecting the fund. Only fundamental investment policy changes need shareholder approval.

These include:

- a proposed merger with another fund
- an increase in management fees
- a significant change in the fund's investment policies
- the addition of a 12b-1 marketing and distribution fee
- a proposal to shut down a fund

Before voting, consider the implication of the proposed action carefully. The fund's management explains in the proxy statement why they believe such an action is necessary. However, just because management endorses a policy change doesn't mean that such a change is in your best interest.

## Buying Funds

Once you've done your research and found a good fund, the next decision you face is where to purchase the fund. There are a number of different fund purchase outlets.

Many investors find it easy and convenient to purchase a fund through a fund family. Others use mutual fund supermarkets. A third option for investors seeking guidance is to use a broker or financial planner.

To purchase a fund directly from a fund family, obtain forms over the phone or from the Internet, fill out the forms, and mail them back to the fund company. Some fund families offer full-service Web sites so that investors can download applications, fill them out and electronically sign them, automating the entire application process.

Mutual fund supermarkets feature thousands of funds from many different fund families. Many large fund families, including Vanguard, Fidelity and T. Rowe Price, offer funds through their own supermarkets, as do discount brokerages such as Charles Schwab and Muriel Siebert. To find other mutual fund supermarkets enter the words mutual+fund+supermarket in an Internet search engine.

The funds offered through a fund supermarket will vary in terms of fees and minimum purchase requirements. Be aware that many funds offered through supermarkets charge investors a distribution fee. This fee compensates the fund supermarket, and is an extra charge that you don't have to pay if you invest directly in a fund through its fund family.

Many fund supermarkets offer investors consolidated statements listing all fund holdings, even if the funds are from different fund families. If you individually purchase funds directly from different fund companies, you'll have to deal with multiple accounts and multiple statements.

If you choose the third option and purchase fund shares through a broker or financial planner, you pay some type of fee to compensate that broker or planner. Such a fee may take the form of a fund with a sales charge, or may be a flat

## INVESTOR PROVILE: ANN MOLISON

*Ann Molison, an NAIC member since 1996, is a former Chapter Director who teaches fund classes to clubs and at chapter events*

### Q. What advice would you give a new mutual fund investor?

I would advise a new fund investor to read as much as he can get his hands on. I would read this book, and attend workshops sponsored by NAIC where mutual fund investing seminars are offered. If my family was already investing in mutual funds through their retirement plans, I would find out what the offerings were, and, after obtaining a copy of this book, I would complete the Check List on each one.

There are some questions I would ask myself—honestly, including what my goals are, how long before I need this money, how do I feel about what has happened in the market, do I trust institutions, what do I know about fund companies, etc. I would also turn off CNBC, not read articles that begin with "The best 10 (or 20 or 100) funds to invest in today" and would avoid buying 'hot' funds and instead look for fund that meet your goals and risk level.

### Q: How has the NAIC Mutual Fund Program helped you?

The NAIC Mutual Fund Program — including the articles in *Better Investing* and this Handbook — are very important tools in my understanding and improvement of my investing skills today. Yes, I still own (in a non-taxed portfolio) 15 stocks, but I have also placed one fund in that portfolio. And, my 403(b) retirement plan now has some diversification outside of where it was three years ago before NAIC developed this program. My confidence level is up. I am able to justify with facts and not emotions to my spouse why one fund meets our needs better than others might.

percentage fee for a fee-based planner. Every dollar that you spend on fund fees is one less dollar you have to invest.

Many fund supermarkets, fund families and brokerages provide online access for mutual fund account holders. Investors access their account statements and fund documents online and may also be able to purchase, exchange and sell fund shares over the Internet.

## Reading Fund Listings

Information about a fund's daily performance is available from many sources. These include daily newspapers, financial Web sites, and fund family and company Web sites.

While this information is widely available, it's a good idea not to become fixated on a fund's daily fluctuations in net asset value. Long-term investors expect fund prices to move up and down on a short-term basis. In the longer term, investors expect superior funds to reward them with solid performance.

Financial newspapers, large daily newspapers and Web sites provide the most complete information regarding a fund's day-to-day performance. This can include total returns for certain time periods, comparison grades to peer funds and expense ratios. Medium and smaller-sized daily newspapers usually give limited information on the most popular funds.

Newspapers generally abbreviate the names of funds to save space. On financial Web sites, funds are listed by their ticker symbol. Fund ticker symbols have five letters, all ending in X.

Newspapers generally list funds by fund family in alphabetical order. Fund listings can be confusing, as the same fund may have several share classes. Fund families created share classes as a vehicle for different types of investors and to accommodate different pricing

---

### FIGURE 3.4: COMMON LISTING SYMBOLS

*Here are some common abbreviations you'll see in fund listings:*

**NAV:** a fund's net asset value. It is the market value of a fund's assets, minus your expenses and any liabilities, divided by the shares outstanding. This is what you will get per share if you sell, minus any back-end loads or redemption fees. The column listing here may also be called "sell."

**Offer Price:** may be labeled "buy." This is what you'll pay to purchase each share—the net asset value plus sales charges. For a no-load fund, the two columns will show the same price or the buy column will have the symbol "NL" for no-load.

**Change:** this column represents how the fund's net asset value has changed since the previous trading day.

**"r":** indicates a fund charging a redemption fee, a fee imposed on short-term shareholders.

**"p":** means that the fund charges a 12b-1 marketing and distribution fee.

**"t":** indicates a fund charging both a 12b-1 marketing and distribution fee and a redemption fee.

**"f":** means that the current net asset value wasn't available.

**"e":** denotes that a capital gains distribution was made and that the fund's net asset value shown does not include it.

**"x":** means that the price does not include the dividend or capital gains distribution, and is the same for a stock listing, indicating an "ex-dividend" price. Ex-dividend means that the dividend has been paid, and the fund's net asset value has dropped to reflect that dividend distribution.

structures. Among funds that carry loads, there are three typical share classes.

Class A shares have a front-end load that is deducted right off the top of an investment in fund shares. Class B shares carry a back-end load; the sales charges are deducted when you sell, and will zero out over a period of years. Class C shares have an ongoing sales charge that is deducted from your fund shares each and every year you own them.

## Fund Record Keeping

Keeping track of what you own is where mutual fund investing gets complicated. Investors who dollar-cost average and who reinvest their fund's capital gains distributions are likely to own shares with differing cost bases.

When you dollar-cost average you buy shares of a fund at many different prices. You buy more shares when the price is low, and fewer shares when the price is high. The price at which you purchase fund shares is known as your cost basis.

While mutual fund companies provide regular statements, many investors choose to supplement these statements with a manual or computerized record keeping system. There are a number of computer programs, including NAIC's Portfolio Record Keeper,

Microsoft Money and Quicken, that track your fund share ownership and your fund's performance.

There are several reasons why you should keep track of your fund investments. First, you'll want to know how your fund has performed. By keeping track of your fund share purchases, sales and capital gains distribution you'll have a better idea of exactly what you own. By keeping accurate records, you'll be able to tell before you sell shares of a fund in a taxable account whether you'll have a gain or loss.

### Tax Consequences

Good record keeping techniques will also help you keep track of the tax consequences of mutual fund distributions. You pay taxes on fund distributions if you hold fund shares in a taxable account, even if you reinvest your fund distributions in more fund shares.

The earlier you find out about the size of a fund distribution, the better your tax planning will be. Many investors have been caught unaware by large fund distributions, and have to dig into savings to pay the resulting taxes.

You'll also owe tax on any sales of fund shares made at a profit. Your profit is determined as the difference between what you paid for your investment—

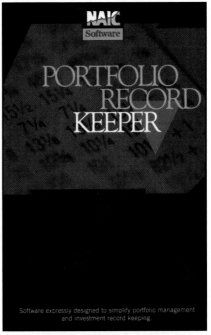

Source: Quant IX Software

the basis—and the price for which it was sold. Even if you didn't sell your fund shares outright, but switched from one fund to another, you will still owe taxes on any profit, provided you hold your shares in a taxable account.

As tax rules frequently change, consult your tax adviser for information on the tax implications of capital gains distributions and of selling fund shares.

Fund companies keep track of much of this information as well, but it's a good idea to maintain your own records as a check-and-balance system on fund company records.

# *Building a Portfolio*

## *Navigate the Road Ahead*

*Investors need a financial plan to guide their investing journey. First consider your goals, and then decide what investing vehicles will help you reach each milestone leading up to your goal.*

*The best mix of investments for your portfolio depends on your risk tolerance, your time horizon and your particular goals. Many investors save for several financial objectives at the same time. Whatever your plan, an appropriate mix of top-quality mutual funds helps you in meeting your investing goals.*

**Financial Plans**

**Diversification**

**Asset Allocation**

**Lifetime Goals**

**Financial Planning Resources**

## Your Financial Goals

Consider your financial goals before selecting specific mutual funds. Decide what you're saving for and figure out approximately how much money it will take to meet those goals.

Many tools are available to help you create a workable financial plan. These include consulting with a financial planner and accessing resources in print and on the Internet.

Once you've decided what you're saving for and have an idea of how much you need to save, allocate your savings among a number of investments. With so many investments—and investment advisers—competing for your dollars, it's difficult to decide where to put your money.

For some investment activities—such as many company-sponsored retirement plans and college savings plans—mutual funds may be the only choice. For other types of investing, mutual funds are only one option among many.

## Creating a Financial Plan

Before you plunge into the world of fund investing, create a financial plan to guide your investing journey. Many people are so caught-up in short-term goals such as paying daily bills and keeping credit card and other payments up-to-date that they neglect long-term savings goals.

By balancing your short and long-term savings needs, you can ensure that you will stay afloat on a daily basis and also have financial security in the future. Short-term goals are beyond the scope of this book. The following is a list of issues to consider when formulating a financial plan:

- Emergency reserves
- Short-term debt
- Retirement planning
- College savings
- Insurance coverage
- Taxes
- Estate planning

When you construct a financial plan, take into account your present financial situation as well as your goals. Gather all of your savings and investing statements and look at what you've saved so far. You may be pleasantly—or unpleasantly—surprised.

Your current and future ability to save is an important

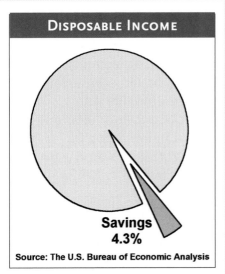

**DISPOSABLE INCOME**

**Savings 4.3%**

Source: The U.S. Bureau of Economic Analysis

*Figure 4.1: Average savings percentage for Americans as a percentage of disposable income.*

variable. People frequently underestimate the amount of money they need to save to reach key lifetime goals. Figure out how much money you'll need to fund your goals, and then determine how much you need to save. Your age is another key factor in making a financial plan. Obviously, a 25-year-old single man will have different financial needs and goals than a 60-year old widow.

Deciding on a workable financial plan requires thought and some study. Think about the "sleep at night factor." Basically, that's a way to assess your appetite for risk. If the risk associated with a particular investment keeps you awake at night, it is most likely too risky for you.

Some investors are comfortable with aggressive investments that might lose as much as 50 percent of their value, because there is also a potential for a large gain. Other investors are less comfortable with aggressive investments and would rather face more moderate losses even if it means less potential for gain.

While no one invests to lose money, risk is an inevitable part of any type of investing. Chapter 2 covered the factors associated with investment risk and explained why it's appropriate for most investors to invest at least some of their assets in the stock market.

Web sites, books and other publications can help you construct a financial plan. There are also many fee-based financial planners that will look at your situation with your goals and create a plan for you to follow over the years. Consult the list of resources at the end of this chapter.

Most investments have tax ramifications. Consult your tax adviser or a financial planner with accounting and taxation credentials for any special tax consequences a particular financial course of action or investment may bear.

### Diversification

NAIC and many investment professionals recommend portfolio diversification for many reasons. Diversification cushions you to a certain degree from the ups and downs of various market segments.

Studies show that investors with a diversified portfolio of stocks and bonds—or of funds invested in stocks and bonds—maximize their investing returns. A diversified portfolio experiences less volatility than a concentrated portfolio. Each person must decide how the various pieces of the asset allocation puzzle fit together.

Diversification works because stocks and bonds—and indeed different types of stocks and bonds—perform differently at different times. For example, when stocks perform well, often bonds do not. And even when stocks are generally performing well, not every company joins the party. A good example is the bull market of the late 1990s. At that time, virtually any company related to technology experienced incredible returns.

Mutual fund managers with the foresight to invest in technology early on were rewarded with breathtaking results, sometimes exceeding

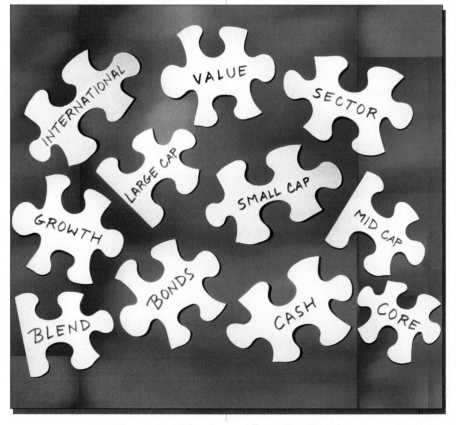

*Figure 4.2: The Asset Allocation Puzzle*

100 percent in one year. However, in that market, the share prices of many companies outside of the technology field, and the funds that invested in them, performed poorly.

Remember, just because a company's stock price doesn't perform well, doesn't mean that the company didn't continue to grow by increasing its sales and earnings. The markets don't always immediately reward company growth with a higher stock price.

Various segments of the market tend to perform well at different times. By constructing a portfolio built around different types of funds, you will participate in the different types of growth the market offers.

## Asset Allocation

Asset allocation refers to the practice of dividing your assets among investing vehicles. Various asset allocation theories and practices suggest methods to divide a portfolio between different types of stock and bond funds. In constructing an asset allocation plan, consider all of your investments—not just your fund investments or your investments in a specific type of account.

For example, if you own stock or bonds directly as well as through a fund, make sure to include your stocks, bonds and funds in any plan you create. Other types of investments—such as direct or indirect ownership of real estate—factor into your plan.

Before deciding on what types of funds you want to invest in, consider whether your portfolio will exclusively focus on stock funds or whether it will include bond funds.

Stock funds offer more growth and total return potential. Bond funds provide current income, which may not be necessary for investors who are many years away from retirement. Retirees, who may need income from their investments to supplement pensions and Social Security, frequently allocate a higher percentage of their portfolios to bonds or bond funds than investors who are still in the workforce.

## INVESTOR PROFILE: JOHN BOGLE

*John Bogle is the founder of Vanguard Group and an index fund pioneer. He is the author of three books, and frequently speaks and writes on fund topics*

### Q. What advice would you give a new fund investor?

Don't look totally at stock funds, but to figure out your asset allocation between bonds and stocks. In fact, before you even begin investing make sure you have some savings in reserve for emergencies.

When picking funds, look at index funds — a low-cost stock index fund and a low cost bond index fund. Costs really add up over time — there is a tyranny of compounding of costs.

Investors can't rely on the government to change how funds operate and to make things easy — they have to do it for themselves. Rely on simplicity and on parsimony. Begin to save now, because later is too late. Keep on dollar-cost averaging through different markets. If you follow a simple strategy such as this, in 20 years you can look back and see that you've done well.

### Q: What common mistakes can fund investors avoid?

A big one is not considering how much they should invest in stocks and bonds. There is risk in having too much in stocks and risk in having too much in bonds. Don't let your emotions get in the way of investing intelligently – pick your asset allocations and stick to them regardless of what the market is doing.

Pay attention to costs and diversification. If you're properly diversified in low-cost index funds, you'll at least get the return that the overall market is earning.

## FIGURE 4.3: ASSET ALLOCATION MODELS

**Aggressive Portfolio suitable for investors in their 20s and 30s**

Stock Funds: 50 percent large cap stock
25 percent mid-cap/small-cap stock
15 percent international stock

Bond Funds: 10 percent high-quality intermediate-term bond

**Moderate Portfolio suitable for investors in their 40s and 50s**

Stock Funds: 40 percent large cap stock
20 percent mid-cap/small-cap stock
10 percent international stock

Bond Funds: 30 percent high-quality intermediate term bond

**Conservative Portfolio suitable for investors either close to retirement or actually retired**

Stock Funds: 30 percent large cap stock
10 percent mid-cap/small-cap stock
10 percent international stock

Bond Funds: 25 percent high-quality short-term bond
25 percent high-quality intermediate-term bond

Even though younger investors don't require the income from bond funds, many financial planning experts recommend that all investors allocate at least a small percentage of their portfolios to fixed-income investments such as bond funds because they diversify a portfolio, lessening its volatility.

Overall asset allocation strategies change as you enter different stages of life. The retirement account portfolio of a 35-year-old many years away from retirement would differ greatly from that of a 60-year-old on the brink of retirement.

*The asset allocation examples in Figure 4.3 illustrate how an investor's profile could change over time. These sample portfolios are included as an illustration of how a portfolio can be managed, and are not an investment recommendation.*

Build your fund portfolio around a few core holdings. Core holdings are high-quality funds investing in large companies. These funds are well-managed and fairly diverse with low costs and relatively low volatility. A core fund forms the bedrock of a solid portfolio.

Large-blend funds are ideal core holdings. These funds invest in companies with both growth and value characteristics. One or more funds can serve as a core holding. For example, a two-fund core holding strategy could include a broad-based, large-blend stock fund and a bond fund.

Other funds in your portfolio play a subsidiary role. These include funds holding small and medium-sized companies and international funds.

Asset allocation may also involve splitting investments among index funds (funds designed to mirror a particular market index) and actively managed funds (funds that hire a portfolio manager). Other plans divide assets between taxable and tax-free investments such as municipal bond funds.

One simple way to diversify a portfolio is to start out with a core fund such as a large-cap blend or growth fund, and build up a $10,000 investment in it. Then, find a superior mid-cap blend or growth fund and build up to a $10,000 investment. The third step is to select an outstanding small-cap blend or growth fund and build up to $10,000.

There are many variations of asset allocation, and the examples mentioned above are a suggestion, not a recommendation. In fact, many investors hold a number of funds simply to take advantage of the variety of options offered in employee retirement plans and college savings plans.

For many investors, it is easy to over-diversify and own too many funds. Not only is it difficult to keep track of many funds, it can be counter productive as well. You may find yourself owning funds with similar goals and objectives, which defeats the idea of diversification.

For example, if you own three large-growth funds, you may think you are diversified because you own three

different funds. But because these are funds with very similar objectives, you really aren't diversified at all. It's better to own three funds with differing objectives than five funds with similar objectives.

*The illustration in Figure 4.4 shows the similarities between the portfolios of the two largest mutual funds in the country, Fidelity Magellan and the Vanguard 500 Index Fund, and how you wouldn't gain much diversification from investing in both.*

Taken to an extreme, asset allocation can involve investing in more than a dozen funds with different investment

objectives. While such a strategy can provide the maximum amount of diversification for your portfolio, it can also get complicated very quickly. You could spend a significant amount of time and energy selecting and following this many funds.

## Lifetime Goals

In the course of a lifetime, you'll set many goals. Frequently, investors save for large purchases and life events, including buying a home, saving for a child's college education and retirement. These goals compete for your savings dollars, forcing you to carefully follow an investing plan.

Typically, funding a child's college education and saving for retirement are the two largest goals you will face in your lifetime. You can meet these important goals by saving a set amount each month and using specific plans designated for both purposes.

### Retirement Savings

With company-funded pension plans on the wane, the responsibility for funding a secure retirement is in your hands. Employees fortunate enough to benefit from a pension plan are wise to supplement those savings.

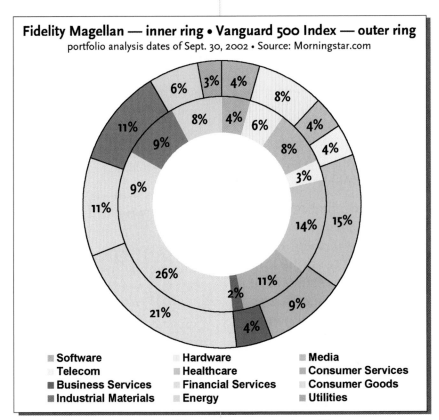

**Fidelity Magellan — inner ring • Vanguard 500 Index — outer ring**
portfolio analysis dates of Sept. 30, 2002 • Source: Morningstar.com

- ■ Software
- □ Telecom
- ■ Business Services
- ■ Industrial Materials
- □ Hardware
- ■ Healthcare
- □ Financial Services
- □ Energy
- ■ Media
- ■ Consumer Services
- □ Consumer Goods
- ■ Utilities

*Figure 4.4: Portfolio Overlap and Diversification*

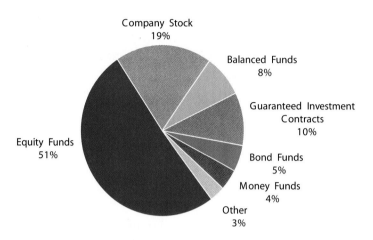

Average Asset Allocation for All 401(k) Plan Balances, 2000

Company Stock
19%

Balanced Funds
8%

Guaranteed Investment Contracts
10%

Equity Funds
51%

Bond Funds
5%

Money Funds
4%

Other
3%

Note: Funds include mutual funds and other pooled investments.
Source: Tabulations from EBRI/ICI Participant-Directed Retirement Plan Data Collection Project

*Figure 4.5 Average Asset Allocation*
Source: 2002 Mutual Fund Fact Book, Copyright ©2002 Investment
Company Institute (www.ici.org). Reprinted with permission.

The federal government created a number of investing vehicles for retirement savings. In February 2003 President Bush proposed a plan to overhaul retirement savings accounts. The fate of that proposal was undecided as this book went to press. As legislation and tax regulations are subject to change, be sure to check on the specifics of retirement savings plans and your eligibility for them with your tax adviser before investing. Under the older retirement plan system and the new proposal, you are responsible for selecting specific investments.

There are two types of retirement plans: employer-sponsored, and individual-sponsored. Many employer-sponsored plans offer a "match" for employee contributions. Individual sponsored plans are those that individuals establish and contribute to on their own, such as Individual Retirement Accounts (IRAs).

Experts project that retirees will need an income very close to their pre-retirement income if they want to continue to enjoy their same standard of living. While some expenses decrease during retirement, others increase.

Retirees also contend with inflation and taxes, two factors that can significantly erode their income over time. With

life expectancies increasing, most people will need more money to fund their retirement than they may expect.

Not only should you save for retirement, you must invest wisely. Without sufficient resources, you will either be forced to remain in the workforce or to cut back significantly on your standard of living.

It makes sense to increase your savings rate rather than rely on optimistic projections of future market returns. While the details of the specific plans available may change, many individuals have a choice between making at least some of their contributions on a before-tax or after-tax basis. Tax-deferred savings plans (those made before taxes are paid) maximize your investment earnings, since the capital gains, dividends and interest from your investments are not taxed until withdrawn at retirement.

Without paying taxes along the way, your investment gains and earnings compound during a period of many years. While you will have to pay taxes on your investments when you withdraw the money at retirement, you will most likely be in a lower tax bracket, meaning that you will pay less tax than you would have during the years you were saving.

After-tax retirement plans offer some significant advantages as well. Because you have already paid taxes on the money contributed, any money you withdraw is tax-free in retirement, as are any dividends, interest and capital gains. If your investments have been profitable, you stand to gain a great deal from not having to pay taxes on this income in retirement.

When investing for retirement, rely on the tools in the NAIC mutual fund program to evaluate the funds offered in your employer's plan. Invest in funds with a solid performance history, long-term management and low costs. If Morningstar doesn't cover some or all of the funds offered in the plan, check the section "Other Sources" in Chapter 7 for ways to gather information on these funds.

Pay special attention to costs associated with variable annuities. Many 403(b) plans offer variable annuities, and costs can be quite high because they include the traditional expenses for a mutual fund plus the cost of insurance. Many variable annuities boast costs of 2 to 3 percent, which can substantially cut into your investment returns.

Consider diversifying your retirement investments, and avoid concentrating too much

of your portfolio in your employer's stock. Too many investors have lost virtually their entire retirement savings when a company's stock crashed.

### College Savings

For anyone with children, the cost of sending those children to college is a major concern. Studies show that college costs are rising nearly twice as fast as inflation. In fact, for the 10 years from 1992 to 2001, general inflation averaged 2.69 percent per year while college costs rose 5.12 percent per year.

Even tuition for state residents, generally far more reasonable than private colleges, is increasing at a more rapid rate as state budgets are pinched by revenue shortfalls. According to the College Board, the average private school's annual cost for tuition, fees, room and board was $25,340 in 2001. The average cost for a state college for residents is still substantially less, but differs significantly from state to state.

Although college is expensive, it pays for itself many times in the long run. College graduates earn significantly more than non-college graduates in a lifetime—as much as $1,000,000, according to the College Board.

As with any type of investing, the earlier you save for a child's college education, the better. A number of cost calculators are

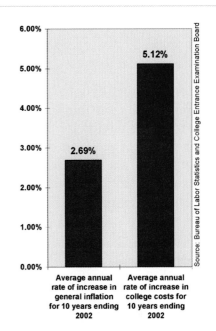

Source: Bureau of Labor Statistics and College Entrance Examination Board

Average annual rate of increase in general inflation for 10 years ending 2002 — 2.69%

Average annual rate of increase in college costs for 10 years ending 2002 — 5.12%

available that can help you estimate the amount you will need to save for each child, depending on when you start saving, how aggressive your investments are and whether you expect to pay for a private or public school.

There are many scholarships, grants and loans available for students, so you probably won't pay the entire bill yourself. For savings you accumulate, several types of special college savings accounts are available. Along with his retirement savings proposal, President Bush also proposed the establishment of Lifetime Savings Accounts that would help fund college and other expenses. Like the current Section 529 and Coverdell Savings Accounts, individuals could contribute funds after taxes, but money could be taken out to fund college expenses tax-free. The fate of this proposal was unknown as this book went to press.

Other investing options are available and contribution limits and eligibility for the above types of accounts do change, so it's a good idea to consult with a tax adviser before investing.

## Financial Planning Resources

There are many helpful financial planning resources. If you need help in devising a financial plan, your options include consulting with a financial planner, or using the wealth of information available in print and on the Internet.

Financial planners help people with overall financial plans and recommend specific investments. While virtually anyone can advertise as a financial planner, certified financial planners (CFPs) are experienced and have completed a specified course of study, which includes a two-day exam.

One way to find a certified financial planner in your area is to use the search feature of the Financial Planner's Association Web site (www.fpanet.org). Ask your friends and business colleagues if they can recommend a CFP.

Financial planners charge fees in two ways: on a commission or fee basis. You pay a commission to a financial planner when you purchase investments that a planner recommends that carry a sales charge. This sales charge, or load, compensates a planner for providing financial advice.

Fee-based planners charge a fee for specific services (such as creating a financial plan) and/or charge a certain percentage of assets to manage clients' investments. Some experts feel that fee-based planners are more unbiased in serving their clients needs, since they don't receive commissions linked to selling specific investments or products. Interview and check references before hiring a planner.

You can also look to the multitude of financial planning information available in print and on the Internet. Some books that provide an overview of financial planning and overall investing considerations are:

- *Personal Finance for Dummies* by Eric Tyson (Hungry Minds, 2000)

- *The Only Investment Guide You'll Ever Need* by Andrew Tobias (Harvest Books, 2002)

- *NAIC's Official Guide* by Angele McQuade (NAIC, 2003)

*Better Investing* magazine, published monthly by NAIC, features a personal finance column as well as articles on mutual fund and stock investing.

Many personal financial Web sites feature articles on a variety of personal finance topics. There are also a number of savings calculators—some on the Web sites listed below—that will help you figure out how much you need to save, and what returns you may earn. Using data that you input regarding your investments, how much you save, your income and your retirement time horizon, these calculators help you figure out how much you need to save to retire comfortably or save for another financial goal.

However, many have limitations and you shouldn't exclusively rely on their results. A few Web sites with useful information include:

- **mPower (www.mpower.com)** features information about all types of retirement plans, including IRAs, 401(k)s and 403(b)s.

- **Saving for College (www.savingforcollege.com)** provides an overview of Section 529 college savings plans and information about other ways to save for college, including Coverdell Savings Accounts and Uniform Gifts to Minors.

- **Morningstar (www.morningstar.com)** features articles on retirement, college savings, personal finance issues and mutual fund and stock investing.

- **The Motley Fool (www.fool.com)** offers articles and savings calculations for a number of personal finance issues, from saving for retirement to refinancing a mortgage.

- **MSN Money Central (www.moneycentral.msn.com)** features a wide variety of resources on personal finance from budgeting to taxes to retirement planning.

# Stock Funds—
# The Key to Growth

## Watch Your Funds Grow

Ownership of stock is the cornerstone of NAIC philosophy. Because stocks have historically returned more than other investments, it makes sense to build your financial plan around them. By investing in quality growth companies and the superior funds that purchase them, you'll have a good chance to meet your financial goals.

To embark on the right investing path, first learn how to navigate the maze of thousands of different funds. Stock funds are the key to growth, but not just any stock fund will do. By learning about the different types of stock funds, and what they aim to accomplish, you'll be better equipped to move forward on the road to profitable investing.

The Ins and Outs of
Investment Style

Investment Objectives

Types of Stock Funds

## The Ins and Outs of Investment Style

An investment style is the direction a fund manager pursues to achieve a fund's investment goals. The three main style categories are growth, blend and value.

Growth and value are generally acknowledged as two different investment styles. Managers of growth funds hope to profit from share price capital appreciation, which happens when the value of the stocks in the fund's portfolio rises. Value fund managers look for companies undervalued by the market at large. In between growth and value are blend funds, which share characteristics of growth and value funds.

As we've mentioned, NAIC has built its investment philosophy around helping investors find growth companies. While many funds describe themselves as growth funds, this doesn't mean that some or even most growth funds share NAIC's definition of what a growth company is and how to find one. There are some growth fund managers who view growth in virtually the same terms as do NAIC investors. Our tools will help you find

managers who purchase NAIC-style growth companies.

We use Morningstar data in this book. In Chapters 8, 9,10 and 11, we'll show you how to draw information from a Morningstar report to fill out the Stock Fund Check List.

Lipper, Value Line, Standard & Poor's and Wiesenberger* Thomson Financial also provide fund data. Different newspaper, television and Web site news outlets rely on one or another of these data providers for fund information.

These companies not only classify funds by investing

style, but also by market capitalization. Fund analysts and investors use market capitalization systems to calculate company size. Mutual funds are frequently classified by the size of company the fund manager primarily invests in.

Fund data providers determine a fund's investing style after evaluating that fund's portfolio holdings over a certain period of time. This classification can change if the portfolio's holdings change substantially.

Analysts, investors and fund companies frequently compare a fund's performance to its peer group. A peer group is a group of funds that share similar characteristics.

Since each fund data provider has its own classification system, a fund may fall into a number of different peer groups depending on the classification used by a fund data provider. What is a mid-cap value fund to one data provider might be a multi-cap core fund to another.

These classification systems are far from perfect because they are so broad and subject to interpretation. Many funds with different investing strategies are lumped together in a peer group where their performance is compared and contrasted.

This results in some very dissimilar funds being compared to one another. In this situation, it is inevitable not all comparisons will be fair or accurate. Take a fund's comparison to its peer group with a grain of salt.

In contrast to a fund's style, a fund's investment objective is an internal designation stated by the fund in its prospectus. A fund with growth as its objective may hold value stocks, just as a fund with a value objective can hold growth stocks.

Let's explore in more detail the meaning of growth, blend and

value. There are many varieties of growth, blend and value, and fund managers, fund data providers and investors apply these terms differently. These investment styles also move in and out of favor in the market. When growth is in favor, frequently value isn't.

## Growth Funds

Managers of growth funds hope to profit from capital appreciation. The managers of traditional or pure growth funds expect that rising sales and earnings will fuel a gain in the stock prices of their holdings.

Growth fund managers pay less attention to a company's price than its growth rate, reasoning that fast-growing companies deserve to command high P/E ratios, and

that if a company fulfills expectations, the price will continue to climb. A P/E ratio is a company's stock price divided by its earnings. Investors view P/E ratios as a measure of a company's growth potential in the market.

Managers of aggressive growth funds, in particular, may purchase rapidly growing companies, many with exceptionally strong sales and earnings growth rates. These companies don't always have established track records.

Growth and income funds, another type of growth fund, invest in both growth and income stocks, providing investors with capital appreciation and income. Income- producing stocks generate dividends and generally have slower growth rates than pure growth companies.

## Value Funds

Value fund managers look for companies undervalued by the market at large. These companies may be young companies that the market has ignored, or "fallen angels" with a history of problems. Managers of value funds expect their funds to profit when the market recognizes the true value of the companies they invest in.

Value funds generally have lower average P/E ratios and lower average portfolio earnings growth rates than growth or even blend funds. A fund's average P/E is the weighted average of the P/E ratios of the companies held by the fund.

The portfolio earnings growth rate is another average, that of the weighted historic—or trailing—earning growth rate. Weighted means that a larger percentage of ownership in a company counts proportionately more than a smaller percentage of ownership in a company. For example, if a fund invests 5 percent of its assets in Home Depot, that ownership position would count more than a 3 percent ownership in Microsoft.

Many value funds own companies that pay dividends. Value funds generally pay out more in dividends than growth funds. Value fund managers vary widely in their stock selection strategies.

## Blend Funds

Managers of funds classified as blend invest in a mix of growth and value companies. In fact, some describe blend funds as "core" funds, meaning that such funds merit consideration as a core investment in your fund portfolio.

These funds steer a middle course between growth and value. While growth funds tend to have higher-than-average P/E ratios and portfolio earnings growth rates, and value funds are lower than average in these areas, blend funds are right smack in the middle.

Blend fund managers may not subscribe to a particular investing philosophy or style, but may select stocks that they believe will perform well in the future, regardless of whether they are steady growers or undervalued opportunities. In fact, blend funds may not have anything in common with each other except that measurements of a number of portfolio metrics, including the portfolio's average P/E ratio and earnings growth rates, fall into a range pre-defined by Morningstar.

Some of the largest funds in the world are blend funds, including Fidelity Magellan and the Vanguard 500 Index Fund, which fall into the large-cap blend category. Blend funds are attractive to many investors because they hold a mix of growth and value companies.

### Growth vs. Value?

Growth or value—which is better? If you own well-managed funds, any variety may do well. It takes two very different types of talent to select growth and value

---

### FIGURE 5.1 A VALUE INVESTING PRIMER

*Deep or absolute value:* managers of these funds adopt a strict methodology focusing on a company's intrinsic worth. Using various measurements, the manager computes the value of a company, and then seeks to purchase it for significantly less than its true worth. The manager expects to profit when the market wakes up and realizes the true value of the company.

*Moderate value:* this approach is also known as the value with a growth twist approach. Managers of these funds adopt a value orientation but are willing to pay more for companies with very strong growth prospects. They are less likely to purchase companies with very poor prospects in the hope of a turn around. These managers may compare a company's P/E ratio to industry benchmarks in an effort to find undervalued opportunities.

*Traditional or pure value:* managers of these funds look for undervalued opportunities but don't go too far down the road of either deep value or growth opportunities. These funds can also be described as middle of the road value funds.

companies. Over a period of time the characteristics of a growth company are easily discerned, and a good growth company is likely to be a solid investment for a fairly lengthy period of time.

It is much more difficult to judge whether the management of a company on the rocks has the talent to turn it around. To really produce continuing value for the investor, the turned-around company must grow and become more valuable or be replaced successfully by a new turn-around situation. When such management is found it can produce a great record, but growth is easier to find and more dependable over the course of time.

NAIC favors growth funds. During its more than 50-year history, NAIC investors have found that the results from growth investing are rewarding and dependable.

## Investment Objectives

A fund's investment objective is the overarching principle under which it is run. Investment objectives are spelled out in a fund's prospectus.

While a fund can follow many different objectives, the wording of those objectives is fairly standard. Here's an example of an objective for a growth and income-oriented stock fund:

Growth and Income Fund XYZ seeks growth of capital and

dividend income. The fund invests at least 80 percent of assets in common stocks of large, well-established companies with a history of paying level or rising dividends. The fund may invest up to one-third of its assets in foreign securities.

That objective reveals quite a bit about the fund in a few sentences. While it contains the word growth in its name, that doesn't necessarily mean the fund is a true growth fund.

Growth & Income Fund XYZ's investment objective suggests that it follows a traditional growth and income strategy, purchasing stocks of large companies with solid histories of dividend payments. The fund also seeks companies

### TOM O'HARA ON GROWTH

"A growth company is generally much easier to recognize by the ordinary investor than is a value company. It is a company that has a record of increasing sales and earnings per share at a fairly regular rate over an extended period of time and its management produces a higher pre-tax profit margin and a higher percent earned on investor capital. NAIC procedures help you recognize these features and also learn how the company produces its growth and judge how long it will continue.

"Prior to the 1990s value companies were called 'under-valued' companies, which is a title still used by some analysts. The value or former under-value results from many factors and some analysts are skilled at discovering these 'unrecognized by the market' values. Sometimes the undervalued company ran into hardships and losses and its price went way down. Over a period of time management has developed new products or greatly trimmed costs and the analysts recognizes that a new period of prosperity for the company is about to appear. These situations are seen as about to produce a period of strong earnings for the company and a consequent stock price increase."

--Tom O'Hara, Chairman Emeritus, NAIC, and Co-Manager, NAIC Growth Fund

that regularly increase their dividends.

Up to one-third of the fund's assets may be invested outside of the United States. By analyzing the company's holdings, you can determine how much of the fund's assets are actually invested overseas.

Some investors are wary of funds that invest a significant proportion of their assets overseas, because it isn't always easy to get information about these companies. Foreign countries have different—and sometimes less strict—disclosure and accounting standards than those in the United States. Some foreign governments are unstable, and such instability could put financial markets at risk. In addition, foreign currencies rise and fall against the U.S. dollar, meaning that the value of an investment can change regardless of its fundamentals.

### Where's the Cash?

Before buying shares in a stock fund, make sure that the fund is indeed investing a large portion of its assets in stock. While funds with the term stock or equity in their name must invest 80 percent of their assets in stock, other stock funds aren't bound by such rules.

Do your homework, and make sure you know the answers to the following questions before investing in a fund:

- Does the fund manager tend to park money in cash during a market downturn?

- Does the manager invest a portion of the fund's holdings in bonds or cash? What type and amount of bonds and cash are in the portfolio?

- How much of the funds total assets can be invested in special securities such as emerging market securities or warrants? Special securities are complex instruments or securities that aren't easily traded. Emerging market securities are bonds or stocks from markets in less developed countries. Warrants are a security that allows the holder the right to purchase a security at a specific price.

If the fund manager has a history of placing 20 percent or more of the fund's investments in cash or cash equivalents (such as a money market fund) during a market downturn, this could mean that this is a manager who practices market timing.

This strategy is quite risky, as no one knows when the market will actually hit a bottom. Many market timers have missed out on substantial rallies, depriving themselves or their shareholders of potential gains in the process.

When you buy shares of a stock fund, you expect to invest in stock. If an examination of the fund's portfolio shows that the fund manager has a track record of investing 10 percent or more of the fund's assets in bonds, cash or other investments, look elsewhere. Unless, of course, you are investing in a balanced fund which splits its assets between stock and bonds.

You are paying a stock fund manager to invest in stock for you, not to dabble in other investments. A stock fund weighed down with substantial investments in bonds or cash will cut the fund's returns, depriving you of potential gains.

Again, when you invest in a stock fund, your money should be invested in stock, not in exotic securities or instruments that you—and maybe even the fund manager—don't really understand. If you don't understand a fund manager's strategy, don't invest in the fund.

Also be aware that a stock fund manager has wide latitude to invest in many different types of securities unless this is specifically prohibited in the fund's prospectus.

## Types of Stock Funds

As the sheer numbers of funds have skyrocketed, so have the different types of funds. While a huge variety of funds are available, distinctions between types of funds have become increasingly blurred. Funds with similar names and objectives may be very different, while funds with very dissimilar names and objectives may be virtually the same.

This has created as many problems for investors as the proliferation of fund types has solved. Investors who invest in three or four funds may think they are diversified, but a closer examination of the funds' portfolio may show that this isn't the case.

It's also possible for one fund—such as an index fund that endeavors to replicate the entire market—to provide virtual one-stop diversification for the stock portion of your portfolio.

We've already covered some of the available fund types. Both growth and value come in

different flavors, while the blend style steers a middle ground between growth and value.

Below is a summary of the various types of stock funds available in the marketplace. This overview begins with balanced funds, which invest in both stocks and bonds. Then we cover index funds, which are passively managed funds endeavoring to replicate the performance of a market index. Next are international and global funds. The overview ends with two types of specialized funds: socially responsible funds and sector funds.

Exchange-traded funds, which are different than traditional mutual funds, bring the chapter to a close.

## Balanced Funds

Balanced funds invest in a mix of stocks, bonds and cash. Managers of such funds pursue an investment objective of capital

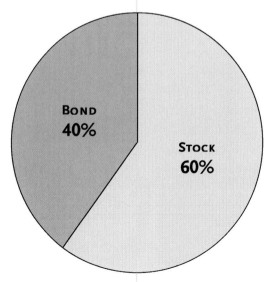

**BOND 40%**

**STOCK 60%**

appreciation and current income. The stock portion of balanced funds will follow either the growth, value or blend style. The bond portion can also be invested in different ways that we'll cover in more depth in Chapters 16 through 20.

There are a number of different types of balanced funds, including traditional balanced funds, funds of funds, life-cycle funds and asset allocation funds. Traditional balanced funds usually maintain a strict balance between the stock and bond portion of the portfolio, with 60 percent stock and 40 percent bonds typical.

A fund of funds invests in other mutual funds to achieve a particular investment objective. These funds may or may not be in the same fund family.

While most funds of funds hold a varied mix of stock, bonds and cash, this combination varies depending on whether the fund is aggressive, moderate or conservative. Funds of funds may sport an expense ratio significantly higher than other balanced funds, charging a traditional fund expense ratio plus an extra fee known as a "wrap" fee on top of those expenses.

Life-cycle funds have a composition that evolves over time. These funds are designed to assist an investor in meeting certain long-term goals, such as retirement or funding a child's college education.

These funds start out with a more aggressive investment mix, then become more conservative as the life-cycle goal nears. They typically convert to nearly 100 percent cash one or two years out from the life-cycle goal to preserve the investor's capital.

Asset allocation funds have portfolios that tend to be more subject to change than other types of balanced funds. An asset allocation fund manager can shift the fund's asset mix to pursue maximum returns with minimum risk of principle, depending on the manager's assessment of the overall market. Because many asset allocation managers use market-timing approaches, this strategy is quite risky.

## Index Funds

Index funds are constructed to mirror a certain segment of the market. Managers of index funds purchase all or most of the securities in a particular index in an effort to deliver results as close to that particular index as possible. There are stock and bond index funds. Some index funds are based on broad market indexes, while others are constructed around more narrow market sector indexes.

The most popular stock fund index is the S&P 500, an index of the 500 largest and most well-known companies in America. One of the largest mutual funds is the Vanguard 500 Index Fund, which opened to investors in 1976.

Many mutual funds benchmark their performance against the S&P 500, or another popular benchmark, a total stock market index. Several indexes endeavor to track the performance of the entire stock market, including the Wilshire 5000 and the Russell 3000. A benchmark is a standard that fund managers or investors compare their performance against. Because the total stock market indexes include many more mid and small-sized companies than the S&P 500 does, the S&P 500 tends to be more volatile than the total stock market index.

Studies have shown that index funds that track a broad-based index outperform the vast majority of actively managed mutual funds. Actively managed mutual funds are those that employ a portfolio manager to buy and sell securities.

Actively-managed funds tend to suffer in relationship to index funds because many have significantly higher costs. These costs weigh the fund down, making it difficult to compete with a low-cost, broadly-based index fund.

This is why the NAIC Mutual Fund Education Program

encourages you to compare the performance of a fund you own or are considering owning to either a broad-based index or an index that closely matches the fund's stated investment objective. If your fund manager can't consistently beat the index, why invest in the fund?

## International Funds

International funds invest exclusively in companies located in countries outside of the United States; global funds invest throughout the world, including the United States.

As in many other investing categories, there are a wide variety of funds under these two broad umbrellas. A number of widely diversified international and global funds invest in companies in a number of different countries. Some funds invest in companies of all sizes, while others focus on a particular type of company such as small, medium or large.

Then there are regional funds, which invest in companies in a specific region, such as Europe or Latin America. Some funds specialize even further, limiting their investing to one particular country.

Regional funds generally invest in either the developed world or undeveloped world. Funds specializing in less-developed countries are known as emerging market funds.

When investing in international funds, remember that overseas securities markets aren't regulated in the same way as in the United States. While securities markets may be fairly and strictly regulated in much of the developed world, in the undeveloped world, there may be little or no regulations. Also, investments in emerging markets can be threatened by revolutions or unstable governments.

A final issue important for investors in international and global funds is currency hedging. Foreign currencies have different values than the U.S. dollar and trade up and down in relation to the dollar. So, a fund could have stocks that are performing well, but if those stocks are held in a currency that is performing poorly against the dollar, investors may actually receive little or no gains from their investments.

Managers of international funds need to decide whether to hedge against the value of currency fluctuations or to ride these fluctuations out. While hedging policies can have a profound effect on a fund in the short term, these variables tend to smooth out over time.

## Socially Responsible Funds

Socially responsible funds appeal to investors who want their investing to reflect their ethical principles. These funds have the objective of investing in companies to promote a certain social or religious agenda.

Many broad-based socially responsible funds avoid investing in companies that manufacture or profit from alcohol, tobacco, gambling and weapons. They may also seek out companies that promote human rights, positive labor relations, community investment and community relations.

Socially responsible investing begins with screening, where fund managers use particular criteria to screen out companies engaging in certain practices and to screen in companies engaging in practices the fund finds desirable. While many funds stop there, other funds take their socially responsible principles a step or two further.

These types of funds may engage in shareholder activism, whereby fund managers will seek to work with company management to change certain policies. Other funds engage in community development activities in an effort to help those in need more directly.

Because many socially responsible funds screen out industrial companies, many invest more of their assets in technology companies. Therefore the funds prosper more when technology is in favor, and suffer more when it is out of favor. However, the portfolios of individual funds vary widely, so do your own analysis of individual funds before investing.

## Sector Funds

Sector funds concentrate on a particular market sector. There are many different types of sector funds. Morningstar segregates the market into three super sectors: the information economy, the service economy and the manufacturing economy. Each of those broad headings has four industry sectors:

- Information economy: software, hardware, media and telecommunications
- Service economy: health care, consumer services, business services and financial services

- Manufacturing economy: consumer goods, industrial materials, energy and utilities

While some sector funds are broadly based, covering a whole industry such as health care, others focus on narrow sub-sectors. The more broadly based funds tend to be less volatile, while narrowly based sub-sector funds can be very volatile.

Before investing in sector funds remember that their lack of diversification can be a big drawback. Also keep in mind that a number of market sectors are represented in mutual funds with broad portfolios.

Many investors were lured into technology sector funds in the late 1990s. Some of these funds soared 100 percent or more in one year. However, when the technology sector rotated out of favor, many investors were left with substantial losses.

## Exchange Traded Funds

Exchange traded funds (ETFs) are index-based baskets of stocks that trade on the stock exchanges like a stock, but boast the unmanaged portfolios and low costs associated with traditional index funds.

Since ETFs trade like a stock, they can only be purchased or sold through a broker for a commission. ETFs are pooled investments that are very

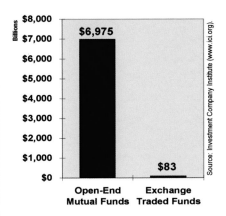

Figure 5.2: Assets invested in traditional open-ended funds vs. ETF assets—data 2001.

similar to mutual funds, but with some differences.

While mutual funds are priced once a day, ETFs trade all day, and their prices fluctuate not only based on the value of the stocks in their portfolios, but also on market supply and demand and investor sentiment.

There are a number of ETFs based on many different types of indexes. ETFs can have different structures depending on their sponsoring brokerage, bank or stock exchange.

While ETFs can be an appropriate investment for an investor with a lump sum of money to invest, they can be very expensive for an investor seeking to dollar-cost average by investing a small sum each month. This is because in addition to the ETF's expense ratio—which is usually quite low—you must pay a brokerage commission each and every time you purchase shares.

These types of funds may engage in shareholder activism, whereby fund managers will seek to work with company management to change certain policies. Other funds engage in community development activities in an effort to help those in need more directly.

Because many socially responsible funds screen out industrial companies, many invest more of their assets in technology companies. Therefore the funds prosper more when technology is in favor, and suffer more when it is out of favor. However, the portfolios of individual funds vary widely, so do your own analysis of individual funds before investing.

## Sector Funds

Sector funds concentrate on a particular market sector. There are many different types of sector funds. Morningstar segregates the market into three super sectors: the information economy, the service economy and the manufacturing economy. Each of those broad headings has four industry sectors:

- Information economy: software, hardware, media and telecommunications

- Service economy: health care, consumer services, business services and financial services

- Manufacturing economy: consumer goods, industrial materials, energy and utilities

While some sector funds are broadly based, covering a whole industry such as health care, others focus on narrow sub-sectors. The more broadly based funds tend to be less volatile, while narrowly based sub-sector funds can be very volatile.

Before investing in sector funds remember that their lack of diversification can be a big drawback. Also keep in mind that a number of market sectors are represented in mutual funds with broad portfolios.

Many investors were lured into technology sector funds in the late 1990s. Some of these funds soared 100 percent or more in one year. However, when the technology sector rotated out of favor, many investors were left with substantial losses.

## Exchange Traded Funds

Exchange traded funds (ETFs) are index-based baskets of stocks that trade on the stock exchanges like a stock, but boast the unmanaged portfolios and low costs associated with traditional index funds.

Since ETFs trade like a stock, they can only be purchased or sold through a broker for a commission. ETFs are pooled investments that are very

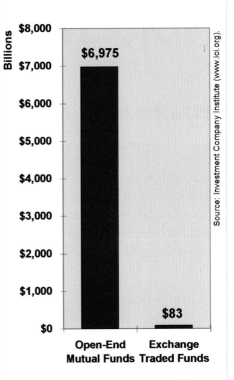

Figure 5.2: Assets invested in traditional open-ended funds vs. ETF assets—data 2001.

similar to mutual funds, but with some differences.

While mutual funds are priced once a day, ETFs trade all day, and their prices fluctuate not only based on the value of the stocks in their portfolios, but also on market supply and demand and investor sentiment.

There are a number of ETFs based on many different types of indexes. ETFs can have different structures depending on their sponsoring brokerage, bank or stock exchange.

While ETFs can be an appropriate investment for an investor with a lump sum of

# How Mutual Funds Work

## *Fund Managers in Action*

When you buy fund shares, you hire a portfolio manager. How that manager runs the fund determines whether you make or lose money. Managers determine which companies to buy and sell. They use different criteria to evaluate companies and manage the fund's portfolio.

The media, individual investors and institutional investors constantly scrutinize the performance of portfolio managers. Many fund managers fail to outperform market indexes. The tools in the NAIC mutual fund program are designed to help you find outstanding managers and the funds they manage.

## How Fund Management Operates

## Portfolio Managers vs. Indexes

## Fund Closings and Mergers

## It's the Management...

The success or failure of fund management makes or breaks a fund. It's as simple—or as complicated—as that.

Whether a fund is a good investment for you depends on its management because the fund manager controls how your money is invested. A fund manager, with information provided by analysts and researchers, decides daily which companies to buy, which to sell and which to hold.

Since you pay a substantial amount for a manager to invest your money, you expect superior performance. Why pay for anything less?

Examine the record of portfolio managers during the past 30 years, and it is clear that many fall short of any definition of superior performance. Studies show that index funds outperform portfolio managers 75 percent of the time over a long period of time.

We'll analyze how portfolio managers select companies and what you are paying for when you invest in an actively managed fund.

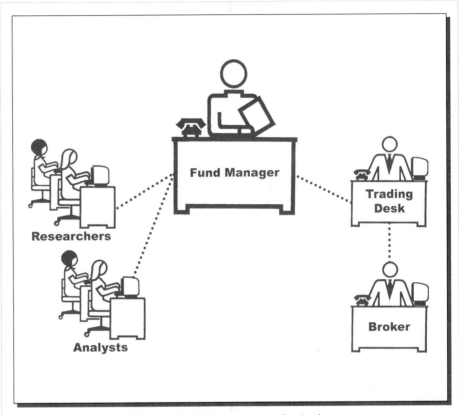

*Figure 6.1: Management in Action*

### How Fund Management Operates

While every fund is different, some common features apply to the operations of most actively managed mutual funds. All funds have a manager or managers that are supported by researchers, analysts, a trading desk and brokers.

*The diagram in Figure 6.1 illustrates how the pieces of the fund management puzzle fit together.*

Researchers, analysts and managers access sophisticated financial data about many thousands of companies. They employ certain criteria, which varies from fund to fund, to sort through these companies.

Most fund companies espouse a fundamental approach to stock selection. Fundamental analysis refers to the practice of examining a company's management, results and methods as opposed to technical analysis, which refers to analyzing overall market trends. The NAIC mutual fund education program also espouses a fundamental approach to evaluating funds in terms of examining their portfolios, management and costs.

Managers rely on researchers and analysts for basic research on a promising company. Analysts from some fund companies roam the globe, interviewing company management and observing company operations. In the office, they scrutinize financial statements, looking at such elements as a company's profitability, cash flow, lines of business, market share and competition.

Portfolio managers themselves devote a significant amount of time to research, examining financial statements, and visiting companies or talking to CEOs on the phone. At many fund companies, analysts and managers engage in lively debates as they discuss the merits of various industries and companies.

Once a manager or management team decides to buy a particular stock, the focus of the operation moves to the trading desk. While management decides how much of a

particular stock to purchase, the trading desk figures out how to make that purchase at the lowest possible cost.

Outside of the drama of what to buy and what to sell, fund managers devote time to staying on top of the businesses of their current holdings, talking to large shareholders and participating in meetings, conference calls and media interviews.

## Management Changes and Blunders

Should you succeed in finding a top-notch portfolio manager with a superior track record, keep in mind that there is no guarantee that manager will stay with a particular fund. A manager may quit, be fired or be reassigned.

*As you can see from Figure 6.2, the average manager remains at a fund for less than five years. NAIC recommends investors seek funds whose managers have a minimum of five years experience managing a particular fund. A manager with less experience is not responsible for the long-term historical track record of the fund.*

Some fund families frequently reassign managers, moving them around from fund to fund like players in a game of musical chairs. Others lose managers who leave to pursue more lucrative opportunities elsewhere.

Despite the limitation of fund objectives, managers in some fund families enjoy considerable latitude in running a particular fund. This can lead to considerable success or failure. Peter Lynch built a stellar record at Fidelity Magellan, while Jeff Vinik left the fund after an ill-fated bet on cash and bonds in 1996.

After Vinik's departure, Fidelity tightened its controls over its portfolio managers so that other managers wouldn't stray as far from their mandates as Vinik did. While this has resulted in less volatility for Fidelity shareholders, it has also meant that most Fidelity funds post returns closer to their tracking indexes. This means while there is less chance that a Fidelity manager will make a Vinik-type mistake, there is also less chance that a manager will enjoy a Lynch-style success.

### Portfolio Managers vs. Indexes

A number of academic studies reveal that index funds regularly outperform the vast majority of actively managed funds. Studies published in the *Journal of Finance* and the *Financial Analysts Journal* more than 25 years ago examined the performance of actively managed funds and concluded that the vast majority of portfolio managers can't outperform market indexes.

Experts attribute the performance gap to fund costs, frequent buying and selling, and a short-term focus. Handicapped by high expenses and high turnover, most portfolio managers can't close the gap with their low-cost, low-turnover, passively managed cousins—index funds.

A few years or quarters of superior performance from an actively managed fund can skew results for years to come, making the fund's long-term performance seem stronger than it actually is. Many portfolio managers trade frequently. This strategy not only increases brokerage costs, but also raises investors' tax liabilities.

The high costs of actively managed funds drags their performance down in

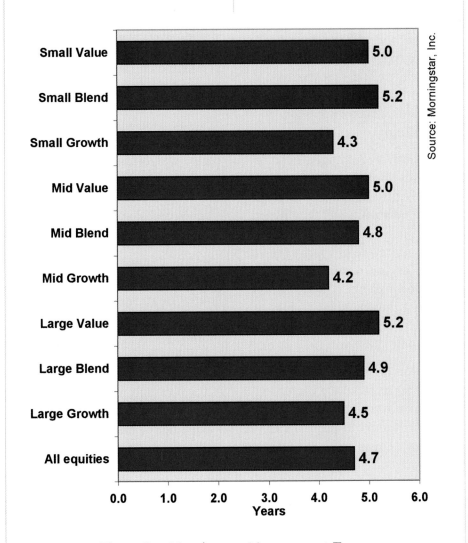

Figure 6.2: Morningstar Management Tenure

relation to low-cost index funds. An example of these higher fees is seen in the average expense ratio charged by large blend mutual funds, which was 1.23 percent in 2000, according to Morningstar.

Contrast this with the expense ratio of a low-cost index fund. An example of an index fund with rock-bottom costs is the Vanguard 500 Index Fund, itself a large-blend fund. This index fund, designed to replicate the performance of the S&P 500, has an expense ratio of .18 percent.

*The bar graph in Figure 6.3 illustrates this gap. Since the category average includes low-cost index funds, the average for actively managed funds is likely higher than the 1.23 percent.*

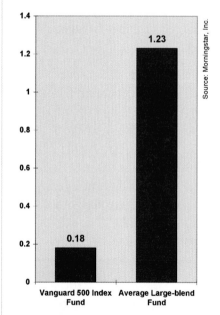

Figure 6.3: Fee Difference

The difference of 1.05 percent translates into $105 of a $10,000 investment that an investor would pay each year of fund ownership. Own $10,000 in shares of a fund with an expense ratio on par with the large-blend category average for five years, and you'll pay $615 in expenses.

If you owned a similar amount of shares in the Vanguard 500 Index Fund, you'd pay $90 in expenses. The difference in costs is $525, money that you could otherwise invest in fund shares. If your fund shares increased in value during that five-year period—as you would expect they would—your expenses would rise accordingly.

If an actively managed fund is not only more expensive than an index fund, but also delivers worse performance, why invest in it? A few active portfolio managers have outperformed an index and manage funds with low expenses. Such funds do exist, but they aren't easy to find. The tools showcased in this book show you how to find these outstanding funds.

Fund managers face increased pressure from shareholders and the media to perform as well as a comparable index. This pressure leads managers to purchase many of the same companies that are in the index so that their fund's

performance won't stray too far from the indexes.

So slavishly do some portfolio managers adhere to index performance measures that their funds become closet index funds. Closet index funds are described as actively managed funds with a portfolio and sector weighting very similar to a particular market index.

This begs the question of why you should pay a portfolio manager to select stocks when you could buy an index fund in the first place. Before you buy shares in an actively managed fund, make sure that manager's approach offers a credible alternative to an index fund. Fund managers with low turnover, high tax efficiency and low expenses generally have a better chance of outperforming their peers and a comparable index fund.

## Fund Closings and Mergers

The performance gap between index funds and most actively managed funds may actually be larger than research shows, given that many of the least successful funds are no longer in business. By closing or merging their least successful funds out of existence, fund companies skew the statistics of actively managed funds, leaving just the records of the most successful to stand against index funds.

Wiesenberger* Thomson Financial, a fund data provider, notes that in 1998, 222 funds were liquidated, while 176 were shut down in the first nine months of 2000. Funds in unpopular sectors, those with poor performance records and funds with assets of less than $50 million, are likely candidates for merger or closure.

Fund companies seeking to merge funds into other funds aren't doing the shareholders of the original funds any favors in most cases. Frequently, funds are merged into other funds with dissimilar objectives.

For example, in 2002 Dreyfus asked shareholders of the Dreyfus Premier Small Company Stock Fund to approve a merger into the MPAM Mid-Cap Stock Fund. Shareholders who originally purchased this fund for its small-cap focus are receiving shares in a mid-cap fund, which is a major change in investment focus.

# Finding Quality Funds

## A Needle in a Haystack?

Look through any personal finance magazine, and you will find ads of every shape and size, promoting the merits of various funds. On the face of it, finding a superior fund seems akin to looking for a needle in a haystack.

Fortunately, there are helpful resources available. Morningstar reports and free screening programs found on many financial Web sites enable you to zero in on the highest-quality funds. Armed with this information, you can sort through the funds competing for your attention and find those that meet your wealth-building requirements.

**The Morningstar Report**

**Other Sources**

**Fund Lists & Screening**

## The Morningstar Report

NAIC bases the tools shown in this handbook on the Morningstar report. Morningstar reports, contained in the publication *Morningstar Mutual Funds,* are widely available at public libraries.

While there are a number of mutual fund data sources, Morningstar's comprehensive coverage of funds and wide availability led NAIC to select it as a basis for its manual tools. You can find Morningstar reports, which are bound in a large dark gray notebook, at your library's reference desk.

Morningstar, which features approximately 1,700 funds, updates its publication every two weeks. Each issue of *Morningstar Mutual Funds*—known as a volume—contains reports on approximately 170 funds. It is published on a 20-week cycle. This means that each covered fund is updated with a new report approximately every five months.

Each of the 10 volumes of *Morningstar Mutual Funds* contains two sections: the Analysis Section and the Summary Section. The Analysis Section has reports on a number of funds in several Morningstar fund categories.

Funds are categorized based on their investment objective and portfolio holdings.

Each category features an overview page with editorial commentary, statistical summaries and specific information about the funds in that particular category. The funds covered in each category are listed in alphabetical order.

The Summary Section serves as an index of all the funds covered in *Morningstar Mutual Funds.* It contains editorial commentary, a focus on featured funds, updates on industry news and trends, a spotlight on new funds, and fund category and benchmark statistics.

*Morningstar Mutual Funds* contains a copy of Morningstar's 48-page Resource Guide, which provides complete explanations of the terms used by Morningstar analysts and an overview of the format of the various analysis sections. The Resource Guide is a separate booklet that should be included in the front or back pocket of the Morningstar fund report notebook.

Sifting through a database of thousands of funds, Morningstar analysts select funds for coverage in *Morningstar Mutual Funds* based on a number of criteria, including funds that have provided investors with a solid risk-reward profile in the past. Analysts also include funds with good performance

records, new funds with strong potential, obscure funds with strong fundamentals and the largest funds.

The scope of Morningstar's services goes far beyond publishing *Morningstar Mutual Funds*. The company sells fund data to fund companies as well as to financial advisers, insurance agents and brokers. Morningstar recently launched a portfolio management program for financial advisers, and a family of stock indexes based on its Style Box methodology.

## Category Overview Sheet

Each category's overview sheet is a valuable resource for fund investors. For an example of a stock category overview sheet, see page 59. Morningstar provides category averages for just about every measurement covered on the fund analysis pages. There is also analyst commentary, highlights covering prominent fund manager changes, fund name changes and Morningstar category changes.

Within limits, category statistical averages provide a yardstick for comparison

## MEET THE EXPERT: DON PHILLIPS

*Don Phillips, a managing director with Morningstar, pioneered the Morningstar Style Box. He's been investing in funds for 27 years.*

### Q. What advice would you give to a new fund investor?

Get started – the key to successful investing is to know yourself as an investor. The only way to learn how you react to the ups and downs in the market is to be in the game. The major thing you'll get from your first investments is not so much capital appreciation, but a better knowledge of yourself as an investor.

### Q: What are the most common mistakes fund investors should avoid?

Buying funds off last year's leaders' list and thinking you're diversified because you have multiple funds. Funds succeed in the same markets because they have similar holdings. Too often investors think they're diversified when they actually own five shadings of the same investment style.

### Q: What steps could funds take to be more shareholder-friendly?

Funds should treat shareholders as owners, not customers. They should report openly and honestly both what has gone right and what has gone wrong. The goal should be to improve the investor's knowledge of the fund so that the investor uses it appropriately.

### Q: What could the SEC do to improve the fund regulatory environment?

They could hold funds, which are investment companies, to the same standards as operating companies. They could make funds openly disclose fund manager's names, compensation and ownership in a fund, so that fund investors can understand fully management's incentives in running the fund.

## ◎ Overview: Large Blend

Large-blend funds often look a lot like the S&P 500 index. That is, they typically have robust weightings in both growth and value sectors, including technology, health care, and financials. Managers in this category often use a growth-at-a-reasonable-price strategy, buying companies with moderate valuations relative to their growth rates.

### Highlights    04-03-02

Vanguard Primecap p.307: Another year, another good return so far.

Fidelity Dividend Growth p.217: No closet indexer, Charles Mangum continues to get the job done.

Vanguard 500 Index p.303: "Bogle's Folly" remains a great core holding.

T. Rowe Price Blue Chip Growth p.291: This fund still holds considerable appeal.

TIAA-CREF Growth & Income p.299: As disappointing as this fund has been lately, we're not ready to give up on it just yet.

### Update    Scott Cooley 04-03-02

Is the large-blend category back from the dead?

For the first time in a while, the group is showing some signs of life. Although the S&P 500 index still sits on a negative three-year return, the market now trades well above the lows it hit following the Sept. 11 attacks. With the Federal Reserve aggressively cutting interest rates and boosting the nation's money supply, stocks rallied sharply in the fourth quarter, with the typical fund in the category returning nearly 11% during the period. The group faltered again during 2002's first two months, declining 4%, but a handful of bullish economic reports have again given stocks a lift in recent weeks, and the category has crawled back to near the breakeven mark for the year to date through March 31.

Our favorite large-blend funds have benefited from the improved market environment. With a passel of economically sensitive tech stocks, Vanguard Primecap gained the most; it has risen more than 20% since the end of September, beating its average rival by 9 percentage points. Fidelity Dividend Growth's Charles Mangum played tech perfectly, loading up on the sector's shares when they were cheap in September, then selling into the sector's fourth-quarter strength. Our other favorites haven't shot out the lights over the past few months, but they have also registered solid, double-digit gains since the end of September.

A lot of investors are asking whether large-cap stocks still have room to run. The truth is that although plenty of folks are willing to offer predictions about the market's short-term movements, no one really knows where stocks are headed. Indeed, few pundits predicted the market's sharp fourth-quarter rally or the rebound in March. That's an argument in favor of building a well-diversifed, low-cost portfolio, then sticking with it for the long haul. We think our picks will help investors do just that.

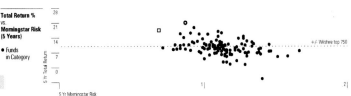

| Total Return % vs. Morningstar Risk (5 Years) | | | |
|---|---|---|---|

● Funds in Category

### Top Funds

| | Best 5 Yr Return% | | Lowest 5 Yr Morningstar Risk | | Highest 5 Yr Morningstar Rating |
|---|---|---|---|---|---|
| ○ | Thompson Plumb Growth | 21.00 | □ Mairs & Power Growth | 0.57 | Fidelity Dividend Growth |
| | Fidelity Exp & Multinatl | 18.72 | Franklin Growth A | 0.60 | Fidelity Exp & Multinatl |
| | Heritage Capital ApprecA | 16.90 | Smith Barney Soc Aware B | 0.66 | Heritage Capital ApprecA |
| | Mairs & Power Growth | 16.79 | Smith Barney Apprec A | 0.67 | Janus Core Equity |
| | Vanguard Primecap | 16.26 | Fidelity Asset Mgr: Grth | 0.70 | Mairs & Power Growth |

| 1991 | 1992 | 1993 | 1994 | 1995 | 1996 | 1997 | 1998 | 1999 | 2000 | 2001 | 03-02 | History |
|---|---|---|---|---|---|---|---|---|---|---|---|---|
| 49.54 | 19.89 | 25.01 | 6.27 | 40.41 | 31.43 | 36.68 | 34.85 | 42.21 | 10.79 | -2.60 | 3.98 | Top Decile Average |
| 32.59 | 8.10 | 11.02 | -0.62 | 32.37 | 21.13 | 27.72 | 22.54 | 20.78 | -6.52 | -13.72 | -0.28 | Total Return % |
| 19.29 | -1.15 | 0.83 | -7.42 | 18.98 | 12.25 | 12.68 | 3.92 | -0.52 | -17.93 | -25.50 | -4.37 | Bottom Decile Average |
| 2.11 | 0.48 | 0.96 | -1.93 | -5.17 | -1.81 | -5.63 | -6.04 | -0.26 | 2.58 | -1.84 | -0.55 | +/-S&P 500 |
| 0.15 | 0.45 | 1.18 | -1.07 | -5.23 | -1.03 | -5.30 | 6.09 | -1.05 | 4.44 | -0.95 | -0.98 | +/-Wilshire top 750 |
| — | — | — | — | — | — | — | — | — | — | — | — | Expense Ratio % |
| — | — | — | — | — | — | — | — | — | — | — | — | Income Ratio % |
| 70 | 68 | 68 | 67 | 73 | 74 | 74 | 71 | 77 | 111 | 96 | — | Turnover Rate % |
| 76.28 | 97.69 | 138.24 | 160.58 | 252.01 | 346.97 | 504.45 | 718.28 | 985.64 | 851.24 | 794.31 | 794.10 | Net Assets $bil |
| 144 | 160 | 190 | 221 | 250 | 280 | 329 | 390 | 448 | 504 | 569 | 572 | # Funds, excluding multiple share classes |

### Performance

| | 1st Qtr | 2nd Qtr | 3rd Qtr | 4th Qtr | Total |
|---|---|---|---|---|---|
| 1999 | 3.67 | 6.73 | -5.93 | 15.69 | 20.78 |
| 2000 | 4.18 | -2.84 | -0.07 | -7.79 | -6.52 |
| 2001 | -12.57 | 5.26 | -15.15 | 10.91 | -13.72 |
| 2002 | -0.29 | — | — | — | — |

### Trailing

| | Total Return % | +/-+/- S&P 500 | Wilshire top 750 | %Rank All Funds |
|---|---|---|---|---|
| 3 Mo | -0.28 | -0.55 | -0.98 | 59 |
| 6 Mo | 10.53 | -0.46 | -1.57 | 42 |
| 1 Yr | -1.61 | -1.85 | -2.45 | 65 |
| 3 Yr Avg | -2.28 | 0.25 | 0.80 | 75 |
| 5 Yr Avg | 8.59 | -1.58 | -1.31 | 32 |
| 10 Yr Avg | 11.50 | -1.75 | -1.32 | 23 |
| 15 Yr Avg | 10.66 | -1.64 | -1.34 | 28 |

### Tax Analysis

| | Tax-Adj Ret% | % Pretax Ret |
|---|---|---|
| 3 Yr Avg | -4.04 | — |
| 5 Yr Avg | 6.47 | 98.3 |
| 10 Yr Avg | 9.13 | 98.1 |

### Risk Analysis

| | Morningstar Return | Score Risk | Morningstar Risk-Adj Rating |
|---|---|---|---|
| 3 Yr | -1.51 | 0.97 | ★★ |
| 5 Yr | 0.80 | 0.92 | ★★★ |
| 10 Yr | 1.00 | 0.91 | ★★★ |
| Wtd Avg | -0.57 | 0.96 | ★★★ |

### Other Measures

| | | | Standard Index S&P 500 |
|---|---|---|---|
| Standard Deviation | 17.63 | Alpha | 0.3 |
| Mean | -2.28 | Beta | 0.95 |
| Sharpe Ratio | -0.47 | R-Squared | 88 |

### Morningstar Category Correlation

| | Style Value | Bend | Growth | |
|---|---|---|---|---|
| | 0.83 | 1.00 | 0.93 | Large |
| | 0.78 | 0.93 | 0.79 | Med |
| | 0.73 | 0.80 | 0.74 | Small |

### Average Expense Ratios

| | | | |
|---|---|---|---|
| Front-End Load | 1.23 | Level Load | 1.91 |
| Deferred Load | 1.86 | No-Load | 0.83 |

### Portfolio Analysis    03-31-02

| Avg number of equity holdings: 205 | % Net Assets |
|---|---|
| General Elec | 2.85 |
| Microsoft | 2.84 |
| Pfizer | 2.33 |
| Citigroup | 2.24 |
| ExxonMobil | 2.01 |
| American Intl Grp | 1.92 |
| Wal-Mart Stores | 1.58 |
| Intel | 1.43 |
| Johnson & Johnson | 1.37 |
| IBM | 1.34 |
| AOL Time Warner | 1.26 |
| Tyco Intl | 1.14 |
| Fannie Mae | 1.13 |
| Bristol-Myers Squibb | 1.01 |
| Philip Morris | 1.00 |

| Most Common Purchases | Value $mil |
|---|---|
| ExxonMobil | 2447.3 |
| First Union | 2445.7 |
| Conoco CI A | 1925.4 |
| ChevronTexaco | 1882.1 |
| Johnson & Johnson | 1849.6 |

| Most Common Sales | Value $mil |
|---|---|
| General Elec | -3543.0 |
| Eli Lilly | -3149.4 |
| Fannie Mae | -2395.3 |
| J.P. Morgan Chase & Co. | -2111.2 |
| Canadian Imperial Bk | -1775.0 |

| Sector Weightings | % of Stocks | Rel S&P 500 |
|---|---|---|
| Utilities | 2.3 | 0.85 |
| Energy | 6.2 | 0.91 |
| Financials | 18.5 | 1.00 |
| Industrials | 11.2 | 0.94 |
| Durables | 1.7 | 0.94 |
| Staples | 6.5 | 0.82 |
| Services | 12.5 | 1.14 |
| Retail | 7.2 | 0.94 |
| Health | 14.6 | 1.02 |
| Technology | 19.4 | 1.12 |

| Investment Style | Stock Port Avg | Rel S&P 500 |
|---|---|---|
| Price/Earnings Ratio | 31.9 | 1.00 |
| Price/Book Ratio | 5.5 | 0.96 |
| 3 Yr Earnings Gr% | 13.9 | 1.25 |
| Price/Cash Flow | 18.4 | 1.03 |
| Med Mkt Cap $mil | 48544 | 0.84 |
| Yield | 0.4% | |

| Market Cap | | |
|---|---|---|
| ● Giant | 47.1 |
| ● Large | 34.1 |
| ● Medium | 16.4 |
| ● Small | 2.1 |
| ● Micro | 0.3 |

| Composition % of assets 03-31-02 | |
|---|---|
| Cash | 4.1 |
| Stocks | 91.5 |
| Bonds | 2.7 |
| Other | 1.6 |
| Foreign (% of Stocks) | 4.2 |

| Cash Inflows | Cash Flow % | % Total Assets Equity | All |
|---|---|---|---|
| 2002 | 3.8 | 28.90 | 19.79 |
| 2001 | 14.1 | 28.69 | 19.92 |
| 2000 | 8.0 | 28.36 | 20.33 |
| 1999 | -18.6 | 30.86 | 22.10 |
| 1998 | -23.6 | 29.84 | 20.40 |

Source: Morningstar, Inc.

during analysis of one fund or a group of funds. In fact, on the Stock and Bond Fund Check List, which are covered in Chapters 8, 9,10, 11, 17 and 18 you compare a single fund's expense ratio to the overall category average.

### Fund Analysis

Morningstar reports pack information, ratios and performance numbers into each fund report. The major sections of the report include manager strategy, portfolio management, performance, historical information, risk analysis, portfolio analysis and analyst commentary. We'll discuss the specific data used in an NAIC fund analysis in the context of the Stock and Bond Fund Check Lists in Chapters 8, 9, 10, 11, 17 and 18.

In the Analysis section, a Morningstar analyst provides a six or seven paragraph commentary on a fund's management, performance and prospects. While a professional analysts' opinion is useful, you should rely more on your own analysis of a fund when deciding whether to purchase shares. Not only is the analyst's report far from comprehensive, an analyst's perspective differs from that of the individual investor. You are best suited to analyze a fund using NAIC fund evaluation tools, taking your own preferences and

financial goals into consideration.

### Morningstar Star Ratings

When a fund receives a five-star rating from Morningstar, its marketing machine generally goes into high gear, touting this rating in print, on television and any other way they can. Before you get carried away and purchase the latest five-star fund, understand how the star system works, and why it is an incomplete measurement of a fund's record and potential.

In assigning star ratings, Morningstar analysts assess a fund's past performance in terms of risk and return. They also take into consideration a manager's skill, overall fund

quality and consistency in fund performance. Analysts use these factors to rank and rate a fund in comparison to its category peer group, eventually arriving at a star rating for each fund covered in *Morningstar Mutual Funds*.

*As seen in Figure 7.1, only 10 percent of all funds covered by Morningstar get a five-star rating. Of the other 90 percent of funds covered, 22.5 percent fall into the four- and two-star categories, 35 percent fall into the three-star category and the bottom 10 percent fall into the one-star category.*

Previously, Morningstar assigned star ratings and category ranking numbers. Beginning in June 2002 the category ranking system was

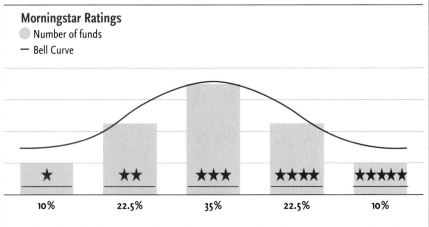

To determine a fund's star rating for a given time period (three, five, and 10 years), the fund's Morningstar Risk score is subtracted from its Morningstar Return score. The resulting number is plotted along a bell curve to determine the fund's rating for each time period. If the fund scores in the top 10% of its category, it receives 5 stars; if it falls in the next 22.5%, it receives 4 stars; a place in the middle 35% earns 3 stars; those in the next 22.5% receive 2 stars; and the bottom 10% get 1 star.

*Figure 7.1: Morningstar Ratings*
Source: Morningstar, Inc.

eliminated, and its function assumed in the star rating system, which was substantially reworked to include category comparisons.

Morningstar itself notes that the star ratings are only a starting place for fund investors. A study of the Morningstar and Value Line fund ratings systems, which was released in early 2003, revealed that funds with high ratings don't necessarily out-perform better than lower-rated funds. Morningstar's system doesn't take into consideration many factors, such as turnover rate, manager tenure and costs, that are important in the NAIC fund analysis program. NAIC recommends that investors subject a fund to a full evaluation with either the Stock or Bond Fund Check List before considering purchasing fund shares.

## Morningstar Stock Fund Style Box

*The Morningstar Style Box is a proprietary tool used to categorize funds. Stock mutual funds are categorized by their investment style and market capitalization. While Morningstar launched the original style box in 1992, it overhauled the methodology in 2002. The updated stock fund Style Box is shown in Figure 7.2.*

The Style Box divides the universe of funds into nine

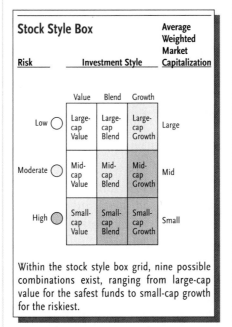

Within the stock style box grid, nine possible combinations exist, ranging from large-cap value for the safest funds to small-cap growth for the riskiest.

*Figure 7.2: Morningstar Stock Style Box*
Source: Morningstar, Inc.

categories: large growth, large blend and large value; mid-cap growth, mid-cap blend, and mid-cap value; and small-cap growth, small-cap blend and small-cap value.

Before placing a fund in a particular section of the Style Box, Morningstar evaluates a fund based on 10 measurements of the individual stocks in the fund's portfolio. These include a company's P/E ratio and dividend yield. The analysis methodology uses both past ratios and projections of future ratios. For example, a company's past four quarter's P/E ratios and an estimate of the next four quarters P/E ratios are taken into consideration.

Morningstar's Style Box analysis classifies a fund based on the stocks in its portfolio rather than the fund's investment objective. Consequently, its Style Box assignment can vary from its stated investment objective. Analysts, fund companies and investors use the Style Box to benchmark a fund against funds in its peer group.

While the Style Box is a useful tool for fund investors, it is limited. It doesn't tell you anything about a fund's management, its costs or other important factors. When considering purchasing a fund, do a full analysis using NAIC's mutual fund program tools, rather than relying on a system such as the Style Box or the Morningstar Star rating system.

### Other Sources

While Morningstar is a comprehensive source of information on many funds, there are thousands of funds that Morningstar doesn't cover. Morningstar provides full-page analysis of approximately 1,700 funds in *Morningstar Mutual Funds;* 2,000 funds (including the ones in the print version) are covered in-depth for premium members on Morningstar's Web site (www.morningstar.com). It also makes "Quicktake Reports" available on 4,000 additional funds at its Web site. While the

Quicktake Reports don't contain all the information necessary to fill out NAIC's analysis forms, much of the needed information is available.

More than 2,000 funds and virtually all variable annuity products are not publicly analyzed by Morningstar. This includes many funds in company-sponsored retirement plans. Morningstar doesn't analyze money market funds, separate share classes of funds, closed-end funds or exchange-traded funds.

### Gathering Information

How do you examine a fund using NAIC methods without the benefit of a full Morningstar report? There are several options.

In addition to *Morningstar Mutual Funds,* some public or college libraries carry Standard & Poor's Mutual Fund Reports, Lipper Mutual Fund Reports, Wiesenberger*Thomson Financial or Value Line Mutual Fund reports. While these reports don't contain exactly the same information as Morningstar, they do include many items that are necessary for an NAIC fund analysis.

Information about funds is available on several personal finance Web sites, including NAIC's Mutual Fund Education and Resource Center (www.better-investing.org/funds), Quicken (www.quicken.com)

and MSN Money (www.money central.msn.com) and on fund company Web sites.

Funds must disclose certain information in their prospectuses and annual and semi-annual reports. These reports, which are available to shareholders and prospective shareholders upon request and via download from the Internet, contain data regarding a fund's performance, management, costs and holdings. Many funds offer fact sheets that provide an overview of the pertinent details of a fund.

For the information that you can't find elsewhere, contact the fund company. (Phone numbers are available on the Internet and from retirement plan administrators or benefits offices.) Ask the customer representatives to fill in the blanks. You may not get every figure, but you'll have enough to do an analysis that will help you choose the best from among the funds your retirement plan offers.

Some retirement plan fund providers contract with Morningstar to provide them with special one-page reports

---

### FIGURE 7.3: OTHER SOURCES

*If Morningstar doesn't cover your fund in its paper version, check out these other potential data sources:*

**In some public libraries:**
- Standard & Poor's Fund Reports
- Value Line Fund Reports
- Lipper Fund Reports
- Wiesenberger*Thomson Financial Fund Reports

**On the Internet:**
- NAIC's Mutual Fund Resource Center
- Standard & Poor's Reports through many on-line brokers
- Fund Company Web sites
- Morningstar Quicktake reports (www.morningstar.com)
- MSN Investor Fund Research (www.moneycentral.msn.com)
- Quicken Fund Evaluator (www.quicken.com)

**In Print:**
- Fund Prospectus
- Fund Annual Report
- Fund Semi-annual Report

**On the Phone:**
- Fund customer service reps
- Retirement plan administrators

that make available virtually the same information as is contained in traditional Morningstar reports. TIAA-CREF, the huge teachers' retirement plan organization, makes such reports available for shareholders in its retirement annuity plans at its Web site (www.tiaa-cref.com).

If your retirement plan fund company doesn't have this arrangement with Morningstar or another data provider, ask for it. Many retirement plan administrators contract with third parties such as Morningstar to provide financial information to plan participants.

You can also request that your retirement plan offer more funds than are familiar to you. Retirement plan administrators have a fiduciary duty toward their plan participants, and are willing to make changes in the plans especially if many employees request such changes.

What if your broker or financial adviser recommends that you invest in an unfamiliar fund not covered by Morningstar? Ask why this particular fund is the best fund for you, and request information about it, such as a prospectus and annual report. If you bought fund shares through a broker in the past and need current information about the fund, call and ask for the details you need.

Many brokers and financial planners subscribe to the Morningstar Principia database and software, which offer comprehensive detail and information about many thousands of funds and variable annuity products far beyond what is contained in a typical Morningstar report. Brokers or planners who subscribe to Principia have the information you need to fill out the NAIC forms at their fingertips.

## Fund Lists and Screens

So that you don't have to pull your hair out examining thousands of funds before you find something suitable, there are lists and screens that cut out many unsuitable funds, leaving you to focus on a more manageable group. Many magazines, books, publications and Web sites offer lists of funds that meet certain criteria. A number of Web sites offer screening tools so that you can use your own criteria to come up with your own list.

### Fund Lists

A number of Web sites and publications feature lists of funds that meet certain pre-determined criteria. Standard & Poor's, for example, touts its

Select Funds (www.standard andpoors.com/onfunds). These funds are a group of funds that demonstrate consistently strong long-term performance with long-term management poised to continue its superior record.

Standard & Poor's also provides lists customized to five different criteria, including top-performing funds year-to-date, largest stock funds and highest yielding bond funds. Morningstar's Web site (www.morningstar.com) offers five pre-set screens built by its analysts and these include screens for solid small-cap funds, superior foreign-stock funds, conservative bond funds and top-performing funds with small asset bases.

Quicken (www.quicken.com) and MSN MoneyCentral (www.moneycentral.msn.com) also offer customized lists. Quicken's list includes funds with low investment minimums while MSN's adds technology funds and funds with strong returns and little risk.

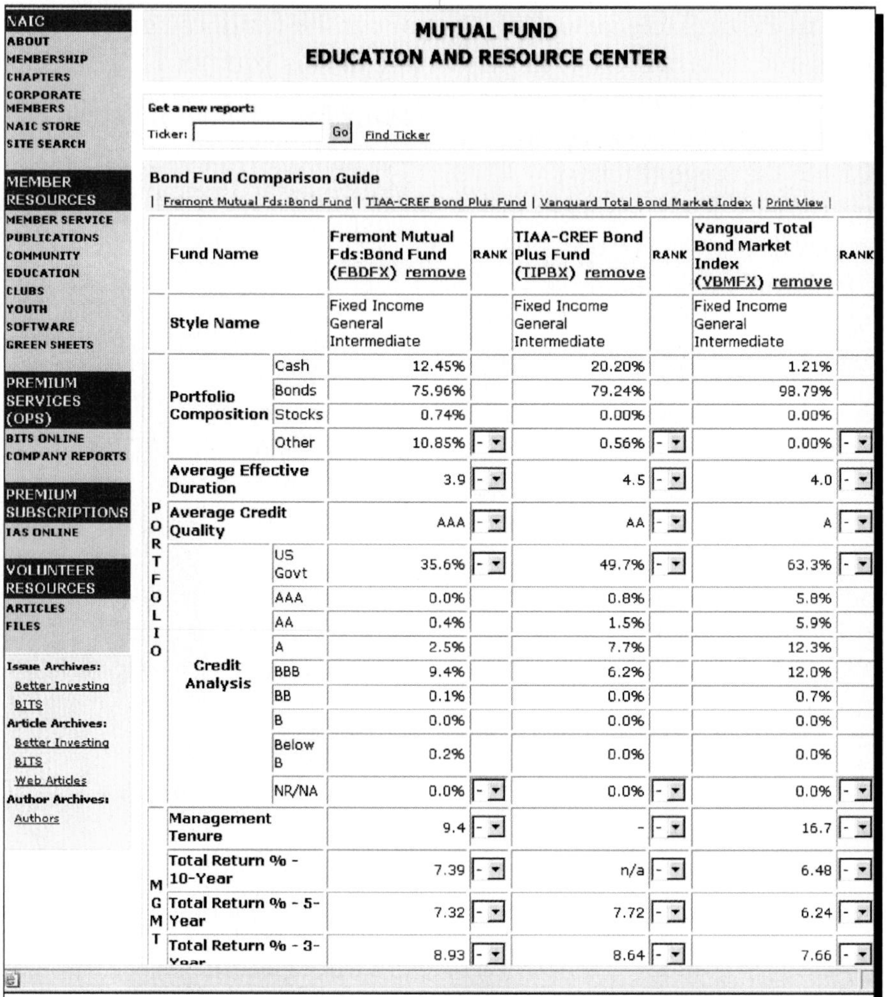

Many magazines, including *Money*, *Kiplinger's* and *Better Investing* publish lists of popular funds or funds that meet certain criteria. Some mutual fund and personal finance books include the author's favored funds. This book doesn't include such a list because we want you to use the NAIC tools to find funds that meet your needs.

Source: Mutual Fund Education Alliance – reprinted with permission. All rights reserved ©2003.

*Figure 7.4: Screen Shot of Mutual Fund Education Alliance Fund Selector*

The flaw with many of these lists is that they don't follow NAIC criteria. NAIC advises investors to seek strong long-term returns and not to be lured into a fund by short-term returns. None of these sites provide lists of funds with low turnover, long-term management and low costs, key NAIC criteria.

However, these lists can be a starting place for further analysis. Select a few funds that seem to meet your investing goals and NAIC criteria and evaluate them using the Stock Fund Check List and Comparison Guide.

## Screening

Many personal financial Web sites deliver screening capability and a number also feature the results of their own screens, customized to various criteria. Screens enable you to sort through the universe of funds and find funds based on certain criteria.

Screens are generally either pre-customized or provide options for you to select criteria important to you. Using NAIC criteria, it is fairly easy to design a screen that will give a list of funds suitable for analysis by the Stock Fund Check List and Comparison Guide.

Customized screens provide lists of funds according to the criteria of the screen builder, whether it be Morningstar's or Standard & Poor's analysts or someone else.

When you build the screen yourself, you choose among a variety of options. These options can include performance measurements, expense parameters, fund investment objective choices and length of management service. Customized screens allow you the freedom to find funds based on your individual objectives.

Many of the Web sites mentioned above offer do-it-yourself screens. These tools vary in usefulness, depending on what criteria you're seeking. Many sites, such as NAIC's Mutual Fund Resource Center, Standard and Poors, and Morningstar, deliver superior screening capability to paying members.

When screening for funds, be careful not to set your parameters too strictly, as this will result in few or no funds meeting your criteria. NAIC criteria are strict, but with a good screening tool you can find funds that may meet your needs after a full Stock Fund Check List analysis.

One variable that will screen out a number of stock funds is to seek funds that beat the S&P 500 or a comparable market index during three, five and 10-year periods. This will narrow the field considerably, and give you a group of candidates that you can then subject to the full NAIC analysis in the Stock Fund Check List.

Below are listed the three, five, 10 and 15-year annualized total return figures for the S&P 500, a benchmark index for large-cap companies. While the S&P 500 isn't the entire stock market, it is useful to see what long-term returns have been for this index.

Web sites, Web site addresses and particular offerings change frequently. At the time of this book's publication, the Web sites listed below offered screening capabilities:

- NAIC Mutual Fund Education and Resource Center: www.better-investing.org/funds

- Morningstar: www.morningstar.com

- Quicken: www.quicken.com

- Business Week: www.businessweek.com

- MSN Money Central: www.moneycentral.msn.com

- Smart Money: www.smartmoney.com

- CBS MarketWatch: www.cbsmarketwatch.com

- Yahoo Finance: finance.yahoo.com

### FIGURE 7.5: S&P 500 RETURNS

| Period | Total Return |
|--------|--------------|
| 3 Years | −11.43% |
| 5 Years | 2.48% |
| 10 Years | 10.08% |

As of August 31, 2003

# Stock Fund Tools

## Building Your Toolbox

We've covered the basics, and now it's time to learn how to use NAIC's mutual fund analysis tools. These tools free you from the mountains of information available about funds so you can focus on their key elements. Three tools — the Stock Fund Check List, the Stock Fund Comparison Guide and the Stock Fund Trend Report — enable you to find, compare and track stock mutual funds to meet your investing needs.

## Stock Fund Check List

## Stock Fund Comparison Guide

## Stock Fund Trend Report

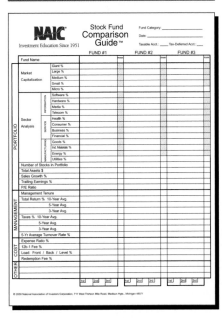

The **Stock Fund Check List** is the cornerstone of the NAIC mutual fund education program. It captures the most vital information about a mutual fund on an easy-to-understand form. This tool focuses on a fund's portfolio, management, performance and costs. Using this information, you cannot only evaluate a fund's past history, but also decide if it will help you meet your investing needs and objectives.

The **Stock Fund Comparison Guide** allows you to compare funds to one another, emphasizing criteria that are most important to you. Using the Comparison Guide, which is built around the same key elements as the Check List, you can compare similar or dissimilar funds to each other. The form places funds on a level footing so you can decide which one will best suit your investing needs.

The **Stock Fund Trend Report** is a tool used after you've purchased a fund. With it, you can follow a fund's key elements over time to see if it still is the same superior fund that you initially purchased.

# Stock Fund Check List— Title Block

## Investment Analysis

The Stock Fund Check List provides an easy way to evaluate a stock fund. The tool focuses on a fund's key elements, beginning with the basic information about a fund and continuing on to its portfolio, management and costs.

The Check List begins with the title block. The first step in fund analysis involves gathering basic information about a fund. With this information in hand, you can proceed to evaluate it as a potential investment.

## Title Block

**STOCK FUND**

# Check List ™

| | |
|---|---|
| Ⓐ Fund Name: | _Dreyfus Appreciation_ |
| Ⓑ Ticker Symbol: | _DGAGX_ |
| Ⓒ Category: | _Large Blend_ |
| Ⓓ Minimum Purchase($): _2500.00_ | Ⓔ Addt'l($): _100.00_ |
| Ⓕ Min Auto Inv Plan($): _100.00_ | Ⓖ Addt'l($): _100.00_ |
| Ⓗ IRA($): _750.00_ | |
| Ⓘ Data Reference: _Morningstar_ | Ⓙ Page No. _____ |
| Ⓚ Current NAV($): _34.59_ | |
| Ⓛ Total Assets($): _3427 (m)_ | |
| M. Taxable: _____ | N. Tax-Deferred: _____ |

## Overview

The Stock Fund Check List is the cornerstone of the NAIC mutual fund education program. This two-sided form has five sections:

- Title Block

- Fund Portfolio Characteristics

- Fund Management Characteristics

- Cost Considerations

- Review

This chapter introduces this key tool and covers the title block portion. Inside the back cover is a foldout page that includes the completed front and back sides of the Stock Fund Check List and two keyed Morningstar reports for Dreyfus Appreciation. We will also reference the Morningstar Overview sheet for the Large

Blend Stock Fund category found in Chapter 7 on page 59.

The Morningstar report, shown twice, is color keyed with numbers and letters from the various sections of the Check List. We did this so you can see where to find the data on the Morningstar report that you need to complete both sides of the Check List. Reference these pages as you work your way through this tool.

In Chapters 8 through 11, we will walk you through each section of the Check List. As we move to a new section a picture of that part of the form is shown, so you can see it while you read the description of the section.

This detailed walk-through of the Check List—and the other fund forms—is provided so that you can familiarize yourself with the material on

the Morningstar report and the Check List before you attempt to complete a Check List on your own. After carefully reading through each section of the completed Check List and becoming familiar with the related material on the Morningstar report, it will be much easier for you to complete a form on your own.

The example fund is Dreyfus Appreciation, categorized by Morningstar as a large blend stock fund. Dreyfus Appreciation is only used as an example in this handbook and no investment recommendation is intended.

The Stock Fund Check List is a snapshot in time of a fund's portfolio, management, performance and costs. By analyzing a fund you can determine if it meets your investment objectives. When

**(A) Fund Name:** _Dreyfus Appreciation_
**(B) Ticker Symbol:** _DGAGX_
**(C) Category:** _Large Blend_
**(D) Minimum Purchase($):** _2500.00_    **(E) Addt'l($):** _100.00_
**(F) Min Auto Inv Plan($):** _100.00_    **(G) Addt'l($):** _100.00_
**(H) IRA($):** _750.00_
**(I) Data Reference:** _Morningstar_    **(J) Page No.** _____
**(K) Current NAV($):** _34.59_
**(L) Total Assets($):** _3427 (m)_
**M. Taxable:** _____    **N. Tax-Deferred:** _____

The title block begins with the fund's name and ticker symbol. While many newspapers list a fund by an abbreviation of its name, Web sites and some magazines list a fund by its ticker symbol.

## Category

Morningstar divides the fund universe into nine categories based on a fund's style and market capitalization. A fund falls into one of three style categories: growth, value and blend, which are fully described in Chapter 5. Market capitalization refers to the size of the companies in a fund's portfolio.

Dreyfus Appreciation is a large blend fund, according to Morningstar. This means that the fund's portfolio is composed of mainly large-sized companies that fall, on average, in between the growth and value styles.

you sit down to complete a Check List, you'll need a blank Check List form, the subject fund's Morningstar report, a pencil or pen, a calculator and the fund's prospectus.

Under normal circumstances, you could find a copy of this report on Dreyfus Appreciation in back copies of *Morningstar Mutual Funds*. However, because Morningstar changed a number of components on its report in July 2002, we used a Morningstar report from the Morningstar Web site (www.morningstar.com) that was produced at a different time from the reports in the notebook. We did this so that this book could be published in a timely manner while reflecting the information on the updated Morningstar report.

Some investors start a file on each fund they are interested in, containing their completed Check List, the fund's Morningstar report, the fund's prospectus, any other important information such as

the fund's annual report, and any notes. If you decide to purchase a fund, consider jotting down some notes about why you chose it. You can refer to these notes in the future when you periodically update your fund study using the Stock Fund Trend Report.

### Fund Name & Ticker Symbol

The first step in fund analysis is an examination of certain basic information about a particular fund. Above is the completed title block for the Dreyfus Appreciation Fund.

**(A) Fund Name:** _Dreyfus Appreciation_
**(B) Ticker Symbol:** _DGAGX_
**(C) Category:** _Large Blend_
**(D) Minimum Purchase($):** _2500.00_    **(E) Addt'l($):** _100.00_
**(F) Min Auto Inv Plan($):** _100.00_    **(G) Addt'l($):** _100.00_
**(H) IRA($):** _750.00_
**(I) Data Reference:** _Morningstar_    **(J) Page No.** _____
**(K) Current NAV($):** _34.59_
**(L) Total Assets($):** _3427 (m)_
**M. Taxable:** _____    **N. Tax-Deferred:** _____

Ⓐ Fund Name: _Dreyfus Appreciation_
Ⓑ Ticker Symbol: _DGAGX_
Ⓒ Category: _Large Blend_
Ⓓ Minimum Purchase($): _2500.00_   Ⓔ Addt'l($): _100.00_
Ⓕ Min Auto Inv Plan($): _100.00_    Ⓖ Addt'l($): _100.00_
Ⓗ IRA($): _750.00_
Ⓘ Data Reference: _Morningstar_    Ⓙ Page No. _____
Ⓚ Current NAV($): _34.59_
Ⓛ Total Assets($): _3427 (m)_
M. Taxable: _____    N. Tax-Deferred: _____

It is not wise to rely on these categories alone when deciding on the right funds to meet your investing needs. You need to dig further to determine just how your money will be invested. We'll give this a closer look in the coming chapters.

## Minimum Purchase Amounts

The minimum purchase amount is the smallest amount of money a fund will accept to open a new account. Many investors allocate a certain sum for the purchase of fund shares. By looking at a fund's minimum purchase requirements at the beginning of your analysis, you eliminate funds with larger requirements than you can afford.

For investors who don't have the $2,500 minimum purchase amount, Dreyfus offers an automatic purchase plan, which allows you to invest a smaller amount upfront, while assuring the fund company that additional share purchases will follow.

## Data Reference, Page Number & NAV

The data reference portion of the title block asks you for your data source. This Check List uses Morningstar data.

The page number is normally listed at the bottom of the Morningstar report and is included for future reference. The page number is not included in the Dreyfus Appreciation report used in this book because it comes from the Morningstar Web site rather than the Morningstar Mutual Fund notebook.

Fill in a fund's net asset value at the time of your fund analysis. Current net asset value information is available in many newspapers and financial Web sites. We have used the NAV directly from the Morningstar report so as not to be confusing.

Ⓐ Fund Name: _Dreyfus Appreciation_
Ⓑ Ticker Symbol: _DGAGX_
Ⓒ Category: _Large Blend_
Ⓓ Minimum Purchase($): _2500.00_   Ⓔ Addt'l($): _100.00_
Ⓕ Min Auto Inv Plan($): _100.00_    Ⓖ Addt'l($): _100.00_
Ⓗ IRA($): _750.00_
Ⓘ Data Reference: _Morningstar_    Ⓙ Page No. _____
Ⓚ Current NAV($): _34.59_
Ⓛ Total Assets($): _3427 (m)_
M. Taxable: _____    N. Tax-Deferred: _____

## Total Assets

Morningstar lists fund total assets last in the annual data section, just below the turnover rate. This number represents the total amount of money invested in a fund by investors.

Fund asset flow affects fund management in several ways. When assets flood into a fund, management is forced to buy stock, as cash by law must be quickly invested.

When shareholders flee a fund, a manager may be forced to sell securities to raise cash to pay them off, and some of these may be sold at a loss. This situation also increases fund portfolio turnover, both of which can impact tax efficiency.

(A) Fund Name: _Dreyfus Appreciation_

(B) Ticker Symbol: _DGAGX_

(C) Category: _Large Blend_

(D) Minimum Purchase($): _2500.00_   (E) Addt'l($): _100.00_

(F) Min Auto Inv Plan($): _100.00_   (G) Addt'l($): _100.00_

(H) IRA($): _750.00_

(I) Data Reference: _Morningstar_   (J) Page No. _____

(K) Current NAV($): _34.59_

(L) Total Assets($): _3427 (m)_

M. Taxable: _____   N. Tax-Deferred: _____

Portfolio turnover is a rough measurement of how often a manager buys and sells stock in a fund portfolio. Tax efficiency is a measure of whether a particular fund impacts investors negatively or positively in terms of the amount of taxes they must pay on their fund's gains. We'll discuss this further in Chapter 10.

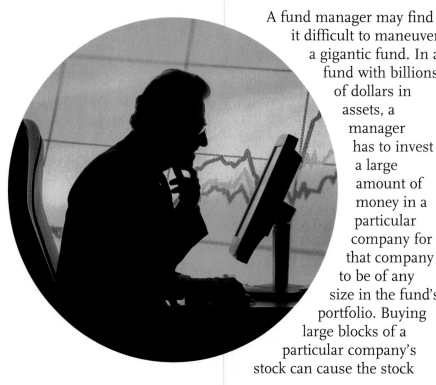

A fund manager may find it difficult to maneuver a gigantic fund. In a fund with billions of dollars in assets, a manager has to invest a large amount of money in a particular company for that company to be of any size in the fund's portfolio. Buying large blocks of a particular company's stock can cause the stock

price to rise, costing the fund more in brokerage fees and a lower potential total return.

Large funds, unless headed by an extremely able manager, tend to perform closer to market averages than smaller funds. Keep an eye on your fund's asset size. Compare it to the average asset size of the funds in the same category on the Morningstar overview sheet.

As of June 2002, Dreyfus Appreciation held $3.25 billion in investor's assets. Looking at the Morningstar report, you can see that the fund's assets took a big jump between 1996 and 1998, when they more than quadrupled. While some of this growth in assets was due to increased investor interest in the fund, some of it was due to the inflation of stock values during the bull market of the mid to late 1990s.

Dreyfus Appreciation is quite a bit larger than its average peer, which has assets of $794.1 million as of March 2002, according to Morningstar. However, compared to some of its largest peers – Fidelity Magellan and Vanguard 500 Index – it doesn't seem so big. Dreyfus Appreciation's Manager, Fayez Sarofim, appears to manage the fund well regardless of its current size.

## Tax Status

Before selecting a fund for investment, you usually have a pretty good idea whether the fund will be in a taxable account or a tax deferred account. In February 2003 President Bush proposed sweeping changes to retirement and college savings plans. The fate of those proposals had not been decided when this book went to press. Consult with your tax advisor regarding the best vehicles for you to save for retirement and college education costs.

Indicate in this area of the Check List which type of account you plan to hold your fund shares in. For a taxable account, keep in mind that you will pay taxes on any dividends and capital gains issued by the fund. Because taxes affect your fund's returns, carefully examine a fund's tax efficiency before buying shares in a fund for a taxable account. However, if your fund shares are in a tax-deferred account, taxes won't be an issue until a later date or not at all, so you can ignore a fund's tax efficiency.

President Bush also proposed a plan to eliminate the taxes that individual investors pay on dividends. The fate of this proposal had not been determined as this book went to press. If this proposal should pass in Congress and be signed by the President, the information in this book regarding the tax treatment of dividends, the advantages of owning dividend producing stock funds in taxable accounts and tax efficiency may not be accurate. Check with your tax adviser regarding these issues.

(A) Fund Name: _Dreyfus Appreciation_

(B) Ticker Symbol: _DGAGX_

(C) Category: _Large Blend_

(D) Minimum Purchase($): _2500.00_    (E) Addt'l($): _100.00_

(F) Min Auto Inv Plan($): _100.00_    (G) Addt'l($): _100.00_

(H) IRA($): _750.00_

(I) Data Reference: _Morningstar_    (J) Page No. _____

(K) Current NAV($): _34.59_

(L) Total Assets($): _3427 (m)_

M. Taxable: _____    N. Tax-Deferred: _____

# Stock Fund Check List— Portfolio

## Investment Analysis

The true analysis work of the Check List begins with a fund's portfolio characteristics. Before investing in a fund, you need to know what type of fund it is, how the fund invests and what it invests in.

We'll guide you step-by-step through these important characteristics and show you where to locate them on the fund's Morningstar report. The fund's investment objective states how the fund plans to invest your money. Other statistics help you verify whether the fund manager is truly carrying out the fund objective.

Investment Objective

Portfolio Composition

Market Capitalization

Holdings

Sector Analysis

Sales Growth

Trailing Earnings

Price/Earnings

## Fund Portfolio Characteristics

An examination of a fund's portfolio characteristics helps you understand more about a prospective investment. In this section of the Check List, we'll take you through each line item, defining terms and illustrating them with our example fund, Dreyfus Appreciation.

### Stated Investment Objective

A fund's stated investment objective—found in its prospectus—in Section 1A tells you a fund's investing strategies, and what types of companies the manager purchases to reach that objective. Section 1A refers to the area of the Check List where you can find this information. While Morningstar formerly included a fund's prospectus objective in its reports, it recently replaced that section with one entitled "Manager Strategy."

This section of the report discusses how fund management carries out the fund's objective, instead of including the objective itself. To determine a fund's objective, either download its prospectus from the fund family Web site or request a copy by mail. You can also call

the fund company and ask a customer services representative. A fund's objective is something you must know in order to fully analyze a fund.

According to our example fund's prospectus, "the fund seeks long-term capital growth consistent with the preservation of capital. Its secondary goal is current income." Capital growth means that investors should expect to see the value of their investment rise based on an increase in the stock prices of the companies in the fund's portfolio. To achieve the fund's objective, management invests primarily in large growth companies and employs a buy-and-hold philosophy.

Note that fund prospectuses may call the investment objective section by different names. For example, Dreyfus titles the objective section "Goal/Approach." Make sure a fund's investment objective matches up with your investing objectives.

---

**1. FUND INVESTMENT CHARACTERISTICS**

(A) Stated Investment Objective: <u>Long-Term Capital Growth</u>
- What are the fund's investment criteria & investment policies?

---

### Portfolio Composition

The portfolio composition data in Section 1B, which you can find on the Morningstar report keyed as 1B on the bottom right-hand side of the page, details how the fund's assets are divided between cash, stock, bonds, other and foreign stocks. When you invest in a stock fund, expect to see a minimum of 90 percent of the fund's assets invested in stock. Dreyfus Appreciation easily exceeds this rule-of-thumb, with 94.7 percent of its assets in stock.

At this time, Dreyfus Appreciation doesn't invest in bonds. A small portion of fund assets— 1.8 percent—is invested in other securities. Other securities include preferred stock, convertible bonds and options. Preferred stock is a class of stock ownership with dividends payable before common stock dividends. Convertible bonds are a type of bond that can be converted into company stock at a certain point. Options offer a buyer the

---

(B) Portfolio Composition:

| Cash | Stocks | Bonds | Other | Foreign |
|---|---|---|---|---|
| 3.4 % | 94.7 % | -0- % | 1.8 % | 4.7 % |

- A cash holding of 20% or more may indicate the manager is trying to time the market...very risky!

right to purchase or sell a security at a certain price.

Dreyfus Appreciation invests 4.7 percent of its stock investments in foreign companies. Many large-cap funds invest a portion of their holdings in large, stable foreign companies.

## Market Capitalization

The market capitalization figures in Section 1C show the percentage of different-sized companies in a fund's portfolio. A company's market capitalization is determined by multiplying its share price by its number of shares outstanding. Morningstar breaks down companies into five market capitalization categories:

- The giant category is the largest 1 percent of U.S. companies.
- The large category is the next 4 percent of U.S. companies.
- The medium category is the next 15 percent of U.S. companies.
- The small category is the next 30 percent of U.S. companies.
- The micro category is the bottom 50 percent of U.S. companies.

True to its investment objective, our example fund invests 99 percent of its stock allocation in giant and large companies.

| C Market Capitalization: | Giant | Large | Medium | Small | Micro |
|---|---|---|---|---|---|
| | 80.2 % | 18.8 % | 1.0 % | -0- % | -0- % |

• Are the assets concentrated according to the stated objective?

It is important to check the actual market cap breakdown of a fund's portfolio to truly determine if a fund invests as the category it is placed in suggests. There are some funds that invest across the entire range of market caps but are placed in a category that doesn't really depict that fact. You may come across a fund that is categorized as a small cap fund yet when you take a closer look at its portfolio you find that it invests 30 or 40 percent of its assets in mid to large-cap companies.

A fund's true portfolio composition in relation to its categorization by a fund data company can dramatically affect how a fund fits into your investing objective. By carefully identifying a fund's market capitalization before you invest, you will be able to diversify your assets with much more certainty than solely relying on its stated category.

## Total Holdings

The total number of holdings in Section 1D for Dreyfus Appreciation is 50. Generally speaking, the more companies held by a fund, the more difficult it will be for a fund to outperform the market as a whole.

While a fund with a concentrated portfolio that holds roughly 50 companies or less has a better chance of outperforming the market, there is more risk that it will under-perform the market as well. Concentrated funds tend to be more volatile than more diversified funds.

How diverse or concentrated a fund is depends also on how many assets it holds. In the case of Dreyfus Appreciation, the fund's $3.25 billion in assets are spread over 50 holdings. This means that the fund takes very substantial positions in the companies in its portfolio.

For example, the fund owns $220.6 million in Pfizer stock, which makes up 6.77 percent of the fund's portfolio. Pfizer, like a vast majority of the holdings of the fund, is a very large company with large amounts of stock available for purchase by investors.

A large blend fund such as Dreyfus Appreciation can easily invest large amounts of money in such companies. Such may not be the case for funds that specialize in small or medium-sized companies.

| D Total # of holdings: | 50 |
|---|---|

## Portfolio Analysis Date

A fund's portfolio analysis date noted in Section 1E is when the fund reported its portfolio holdings to the public. This Morningstar report includes information on Dreyfus Appreciation's portfolio as of March 31, 2002.

This means that all the data related to the portfolio— including the portfolio holdings, investment style analysis, sector weightings, portfolio composition and market capitalization—is based on what the portfolio owned at the end of March, 2002.

In 2002 and earlier, the Securities & Exchange Commission required disclosure of fund portfolio holdings twice a year. The SEC also allowed fund companies a full two months to release their holdings after the reporting period is ended. The SEC was considering requiring fund companies to report holdings quarterly in early 2003, but had not made a final decision when this book went to press.

Because of this lag time, portfolio information in Morningstar reports is usually fairly dated. In fact, by the time

> E Portfolio Analysis Date: _3/31/02_

Morningstar publishes its report, data could be up to eight months old. Morningstar's five-month reporting cycle adds an additional delay, so by the time you read a fund report the data can be more than a year old.

If you do want more up-to-date information, check a fund company's Web site. Some funds update information more frequently there and provide other useful information on their funds.

## MEET THE EXPERT: KEN JANKE

*Ken Janke, currently serves as chairman of NAIC and co-manages the NAIC Growth Fund, a closed-end fund.*

### Q. What is the major difference between NAIC's investing practices and other investing practices?

We are much more long-term oriented. NAIC investors hold onto a company for a number of years, as long as the company continues to do well, no matter what the stock price is doing.

### Q: What common mistakes can fund investors avoid?

As long-term investors, NAIC members shouldn't be too concerned with short-term market moves. Don't sell a company just because its stock price has gone down!

Many fund investors simply look at last year's performance numbers when they pick a fund. You need to look at five or 10 years of performance, not just the most recent year.

Don't chase the hot funds. Look how wrong investors went who invested in the top performing funds from 1999—those were all technology funds, and they fell hard in 2000, 2001 and 2002. You can lose a lot of money by emphasizing short-term performance.

### Q: What are the differences between being an individual investor and a fund manager using the same NAIC investing philosophy?

The approach I use to look at companies hasn't changed—I invest the same way as a fund manager as I do as an individual investor. But as a fund manager, I am a custodian of other people's money, and it's easy to second-guess myself, in terms of trying to buy a good company at the lowest possible price. I'm personally accountable for the performance of the Growth Fund, and I have people and their families depending on how well we do here.

## Top 10 Holdings

Dreyfus Appreciation's top 10 holdings, noted in Section 1F, comprise 43.86 percent of the fund's entire portfolio. It is these top 10 holdings that the fund manager is relying on to drive a large portion of the fund's returns.

As we mentioned earlier, Dreyfus Appreciation is a fairly concentrated or focused fund in that it invests in a fairly small number of companies. If these companies prosper and perform well, the fund will do likewise. If they perform poorly and their stock prices fall, the fund's net asset value will fall as well.

The largest holding is Pfizer, the giant pharmaceutical company. While Pfizer makes up a larger portion of the portfolio than any other holding, this percentage isn't significantly larger than the next holding, Johnson &

Johnson at 5.28 percent of assets, another pharmaceutical and health care company.

Watch to see if one holding makes up a far greater percentage of the fund's assets than the rest. If one does, does this make you uncomfortable? When one holding is overly large, you may not be as diversified as you had previously thought.

This could be a holding that has been very successful that the manager purchased many years ago. Such a large holding can make a fund more volatile. Are the fund's assets concentrated too much in just these top 10 holdings?

When looking at a fund's top 10 holdings, see if any of them

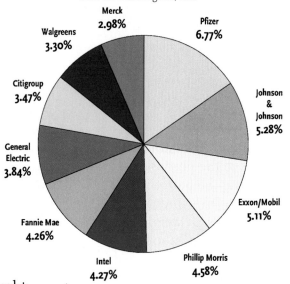

*Figure 9.1: Dreyfus Appreciation's top 10 holdings by percentage of assets in the total portfolio:*
Source: Morningstar, Inc.

Merck 2.98%
Pfizer 6.77%
Walgreens 3.30%
Citigroup 3.47%
Johnson & Johnson 5.28%
General Electric 3.84%
Exxon/Mobil 5.11%
Fannie Mae 4.26%
Phillip Morris 4.58%
Intel 4.27%

are familiar. With a large-cap blend fund such as Dreyfus Appreciation, it is likely you will have heard of at least a few of the companies. This may not be the case with funds that focus on smaller or on international companies. You need to decide if being familiar with the companies in a fund's portfolio is important.

Farther down the top 10 list is another pharmaceutical company, Merck. Merck is the tenth holding and makes up 2.98 percent of the portfolio. So three companies in the health care sector—Pfizer, Johnson & Johnson and Merck—make up 15.03 percent of the entire portfolio. Think about the implications of this for your investing strategy.

You may be investing in a fund with more than 100 holdings

F Top 10 Company Holdings:

| No. | Company Name | Sector | Assets |
|-----|--------------|--------|--------|
| 1 | Pfizer | Health | 6.77 % |
| 2 | Johnson & Johnson | Health | 5.28 % |
| 3 | Exxon Mobil | Energy | 5.11 % |
| 4 | Philip Morris | Goods | 4.58 % |
| 5 | Intel | Hardware | 4.27 % |
| 6 | Fannie Mae | Financial | 4.26 % |
| 7 | General Electric | Ind. Materials | 3.84 % |
| 8 | Citigroup | Financial | 3.47 % |
| 9 | Walgreen | Consumer | 3.30 % |
| 10 | Merck | Health | 2.98 % |
| | | | 43.86 % Total |

• Does any one holding make up a far greater percent of assets than the others?

thinking you are amply diversified. But if the fund has a large portion – say 30 or 40 percent – of its assets invested in just the top 10 holdings, are you as diversified as you think? In such a situation, the bottom 10 or 20 holdings will have little impact on the fund's overall performance.

*The pie chart in Figure 9.1 illustrates how the top 10 holdings are divided by percentage of holdings. Dreyfus Appreciation's top 10 holdings include many well-known companies.*

### Sector Analysis

Broadening out our examination of a fund's portfolio, the sector analysis in Section 1G, the last section of the front side of the Check List, analyzes a fund's entire portfolio by market sector. Morningstar divides the stock universe into three super sectors, which include four specific sectors.

The Information Economy encompasses various technology industries; the Service Economy covers a wide variety of service-oriented industries; the Manufacturing Economy includes companies making basic materials and consumer goods and services.

A look at a fund's sector weightings is another way of assessing the diversification of a fund's portfolio. A

## FIGURE 9.2: SECTORS & SUPER SECTORS

### Information Economy:

**SOFTWARE:** companies that design and market computer operating systems and other applications.

**HARDWARE:** companies that manufacture computer hardware, semiconductors and other equipment and components.

**MEDIA:** companies that own and operate television networks and/or provide news and entertainment content.

**TELECOMMUNICATIONS:** companies engaged in either fixed line or wireless communication services.

### Service Economy:

**HEALTH CARE:** covers a varied assortment of health care companies, including pharmaceutical and biotechnology companies, hospitals, medical services and supply companies.

**CONSUMER SERVICES:** retail stores, home builders and suppliers, education companies, personal services, etc.

**BUSINESS SERVICES:** companies that provide advertising, publishing, security, distribution, waste management and business support services, among others.

**FINANCIAL SERVICES:** banks, savings and loans, insurance companies, money management firms, brokers and accountants, among others.

### Manufacturing Economy:

**CONSUMER GOODS:** companies that provide or manufacture a wide variety of goods, including cars, household products, clothes and consumer electronics.

**INDUSTRIAL MATERIALS:** companies involved in defense and aerospace and in producing chemicals and machinery.

**ENERGY:** gas and oil services, oil-related services including drilling, distribution, pipeline and service stations.

**UTILITIES:** gas, electric and water utility companies.

portfolio spread over a few sectors is likely to be more volatile than a portfolio spread over many sectors.

Examining Dreyfus Appreciation's weightings in Morningstar's super sectors, nearly half of the portfolio's

assets are invested in the service economy. The fund has traditionally underweighted technology, which can be seen in the percentage of assets devoted to information services. While this held the fund's performance back in 1998 and 1999, it helped the

---

Ⓖ Portfolio Sector Analysis (%):
Info __17.6__ : Software __2.4__ Hardware __6.3__ Media __3.9__ Telecom __5.1__
Service __47.9__ : Health __19.9__ Consumer __7.3__ Business __0.9__ Financial __19.7__
Manufacturing __34.5__ : Goods __17.7__ Ind Mtrls __6.9__ Energy __9.9__ Utilities __0__

• The fewer number of holdings and sectors that the fund s assets are spread over the greater likelihood for volatility within the portfolio.

fund in 2000 and 2001 when tech stocks sank.

In its top 10 holdings, Dreyfus Appreciation covers seven out of the 12 Morningstar sectors. The fund's entire portfolio is spread over 11 sectors. The only sector that the fund doesn't own stock in is the utility sector. The largest concentration of assets is in the health care services, financial services and manufacturing goods sectors.

It isn't necessary for a fund to own stocks in every sector. Some fund managers favor certain sectors in their stock selection process, while others purchase good companies regardless of their market sector.

By studying the data in the different sections we covered so far, you'll be able to identify how the fund invests and what it invests in. Looking at a fund's sectors, see if the fund focuses on growth sectors, such as the sectors in the information and service super sectors, rather than the cyclical industries that make up the manufacturing sector.

## Sales Growth Rate

Sales growth, recorded in Section 1H of the Check List, is an integral part of the way NAIC investors evaluate growth companies. Morningstar calculates the sales growth of the companies

(H) Sales Growth ___12.0___ %

in the fund's portfolio during the past four years, weighting the companies by the size of their position in the portfolio.

Because companies must sell goods or services to produce earnings for shareholders, a fund's portfolio sales growth rate is an important indicator of how the companies have grown their businesses in the past. While past growth isn't always a reliable predictor of future growth, companies that have grown their businesses steadily in the past are more likely to do so in the future.

Dreyfus Appreciation's average portfolio sales growth rate is 12 percent. Because the fund is mainly composed of large companies, the portfolio sales growth rate will be lower than funds with portfolios of smaller companies.

In general, look for growth about 7 percent per year for a giant company to 12 percent or more for a small company. Aim for an average growth rate of 15 percent for your entire portfolio.

Sales growth rates also vary depending upon the underlying economy. In times of economic expansion, superior growth companies will experience faster growth. During recessions, even the best growth companies may

find their growth slowing significantly. Some may not even grow at all if conditions are particularly difficult. Keep these variables in mind when evaluating a fund's portfolio sales growth rate.

## Trailing Earnings

A fund's trailing earnings growth rate, recorded in Section 1I of the Check List, is a weighted average of the last four years of growth rates for the companies in the fund's portfolio. In general, earnings growth leads to higher stock prices, which leads to an increase in fund net asset value.

Earnings growth should be strong and consistent. This demonstrates that a company's management is able to turn sales and marketing success into steadily growing profits for individual investors. The end result: increased shareholder value.

Dreyfus Appreciation's trailing earnings growth rate is 11 percent. The management of Dreyfus Appreciation seeks companies with strong earnings growth rates.

According to the fund's prospectus, "The fund focuses on 'blue chip' companies with total market values of more than $5 billion. These

(I) Trailing Earnings ___11.0___ %

established companies have demonstrated patterns of profitability, strong balance sheets, an expanding global presence and the potential to achieve predictable above-average earnings growth.

"In choosing stocks, the fund looks for growth companies. The fund first identifies economic sectors that it believes will expand over the next five years or longer. Using fundamental analysis, it then seeks companies within these sectors that have proven track records and dominant positions in their industries."

## Price/Earnings

The average price-to-earnings ratio (P/E) recorded in Section 1J for a fund is the weighted average P/E ratio of all of the stocks in the fund's portfolio. A company's P/E ratio is its price divided by its earnings. Weighted means that the companies making up the larger positions in the fund portfolio have more influence on the calculation than the smaller positions do.

When Morningstar revised the portfolio statistics section of the stock fund reports, it changed the average P/E measurement from a historical measurement to a projected measurement. The P/E ratio "represents the amount

| J | Price/Earnings Ratio __25.0__ |

investors are paying for each dollar of expected earnings per share," according to the *Morningstar Mutual Funds* Resource Guide Addendum. The projected earnings are derived from leading analysts' estimates as provided by Zacks (www.zacks.com), an investment research firm.

We use the price projected earnings ratio for a fund's portfolio because Morningstar provides no other P/E measurement on their stock fund report. Morningstar also includes a projected earnings growth rate measurement, but we elected to use the trailing earnings growth rate measurement because it is an actual figure, not one based on analysts' estimates. Analysts tend to be optimistic, and may be swayed by other relationships that their employing firm has with the companies they are covering. Hence, analysts' estimates are not without bias.

An individual company's P/E ratio is frequently used to determine if that company is a good value at a particular price. Companies with high growth rates generally have high P/E ratios.

If a company is growing fast or has recently gone public, a rising P/E ratio may mean that investors have high expectations for the company. Investors may award

companies that have consistently increased sales and earnings rates quite high P/E ratios.

Higher growth rates generally suggest higher P/E ratios. Well-managed growth companies generally sport higher P/E ratios than other types of companies. A high P/E usually indicates that the market is willing to pay a higher price to own a stake in a business, while a low P/E indicates that the market has less confidence that a company's earnings will increase.

Dreyfus Appreciation's P/E ratio is 25, slightly higher than the P/E ratio of the S&P 500 index. As of Oct. 31, 2002, the average P/E ratio of the S&P 500 Index was 22. During the 30-year period from Oct. 1969 to Oct. 1999, the average P/E for the Index was 14.7, with a high of 35.4 and a low of 6.6. In Oct. 1999 the P/E ratio was 33.2.

# Stock Fund Check List— Management

## Focus on Quality

Now that you know how the fund invests and what it invests in, turn your attention to management quality. As an informed investor, your goal is to buy the highest quality fund at the lowest possible cost.

Judge management by its accomplishments, not by market hype. Examine past performance and tenure. Analyze tax efficiency and portfolio turnover rates. With concrete evidence in hand, decide if fund management makes the grade.

Fund Manager

Management Record

Net Asset Value

Total Return

Tax Analysis

Turnover

## Overview

We can't stress this enough; when you buy shares in a fund, you pay a portfolio manager to invest your money. While portfolio managers use differing money management techniques, their results are quantifiable. Look at a manager's track record.

Besides performance numbers, an examination of a fund's turnover and tax efficiency tells you how the fund is managed. Each piece of the puzzle adds up to an overall picture. With a comprehensive assessment of the fund in hand, you can decide if it's right for you.

## Fund Management Characteristics

A fund's management quality, track record and longevity are some of the most important variables in assessing a fund's soundness. You can measure a fund manager's past record by assessing performance using the Check List.

## Fund Manager & Date Fund Started

Section 2A1 of the Stock Fund Check List asks for the fund manager's name and length of service with the fund.

---

| 2. FUND MANAGEMENT CHARACTERISTICS |
| --- |
| (A)(1) Fund Manager: _Fayez Sarofim_   Years: __12__   (2) Date Fund Started: _1/84_ |
| • If manager has been with the fund less than five years, give name of previous fund managed, length of service and investment style: _____ |

---

The manager of the Dreyfus Appreciation Fund is Fayez Sarofim, who has been with the fund for 12 years as a sub-adviser for Dreyfus.

Sarofim's money management experience stretches back to 1958, when he founded the Houston-based Fayez Sarofim & Co. A sub-adviser is a management company chosen from outside the fund company. Sub-advisers are fairly common in the fund industry.

It makes little difference to you as a fund investor whether the fund is directly managed or sub-advised, as long as the sub-adviser has at least five years of experience running the fund. If you find a sub-adviser or manager has been with the fund for fewer than five years, in most cases you can stop your analysis at this point and turn to another fund.

Why does NAIC believe that managers must have a minimum of five years of experience? Fund managers who lack five years of experience at the same fund bear little responsibility for a fund's long-term performance.

When you buy shares in an actively managed fund, you are making an investment in the fund manager 's expertise in piloting a particular fund. Why invest your hard-earned money in someone with little experience?

An exception to this rule is when a long-time assistant manager takes over for a departing head manager. If these two have worked closely together, and the former assistant plans to continue investing in the same way as the former head manager, the fund's makeup isn't likely to change much.

In Section 2A2 is the date the fund began operations. Dreyfus Appreciation started in January 1984.

## Management Record

In Section 2B of the Check List, we evaluate a fund's past performance, looking at its net asset value, annual total return, total return against the S&P 500 index and total return compared to another market benchmark.

| B Management Record: | | Initial Year | | | | | | | | | |
|---|---|---|---|---|---|---|---|---|---|---|---|
| ① Current Management Period: enter all years | | 1992 | 1993 | 1994 | 1995 | 1996 | 1997 | 1998 | 1999 | 2000 | 2001 |
| ② Net Asset Value (NAV): | | 15.15 | 14.92 | 15.17 | 20.55 | 25.58 | 32.38 | 42.07 | 45.73 | 42.94 | 38.02 |
| ③ Annual Total Return%-Subject Fund: | | 4.28 | 0.71 | 3.62 | 37.89 | 25.67 | 27.86 | 30.85 | 9.97 | 1.80 | -10.75 |
| ④ +/- Total Return% - S&P 500 Index: | | -3.34 | -9.35 | 2.31 | 0.35 | 2.73 | -5.50 | 2.27 | -11.07 | 10.90 | 1.13 |
| ⑤ +/- Total Return% - Other Index: | | -3.37 | -9.13 | 3.17 | 0.29 | 3.51 | -5.17 | 2.22 | -11.86 | 12.76 | 2.02 |

• Has the current manager consistently out-performed the index?

## Current Management Period

A fund's current management period, shown in Section 2B1, includes only the years that current management has been in charge. Portfolio managers should only get credit for their own accomplishments, not those of past management.

For example, if a manager has been with a fund for six years, include only the last six years of information in your analysis. Don't use the full number of years listed in the Morningstar report.

## Net Asset Value

A fund's net asset value, shown in Section 2B2, is the value of all the securities in the portfolio, less fund expenses and liabilities and then divided by the number of fund shares outstanding.

While fund net asset value doesn't reflect a fund's total return to shareholders, it does tell you whether fund shares have generally increased in value. Net asset values don't reflect distributions made to shareholders.

The net asset value history for Dreyfus Appreciation shows that the fund has appreciated substantially between 1992

and 2001. The Morningstar report reveals that the fund distributed $3.22 per share to shareholders in 2000 after the fund sold appreciated securities. The amount of that distribution was subtracted from the fund's net asset value, as shareholders received it either in additional shares through a dividend reinvestment program or in cash.

## Annual Total Return

Since you can't rely on net asset value for a complete picture of

a fund's returns, look at a fund's total return percentage as shown in Section 2B3. Total return factors in management fees, administrative expenses, 12b-1 marketing and distribution fees, and other costs automatically deducted from a fund's assets.

*However, Morningstar doesn't adjust total return for sales charges and distribution fees. If such fees are imposed on a fund, they can substantially cut into its total return. Dreyfus Appreciation doesn't have a load. In Figure 10.1, see the Dreyfus Appreciation Fund performance peaks and valleys.*

Morningstar provides 11 years and three months of returns for Dreyfus Appreciation. Entering the data on the form, you see

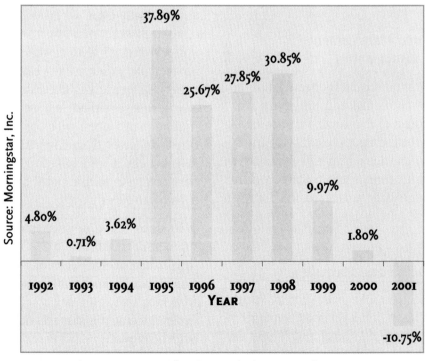

*Figure 10.1: Dreyfus Appreciation's Total Return*

| B | Management Record: | Initial Year | | | | | | | | | |
|---|---|---|---|---|---|---|---|---|---|---|---|
| 1 | Current Management Period: enter all years | 1992 | 1993 | 1994 | 1995 | 1996 | 1997 | 1998 | 1999 | 2000 | 2001 |
| 2 | Net Asset Value (NAV): | 15.15 | 14.92 | 15.17 | 20.55 | 25.58 | 32.38 | 42.07 | 45.73 | 42.94 | 38.02 |
| 3 | Annual Total Return%-Subject Fund: | 4.28 | 0.71 | 3.62 | 37.89 | 25.67 | 27.86 | 30.85 | 9.97 | 1.80 | -10.75 |
| 4 | +/- Total Return% - S&P 500 Index: | -3.34 | -9.35 | 2.31 | 0.35 | 2.73 | -5.50 | 2.27 | -11.07 | 10.90 | 1.13 |
| 5 | +/- Total Return% - Other Index: | -3.37 | -9.13 | 3.17 | 0.29 | 3.51 | -5.17 | 2.22 | -11.86 | 12.76 | 2.02 |

• Has the current manager consistently out-performed the index?

that the fund has had its ups and downs. In 1995, it notched a total return of 37.89 percent, while it lost 10.75 percent in 2001. It's a good idea to use this section to assess your tolerance for those ups and downs. Are you comfortable with a possible yearly loss of 10 percent or more? Investing in stock and stock funds carries risk, and long-term investors should be prepared to endure bear markets just as they profit from bull markets.

Such peaks and valleys are common, and are one reason why we don't totally rely on yearly total return figures to tell the whole story behind a fund's performance. In Section 2C — Total Return and Tax Analysis —we look at a fund's average total return for three, five and 10 years. This view smoothes out the highs and lows and gives us a couple of longer-term numbers to examine.

## Total Return vs. The S&P 500 Index

Comparing a fund's total return to a well-established market benchmark will quickly sort out the wheat from the chaff. While you can't expect your fund to outperform the index every year, it should demonstrate superiority over a period of years.

Examine a fund's record on a year-to-year basis against the index, as we do in Section 2B4. Dreyfus Appreciation, like virtually all actively managed funds, has a mixed record in comparison to the S&P 500. Our analysis shows that it beat the index six years out of 10.

Look also at the three, five and 10-year total return numbers verses the index as seen in the Performance section of the Morningstar report. Dreyfus Appreciation beat the S&P 500 index in all three time periods. The margin is most pronounced during the three-year annual total return period, when the fund beat the index by 3.93 percent.

Keep in mind that when we refer to three, five and 10-year total return figures we are speaking of yearly averages. For example, the Dreyfus Appreciation Fund's five-year total return of 4.78 percent

means that the fund's average return over five years was 4.78 percent, not that it was 4.78 percent each and every one of those individual five years.

Remember there are index funds that will track various segments of the market. If a fund can't outperform a comparable market index during a long period of time, it most likely isn't a superior fund. And why invest your hard-earned money in anything less than a superior fund?

## Total Return vs. Other Index

The Check List provides a second opportunity to compare a fund to a benchmark index in Section 2B5. While the S&P 500 is an acceptable benchmark for Dreyfus Appreciation and many other large-cap blend funds that build their portfolios around big companies, it isn't a good basis of comparison for other types of funds.

The Morningstar report provides a second index comparison. According to the *Morningstar Mutual Funds* Resource Guide, "We also provide a comparison with a secondary, specialized benchmark. Because the S&P 500 index is composed almost entirely of large-cap domestic

| B | Management Record: | Initial Year | | | | | | | | | |
|---|---|---|---|---|---|---|---|---|---|---|---|
| 1 | Current Management Period: enter all years | 1992 | 1993 | 1994 | 1995 | 1996 | 1997 | 1998 | 1999 | 2000 | 2001 |
| 2 | Net Asset Value (NAV): | 15.15 | 14.92 | 15.17 | 20.55 | 25.58 | 32.38 | 42.07 | 45.73 | 42.94 | 38.02 |
| 3 | Annual Total Return%-Subject Fund: | 4.28 | 0.71 | 3.62 | 37.89 | 25.67 | 27.86 | 30.85 | 9.97 | 1.80 | -10.75 |
| 4 | +/- Total Return% - S&P 500 Index: | -3.34 | -9.35 | 2.31 | 0.35 | 2.73 | -5.50 | 2.27 | -11.07 | 10.90 | 1.13 |
| 5 | +/- Total Return% - Other Index: | -3.37 | -9.13 | 3.17 | 0.29 | 3.51 | -5.17 | 2.22 | -11.86 | 12.76 | 2.02 |

• Has the current manager consistently out-performed the index?

stocks, it is a good performance measure for large-cap domestic stock funds and the overall market, but other comparisons are less useful.

"Comparing a foreign stock fund with the S&P 500 index, for example, does not tell the reader how the fund has done relative to foreign stock markets," the Morningstar Guide continues. Morningstar compares the fund's performance with one of fifteen narrower indexes.

In the case of Dreyfus Appreciation, Morningstar

provides a comparison with the Wilshire top 750. According to the Wilshire Web site (www.wilshire.com), the Wilshire 750 is composed of the 750 largest companies in the Wilshire 5000 index, a total stock market index.

A comparison of lines 4 and 5 of Section 2B shows little difference in the returns of Dreyfus Appreciation versus these two indexes. Just as with the S&P 500, the fund outperforms the Wilshire 750 six out of the past 10 years. It's

up to you to decide whether to compare a fund to a second index or to rely on the S&P 500 index comparison.

As with the comparison of individual year returns, you can also examine long-term total returns for three, five and 10-years for the other index. In the case of the Wilshire Large 750, Dreyfus Appreciation beat the index during all three time periods, by slightly larger margins than it beat the S&P 500: 4.34 percent for the three-year period, 1.32 percent

## MEET THE INVESTOR: GARY SIMMS

*Gary Simms, an NAIC Chapter Director with the Heart of Illinois Chapter, teaches a variety of fund classes based on the NAIC fund tools.*

**Q. What is the major difference between NAIC's investing practices and other investing practices?**

NAIC's program works. I believe that long-term investing requires placing my money with growing companies and allowing them to do their thing.

**Q. What common mistakes should fund investors try to avoid?**

They chase last year's hot funds and try to catch the high returns, but wind up losing money when the overvalued fund returns to its more average performance. I always compare my funds to index funds. Heck, my funds are index funds. I don't chase returns anymore.

Don't pay loads. Watch expenses. Eat alphabet soup – don't invest in it. Funds offer Class A, B and C shares, which let you pick the way you'll be overcharged.

**Q: How has the NAIC Mutual Fund Program helped you?**

It lets me do a side-by-side comparison of the funds I'm considering. This is extremely important. There is nothing like it that I know of.

I was taking my first Stock Selection Guide course back in March of 1996 when our instructor handed out a copy of the January 1995 *Better Investing* which had the original mutual fund article by Helen McLane on the Mutual Fund Equity Guide. It had the three main categories: Risk, Return and Cost. These are John Bogle's Eternal Triangle of Investing. I knew I was on to something important. I've used this sheet ever since then. It has evolved since then, but that basic form remains today.

I've been able to buy mutual funds knowing how one fund's return, risk and costs compare to other funds and to the category averages.

| C | Total Return & Tax Analysis: | 3 Yr. | 5Yr. | 10 Yr. |
|---|---|---|---|---|
| | 1. Fund Total Return%: | -5.24 | 4.78 | 11.51 |
| | 2. Fund Tax- Adjusted Return%: | -6.04 | 4.11 | 10.82 |
| | 3. Taxes(%): | .80 | .67 | .69 |

for the five-year period and .44 for the 10-year period.

## Total Return & Tax Analysis

In Section 2C of the Check List, you examine a fund's long-term total return and tax-efficiency.

A fund's long-term total return is extremely significant. While past performance is no guarantee of future results, funds that have performed consistently well for a long period of time in the past are more likely to do so in the future.

All of the total return figures show a fund's average total return for a particular period of time, smoothing out short-term performance gains or declines. For our purposes, the 10-year total return figure carries the most weight as the figure covering the longest period of time. NAIC members buy stocks and funds planning to hold onto them for the long-term, unlike many other investors who plan to quickly sell securities for a quick profit.

The five-year and, in particular, the three-year total return numbers are more short-term. You'll notice that we don't include the one-year total return figure, although it is available from Morningstar, because it is far too short-term in nature.

When available, to get more of a long-term perspective, it's useful to consider the 15-year performance figures that Morningstar includes for a fund, provided that it's been around that long with the current manager—many haven't.

Recent figures show the impact of the bear market of 2000-2002, with five-year total returns dropping to 4.78 percent from a 10-year total return of 11.51 percent, and three-year figures falling into negative territory at −5.24 percent. Keeping all of this in perspective, we see that although the fund's performance doesn't look good in recent years, it still beats the S&P 500 index in terms of three, five and 10-year total return.

It's important to put into perspective a fund's long-term total returns and what the current market cycle is — growth and value can peak at different times. When growth is in favor, most growth funds look good, even ones that aren't particularly well-managed. The same holds true when value funds are in favor for those types of funds.

For fund investors who hold shares in a taxable account, taxes are a major issue. The SEC estimates that the average fund investor holding fund shares in a taxable account loses between 2 and 3 percent of gains to taxes. That can add up over a long period of time, taking a significant bite out of your fund profits.

Section 2C of the Check List provides an analysis of a fund's tax efficiency because of the potential impact of taxes on fund returns.

To figure out how tax efficient a fund is, determine the spread between a fund's tax-adjusted return and its total return for a specific time period. This will give you a number that approximates what percentage of the fund's interest, dividends and capital gains you will pay in taxes. The lower the resulting number, the more tax efficient a fund is; the higher the number, the more tax liability you will incur.

*To get another take on tax efficiency, divide the percentage of taxes by a fund's total return. This shows you what percentage of a fund's total return you would have paid in taxes. Let's zero in on the significance of both numbers in the example in Figure 10.2.*

Fund managers have some control over a fund's tax efficiency. When selling securities for a profit, they can also sell stocks at a loss to offset the gains from profitable securities sales. However, if you seek income through your fund investments, remember that income-oriented funds are by nature tax-inefficient.

Managers can also keep track of their cost basis in the stocks they own, and sell stocks with a higher basis first to keep tax liabilities as low as possible. A cost basis is what it costs a manager to purchase a particular stock.

However, because of the way funds are structured, managers can do only so much to minimize shareholder's tax liabilities. If a fund manager decides to sell an overvalued stock to lock in profits, the fund will book a gain that will be passed on to fund investors. Would it be better for the fund manager to forgo that gain, and risk the stock price falling so that fund investors wouldn't have to pay tax on that gain? No—gains are certainly preferable to losses.

Keep in mind that the current three-year long bear market means that many funds have negative total returns. Even if a fund has greatly outperformed its benchmark, if its total return is negative, this means that an investor who owns shares in that fund lost money. For funds with poor tax efficiency, the investors loses even more money on top of the negative total return.

Here's how it works: say that you own shares in XYZ Blend Fund, which performs exactly the same as the average large blend fund. Your total return for the past three years has been –2.28 percent. This means that you lost 2.28 percent on average off the value of your fund shares each year for that three years. Add the fund's tax-inefficiency on top of that, and your loss actually widens to an average of –4.04 percent, or 1.76 percent more per year.

How is that possible? It's possible because fund companies must distribute all income, dividends and capital gains to their shareholders. XYZ Blend Fund either received interest or dividends or the fund manager produced capital gains by selling appreciated stock. These distributions produced a taxable event for all shareholders who hold shares in taxable accounts, increasing their loss.

This doesn't mean that dividends, interest and capital gains distributions are bad. We are just making you aware that investing outside of a tax-deferred account will have a negative impact on your return, especially if the fund is tax inefficient.

In early 2003, President George W. Bush proposed a plan to eliminate the taxes that individual investors pay on dividends. The fate of this proposal had not been

## FIGURE 10.2: TAXING CALCULATIONS

If you had invested in Dreyfus Appreciation in 1992 (10 years ago), how much of your profits would have gone to pay taxes?

| | |
|---|---|
| Fund Total Return | 11.51 |
| Fund Tax-Adjusted Return | 10.82 |
| Taxes (%) | .69 |

By examining the difference between the fund's tax-adjusted return (10.82 percent) from its total return (11.51) we find the percent of returns paid out in taxes (.69 percent). The lower this number is, the better. Dreyfus Appreciation is a fairly tax-efficient fund for the 10-year period.

Now let's look at the next piece of the tax efficiency puzzle. How much of the fund's positive total return actually goes to pay taxes?

**.69 percent (taxes %) divided by 11.51 (fund total return) = 5.99 percent**

This 5.99 percent is the average amount you, as an investor in Dreyfus Appreciation, would have paid out of your profits and distributions on fund shares in taxes.

So, if you had a $2,000 profit in Dreyfus Appreciation in a given year, you would have paid on average $119.80 in taxes on that profit for the year.

determined as this book went to press. If this proposal should pass in Congress and be signed by the President, the information in this book regarding the tax treatment of dividends, the advantages of owning dividend producing stock funds in taxable accounts and tax efficiency may not be accurate. Check with your tax adviser regarding these issues.

## 5-Year Average Turnover Rate

The portfolio turnover rate, recorded in Section 2D of the Check List, is a rough measurement of how often a fund manager buys and sells securities in a fund's portfolio.

| D 5-Year Avg. Turnover Rate (%): | Years: | Initial Year 1997 | 1998 | 1999 | 2000 | 2001 | Total | Average | Average = (Total All Turnover Rates) / # of Years Entered |
|---|---|---|---|---|---|---|---|---|---|
| | Turnover Rate: | 1 | 1 | 12 | 4 | 5 | 23 | 4.6 | |

- A turnover rate of 20% or less indicates management follows a buy & hold investment style
- High turnover rates lead to higher brokerage costs & can increase your tax liability

NAIC investors seek funds with five-year average turnover rates of 20 percent or less. This indicates whether a fund manager follows a buy-and-hold investing philosophy.

As with other important measurements of fund performance, the turnover rate shouldn't be viewed in isolation. Average the most recent five years of turnover data and see if the average is above or below 20 percent.

Dreyfus Appreciation's five-year average turnover rate is 4.6 percent. This rate is exceptionally low, both when compared to the NAIC benchmark and the fund's large blend peers. According to Morningstar, the average large blend fund's five-year average turnover rate is 96 percent.

Some fund managers believe that frequent buying and selling will be more profitable to the fund than buying and holding stocks for the long term. Research shows that frequent buying and selling doesn't necessarily lead to superior performance.

Rapid turnover increases fund brokerage costs, which are paid by fund investors. In addition, if securities sales are profitable to the fund, the fund passes

these profits along to shareholders in the form of capital gains distributions. High turnover is reflective of a manager whose style is more like a trader as opposed to an investor. With frequent turnover it is impossible for you to get a feel for the companies the manager invests in because the holdings change too rapidly.

On the other hand, when you invest in a fund with a buy-and-hold philosophy, you'll see virtually the same companies in the portfolio quarter after quarter, allowing you to become familiar with them. If you decide to take your investing research to the next level, you can evaluate if they are true growth companies that will lift the performance of the entire fund portfolio.

In your search for a sound fund you will find that a large majority of funds don't meet NAIC criteria on turnover rates. It can be quite difficult to find funds with five-year average portfolio turnover rates of 20 percent or less. Keep in mind that lower turnover rates are better than higher turnover rates, even if they are higher than 20 percent.

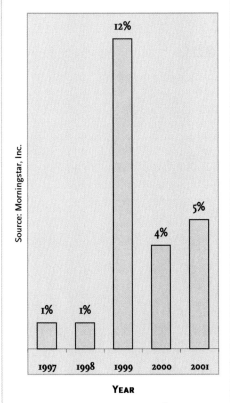

Source: Morningstar, Inc.

12%

1% 1% 4% 5%

1997 1998 1999 2000 2001

**YEAR**

*Figure 10.3: Dreyfus Appreciation's Turnover Rate*

# Stock Fund Check List— Costs and Review

## Counting the Costs

If a fund's portfolio and management satisfy your requirements, then it's time to put its costs under a microscope. Every dollar you spend on fund fees is one less dollar you can invest.

The number and variety of fund fees is bewildering. From management fees to brokerage commissions, these virtually invisible charges can cost you dearly.

There is no proven relationship between high costs and better returns; in fact, funds with higher costs must perform better than low cost funds just to stay even.

In the last part of the Check List, re-examine your understanding of a fund's key elements. Do you understand how your money will be invested? Are the fund's costs reasonable? A thoughtful consideration of these and other questions will help you decide if a particular fund will meet your wealth-building needs.

**Expense Ratio**

**Loads**

**Other Fees**

**Review**

## Overview

Costs matter. It's a simple fact, but one that bears repeating—the more you spend on fund fees, the less money you have to purchase fund shares. And the more of your return that you lose to fund costs, the less you have to meet your financial goals.

Mutual fund costs aren't easy to understand, because many of these fees are virtually invisible. When you buy shares of stock, your order confirmation tells you the exact amount of the commission and fees. With funds, there is no such handy piece of paper. Funds have many different fees and costs, which are either deducted from your account on a percentage basis or which are virtually impossible to quantify. To complicate the issue further, not all of the fees apply to every fund.

Fund costs can be divided into two categories: fees that cover fund operating expenses, and sales charges that compensate brokers and financial advisers. The most visible fund operating charge is the expense ratio, which expresses the percentage of your assets invested in the fund deducted each fiscal year to cover expenses. Sales charges are also known as loads.

*There are no studies proving that load funds outperform no-load funds. Because there are so many no-load funds with equal or better performance to load funds, many investors eliminate load funds from consideration. These do-it-yourself investors choose to focus their energy on finding a top-notch, no-load fund that will meet their investing needs. Figure 11.1 is a brief primer of fund fees.*

### FIGURE 11.1 FUND FEE PRIMER

*Fees included in the expense ratio:*

**Management Fee:** a percentage of assets paid by investors for fund portfolio management services.

**Administrative Fees:** those related to processing fund share purchase and redemption orders, possession of the fund's securities, customer service functions, and bookkeeping and audit of fund accounts.

**12b-1 Fee:** a marketing and distribution fee charged by some funds. If the fee is .25 percent or more, a fund must break it out and identify it as a 12b-1 fee.

*Fees not included in the expense ratio:*

**Brokerage Commission:** the costs involved when a fund buys and sells stock or other securities.

**Redemption Fee:** a short-term fee imposed to discourage investors from rapidly jumping in and out of a fund. These fees are time limited, and usually expire after a number of months or one year's ownership of fund shares.

**Front-end Load (Class A Shares):** fund shares sold by brokers or financial advisers that carry an up-front sales charge that is deducted from the amount of money invested prior to the actual purchase of shares.

**Back-end Load (Class B Shares):** also known as contingent deferred sales charges, also sold by brokers or financial advisors. This fee is assessed if the owner of fund shares sells shares before a certain period of time has elapsed. This fee is generally assessed on a sliding scale.

**Level Load (Class C Shares):** fund shares sold by brokers or financial advisers that levy a certain percentage fee each and every year that an investor owns this class of shares.

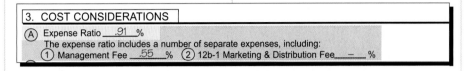

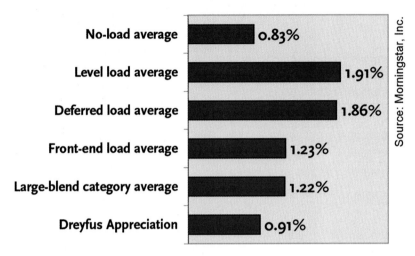

*Figure 11.2: Expense Ratio Comparison*

## Expense Ratio

A fund's expense ratio and it's comparison to a peer group average are covered in Sections 3A and 3B. Dreyfus Appreciation's expense ratio is .91 percent. It compares well to the fund's large-cap blend peer group, which has an average expense ratio of 1.22 percent (not listed on the Morningstar Overview sheet). If you invested $10,000 in shares of Dreyfus Appreciation, your expenses for one year would be $91, $32 less than if you bought $10,000 of shares in the average large blend fund.

*The bar graph in Figure 11.2 compares Dreyfus Appreciation's expense ratio with that of the average large blend fund as well*

*as averages of different share classes of large blend funds.*

Because most fees are assessed on a percentage basis of assets—and are subtracted from total fund assets—many investors don't realize how much they are paying to own shares in their mutual funds. In addition, as your investment grows in a fund through continued contributions or capital appreciation, or both, your fund fees rise.

For example, if you invest $10,000 in a fund with a .75 percent expense ratio you would pay $75 annually for

these expenses. If you purchase more shares, and your account appreciates, growing to $15,000 in three years while the expense ratio stays the same, your expenses will climb to $112.50.

And that just includes the expense ratio, not the brokerage commissions or any redemption fees or loads. These expenses are assessed each and every year that you own fund shares. This isn't the case for direct ownership of stock, where you pay commissions only when you buy or sell shares.

Before buying a fund, it's a good idea to calculate approximately how much of your investment will go to pay fund fees. To get a good idea of how much your fund fees will cost, take a look at the SEC's Cost Calculator at www.sec.gov. Think about how much you plan to invest, and the fee levels of the different funds you are considering.

## Management Fee

The management fee, in Section 3A1, is part of the expense ratio. The management fee is paid to the fund management company, also known as the fund adviser, for portfolio management

3. COST CONSIDERATIONS
(A) Expense Ratio ___.91__%
The expense ratio includes a number of separate expenses, including:
(1) Management Fee ___.55___% (2) 12b-1 Marketing & Distribution Fee___–___%

services. Dreyfus Appreciation's management fee is .55 percent.

Management companies employ fund managers, researchers and analysts. They also pay for company data these employees analyze and for the expenses involved in running a trading desk. It's reasonable to expect to pay for this service but each investor needs to decide if the price they are paying is worth what they are getting in return.

## 12b-1 Fee

All funds have marketing and distribution costs, but not every fund levies a 12b-1 fee, which is covered in Section 3A2 of the

```
┌──────────────────────────────────────────────────────────────┐
│  3.  COST CONSIDERATIONS                                       │
│ Ⓐ Expense Ratio ___.91__ %                                    │
│   The expense ratio includes a number of separate expenses, including: │
│   ① Management Fee __.55__ %  ② 12b-1 Marketing & Distribution Fee___–___ % │
└──────────────────────────────────────────────────────────────┘
```

Check List. Dreyfus Appreciation has no 12b-1 fee. Marketing and distribution costs include printing and mailing prospectuses and annual and semi-annual reports. Other costs that fall under this area include advertising (on television, in print and on the Internet) and Web site maintenance.

12b-1 fees not only cover certain marketing and distribution costs, but they also compensate brokers and financial advisers for selling fund shares. If a broker sold you a fund with a back-end load, you wouldn't be charged that load until you sold your fund shares. But your broker would receive at least part of a 12b-1 fee that you paid as part of your expense ratio, as a commission, each and every year that you owned fund shares.

These fees also compensate fund supermarkets for listing and selling shares in a wide variety of funds. This is why it is generally cheaper to purchase fund shares directly from a fund company than through a fund supermarket.

## INVESTOR PROFILE: CANDIS KING

*Candis King, an NAIC lifetime member, served as a Chapter director for many years. She writes and teaches about mutual fund and stock investing.*

### Q: How long have you been investing in mutual funds?

Perhaps the question should be how long have I successfully been investing in mutual funds. At one point I had invested in a mutual fund recommended to me by a former co-worker, friend and now broker. This was around 1986 when the market was pretty strong. The load on the fund was astronomical. The fund ended up costing me a small fortune in fees and non-performance. After that experience, I deferred investing in any mutual funds for several years, until my first child was born in 1991. I invest only in no-load funds now.

### Q: How has the NAIC Mutual Fund Program helped you?

By offering a systematic approach to analyzing mutual funds, it has helped to de-mystify mutual funds and has helped me become aware of the variety of differences in mutual funds. Knowledge is power in the pocketbook.

### Q: In your opinion, what is the major difference between NAIC's investing philosophy and other investing practices?

The difference is night and day. The NAIC investing philosophy allows one to acquire and develop knowledge and to de-mystify money. Many other investing practices require that one turn all decisions over to an 'expert' and don't increase knowledge of the subject of money. And knowledge is power in the pocketbook.

Before purchasing shares in a fund with a 12b-1 fee, think about the pros and cons of paying a marketing and distribution fee. As listed above, the major disadvantage is increased costs, while there are no readily apparent advantages.

## Loads

Fund Loads are covered in Section 3C of the Check List. Dreyfus Appreciation is a no-load fund. Investors can purchase shares in Dreyfus Appreciation directly from Dreyfus and pay no sales charges. While Dreyfus Appreciation carries no sales charges, many funds do.

*Loads are also known as sales charges. They are charged to fund investors in exchange for investing advice. There are several different types of loads investors may encounter, as detailed in the Fund Fee Primer in Figure 11.1.*

Here is an example of how a back-end load might work. Back-end loads are fees deducted when investors sell fund shares, but decrease the longer fund shares are owned, eventually zeroing out. Fund companies structure back-end load fees differently.

If you purchased shares in a back-end load fund with a 5

percent load, you would pay that 5 percent if you sold your shares with in the first year, 4 percent if you sold in the second year, 3 percent in the third year, 2 percent in the fourth year, 1 percent in the fifth year, and nothing if you held your shares to the sixth year and beyond.

Keep in mind, if you are using an automatic investment plan to purchase back-end loaded shares, you will own many

different lots of shares with different schedules under which the load expires. Fund companies offer automatic investment plans to investors who want to invest a certain sum each month in fund shares.

For example, if you bought $1,000 of shares through an automatic investment plan in 2000 under the back-end load described above, those shares would be free of the load by 2006. However, if you purchased an additional

---

## FIGURE 11.3 LOAD IMPACT

**Front-end load**

- Fee is deducted from initial money used to purchase shares.
- $10,000 invested with a 5 percent front-end load.
- Load charged: $500.

**Back-end load**

- Fee is deducted when shares are sold.
- $10,000 invested, shares sold after two years and shares value has grown to $12,000, initial 5 percent fee declines to 3 percent.
- Load charged: $360.

**Level Load**

- Fee is deducted each and every year you own fund shares.
- $10,000 invested for three years, with share value increasing to $11,000 in first year and $12,000 the second year. The level load fee is 1 percent per year.
- Load charged: $330 for entire three-year period.

**No Load**

- No fee deducted at any phase of investment.
- $10,000 invested for the long term.
- Load charged: $0.

$1,000 of shares in 2001, those shares wouldn't escape a load until 2007.

Level load shares are the most damaging and expensive of all loads for the long-term investor because they are assessed annually.

*The example in Figure 11.3 illustrates the points made above, showing with real examples how much you would pay in sales charges under four different scenarios.*

Think carefully before purchasing shares with a sales charge. The loads you pay will cut into your return for years to come, holding the performance of your fund below a comparable no-load fund.

### Redemption Fees

A redemption fee, covered in Section 3D, is a short-term fee that fund companies occasionally charge when shareholders redeem—or sell—fund shares. Fund companies typically impose redemption fees to discourage investors from jumping in and out of funds.

Market timers, investors who move from fund to fund seeking a quick profit, can be very disruptive to a fund's cash flow situation. Redemption

fees usually last for a set period of time, such as three months, six months or a year. The SEC limits redemption fees to no more than 2 percent. Dreyfus Appreciation doesn't charge a redemption fee.

### Brokerage Commissions

Brokerage commissions are passed on to fund investors. It is difficult for fund investors to quantify exactly how much they pay in brokerage commissions.

A fund's annual report and Statement of Additional Information includes figures on how much the fund as a whole pays for brokerage commissions. However, this information isn't stated in terms of how much per each share of stock bought or sold is paid or how much the typical investor pays. Brokerage commissions are a significant cost for funds and fund investors, as fund managers typically buy and sell

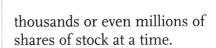

thousands or even millions of shares of stock at a time.

A large fund with assets in the billions could easily run up more than $10 million in brokerage commissions a year. Funds with high turnover rates tend to have higher commission costs than funds with lower turnover rates.

Fund managers and boards of directors are not required to seek the lowest broker, but decide which brokers to use based not only on the cost of commissions but services that the brokerage may provide in exchange for fund business. Many funds use several different brokerages, and may also use brokerages that are affiliated with the fund company in some way.

---

Ⓓ Redemption Fee ___ – ___ %

Note: Investors also pay fund brokerage commissions

### Fee Wrap-Up

The importance of fund fees can't be overemphasized. You can't control a fund's future performance, but you can control how much you pay in fund expenses. By choosing an inexpensive fund over an expensive one, you'll save hundreds of dollars in fees. Make sure that an inexpensive fund delivers the top-notch performance you're expecting.

*Figure 11.4 illustrates the difference in the expenses you would pay if you invested $10,000 in three funds: one with a .20 expense ratio, one with a 1.00 percent expense ratio and the third with a 2.00 expense ratio. The example uses a compound annual return of 8 percent.*

An NAIC investor adopting a "do-it-yourself" approach and using the tools and information in this book can find superior funds with reasonable fees. You work hard for your money, and it makes sense to spend time learning how to invest it wisely for the long-term. Such knowledge can pay off handsomely in the future.

### Reviewing the Check List

With a Check List, a Morningstar report and a pencil, you can complete an analysis of a stock mutual fund fairly quickly, gaining an understanding of a fund's important elements.

NAIC's tools and analysis methodology make the evaluation of funds accessible to individual investors.

The review questions in Section 4 help you focus both on the fund you're examining and your investment needs. Of the thousands of funds available, just how many are suitable candidates for your portfolio? By setting your standards high, and knowing what you want in a fund before you invest, you'll have a better chance of investing successfully.

### Review Questions

The final section of the Check List is a seven-question review, designed to help you figure out if the fund you've just analyzed will meet your investing needs.

● **Do you understand how fund management invests your money?**

When you buy shares in a fund other than an index fund, you pay a professional manager to invest your money. It is vital that you understand the fund's investment objective and the

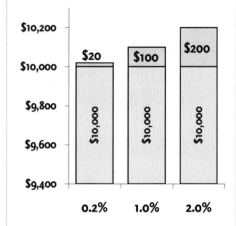

*Figure 11.4: Rising Expenses*

strategies the manager uses to carry out the objective.

Take a few minutes to re-read the fund's investment objective as stated in the prospectus. Not only does the prospectus state the fund's overall objective, but it also lays out management's strategies and the expected risks involved. How do the objective, strategies and risks fit in with your investing goals and needs?

● **Are you familiar with the types of companies the fund manager purchases?**

If you aren't familiar with the types of companies in the fund portfolio, take a few

---

**4. REVIEW**

- Do you understand how fund management invests your money?
- Are you familiar with the types of companies the fund manager invest in?
- Has fund management been in place for five years or more?
- Does fund management follow a buy-and-hold investing style?
- Does the fund consistently out-perform an appropriate market index?
- Is the fund so tax-inefficient that it belongs in a tax-deferred account?
- Are the fund's costs reasonable?

Completing the Check List provides you with a better understanding of how a fund invests, what it invests in, how effective current management is, and what percentage of your investment dollars pay fund expenses.

## Dreyfus Appreciation Fund, Inc.

Seeks long-term capital growth by investing in common stocks

**PROSPECTUS** May 1, 2002

YOU, YOUR ADVISOR AND

**Dreyfus**
A MELLON FINANCIAL COMPANY

As with all mutual funds, the Securities and Exchange Commission has not approved or disapproved these securities or passed upon the adequacy of this prospectus. Any representation to the contrary is a criminal offense.

Source: Dreyfus, 2003. Used with Permission.

minutes to familiarize yourself with them. Type the ticker symbol into a personal finance Web site and find out some basic information about the company. How large is it? Is management increasing sales and earnings?

● **Has fund management been in place for five years or more?**

Management with less than five years of experience with a particular fund bears little responsibility for a fund's record. Look for funds with long-term managers who have a demonstrated commitment to the fund.

● **Does fund management follow a buy-and-hold investing style?**

Low turnover not only keeps your tax and brokerage commission expenses down, it also helps you know what you own.

● **Does the fund consistently outperform an appropriate market index?**

If a particular portfolio manager can't outperform a benchmark market index over a long period of time, why continue to invest? You can get performance that matches the market by purchasing shares in a broadly-based, low-cost index fund.

● **Is the fund so tax inefficient that it belongs in a tax-deferred account?**

Not all superior funds are tax efficient. If you want to buy shares in a well-managed, tax-inefficient fund, purchase those shares in an IRA or 401(k) account where they will be sheltered from taxes. Tax-inefficient funds exact a high price, as a higher percentage of your total return goes to pay taxes instead of adding to your nest egg. One exception is if you are purchasing funds to provide income.

● **Are the fund's costs reasonable?**

Watch out for expensive funds. Some funds—those with expense ratios and fees over 2 percent—cost as much as a private money manager. Strive to find the best fund you can for the lowest possible cost.

# Stock Fund Comparison Guid —Title Block and Portfolio

## Compare the Best Funds

The Stock Fund Check List provides an overview of a single fund. To find the fund that meets your wealth-building needs, you want the best of the best. The key to locating that one fund in 10,000 is to compare several top-notch funds.

Using the Stock Fund Comparison Guide, you contrast the key elements of up to three funds.

You examine the qualities NAIC emphasizes in fund analysis: portfolio, management and costs.

Before comparing your selected funds, consider what qualities are most important. For some investors, total return is the key factor. For others investing in a taxable account, tax efficiency is number one. Decide which factors are most important to you and then pick the fund that most closely meets those criteria.

**Title Block**

**Rankings**

**Portfolio**

## Overview

The Comparison Guide is a one-page form. You draw information for the Comparison Guide from previously filled-out Check Lists or directly from Morningstar reports.

The Comparison Guide follows the same format as the Stock Fund Check List. However, not all items from the Stock Fund Check List are included on the Comparison Guide. Portfolio Composition, which was also formerly included in an older version of the Comparison Guide, was eliminated to make room for more relevant analysis items. If an element that is important to you—such as portfolio composition—is not included in the Comparison Guide, you can use the section called Other at the bottom of the form to add that element to your comparison.

## Stock Fund Comparison Guide™

Investment Education Since 1951

Fund Category: _Large Blend_

Date: _7/27/02_

Taxable Acct.: _X_ Tax-Deferred Acct.: ____

|  |  |  | FUND #1 | RANK | FUND #2 | RANK | FUND #3 | RANK |
|---|---|---|---|---|---|---|---|---|
| | Fund Name | | Fund #1 | | Fund #2 | | Fund #3 | |
| PORTFOLIO | Market Capitalization | Giant % | 38 | | 54.0 | | 15.0 | |
| | | Large % | 52 | | 42.3 | | 58.0 | |
| | | Medium % | 7.8 | | 3.7 | | 20.6 | |
| | | Small % | 2.2 | | 0 | | 6.1 | |
| | | Micro % | 0 | 1 | 0 | 1 | 0 | 2 |
| | Sector Analysis | INFORMATION Software % | 3.2 | | 4.0 | | 9.2 | |
| | | Hardware % | 10.0 | | 8.6 | | 6.0 | |
| | | Media % | 11.2 | | 2.9 | | 20.0 | |
| | | Telecom % | 3.0 | | 6.4 | | 18.1 | |
| | | SERVICE Health % | 11.9 | | 16.3 | | 0 | |
| | | Consumer % | 12.0 | | 6.7 | | 17.4 | |
| | | Business % | 6.1 | | 1.3 | | 3.2 | |
| | | Financial % | 17.9 | | 20.7 | | 14.6 | |
| | | MANUFACTURING Goods % | 9.0 | | 10.0 | | 0 | |
| | | Ind. Materials % | 7.9 | | 11.1 | | 11.5 | |
| | | Energy % | 5.0 | | 7.9 | | 0 | |
| | | Utilities % | 2.8 | 1 | 4.1 | 2 | 0 | 3 |
| | Number of Stocks in Portfolio | | 98 | 2 | 122 | 1 | 37 | 3 |
| | Total Assets $ | | 2,815m | -- | 552m | -- | 25,176m | -- |
| | Sales Growth % | | 8.0 | 3 | 16 | 1 | 12.5 | 2 |
| | Trailing Earnings % | | 8.0 | 3 | 14.5 | 1 | 11.0 | 2 |
| | P/E Ratio | | 25.0 | 1 | 31.0 | 3 | 28.0 | 2 |
| MANAGEMENT | Management Tenure | | 10 | 1 | 3.5 | 2 | 7.5 | 1 |
| | Total Return % 10-Year Avg. | | 12.7 | 1 | -- | -- | -- | -- |
| | 5-Year Avg. | | 11.2 | 2 | -- | -- | 13.0 | 1 |
| | 3-Year Avg. | | 4.5 | 3 | 7.0 | 1 | 5.8 | 2 |
| | Taxes % 10-Year Avg. | | 0.73 | 1 | -- | -- | -- | -- |
| | 5-Year Avg. | | 0.84 | 1 | -- | -- | 2.0 | 2 |
| | 3-Year Avg. | | 0.29 | 1 | 0.90 | 3 | 0.69 | 2 |
| | 5-Yr Average Turnover Rate % | | 18 | 1 | 35 | 2 | 61 | 3 |
| COST | Expense Ratio % | | 0.65 | 2 | 0.42 | 1 | 1.03 | 3 |
| | 12b-1 Fee % | | 0 | 1 | 0 | 1 | 0.25 | 2 |
| | Load: Front / Back / Level % | | 0 | 1 | 3 (front) | 2 | -- | 1 |
| | Redemption Fee % | | 0 | 1 | 0 | 1 | 1.0 | 2 |
| OTHER | | | | | | | | |
| | | | | | | | | |
| | | | | | | | | |

| 1st 12 | 2nd 3 | 3rd 3 | | 1st 8 | 2nd 4 | 3rd 2 | | 1st 3 | 2nd 9 | 3rd 4 |

The Portfolio Section of the Comparison Guide examines several factors in the funds' portfolio, including market capitalization, sector analysis, number of stocks, total assets, sales growth, trailing earnings and price/earnings. The Management Section looks at management's length of service, total return, tax efficiency and turnover. The Cost Section analyzes a fund's costs, including the expense ratio and sales charges. This chapter focuses on the Title Block and Portfolio Section of the Comparison Guide; the Management and Cost Sections are covered in Chapter 13.

The example funds used in this handbook for the Comparison Guide are not real funds, but funds constructed for teaching purposes. Throughout this chapter, the example funds are referred to as Fund #1, Fund #2 and Fund #3.

## Title Block

Use the Comparison Guide's Title Block Section to fill in the funds' basic information. The title block asks for the category of the funds that you are examining.

An analysis of funds in the same category tells you which fund in the category is superior, according to the

elements that mean the most to you. This Comparison Guide examines three large blend funds. This provides an apples-to-apples comparison of the three funds and is the way that most investors make the best use of the form.

This is only one of the uses of the Comparison Guide. You can use the Comparison Guide in several different ways. For example, you could compare funds with different investment styles to each other to gain a better overall understanding of

the growth, blend and value investment styles.

You could also compare funds in different categories or with different market capitalizations. You might want to compare two funds in one category to a low-cost index fund in the same category or you could compare a fund that bills itself as a tax-efficient fund to a regular fund.

The Comparison Guide asks you to fill in the date you prepared it. The final item in the Title Block asks you to decide whether you will hold the selected fund in a taxable or tax-deferred account. Investors in taxable accounts may give greater weight to a fund's tax efficiency than investors in tax-deferred accounts. In this Comparison Guide we're examining a fund in a taxable account, so that box is checked.

## Rankings

The rankings in the Comparison Guide are intended to serve as a broad guideline, not as a mechanical system that will automatically designate the top-ranking fund. Because many of the elements

| NAIC® Investment Education Since 1951 | Stock Fund Comparison Guide™ | Fund Category: _Large Blend_ |
| --- | --- | --- |
| | | Date: _7/27/02_ |
| | | Taxable Acct.: _X_  Tax-Deferred Acct.: ___ |

in the Comparison Guide are subjective, you must first think about which elements are most important towards meeting your investing objectives before ranking each fund.

For example, if you're looking for a fund with a concentrated portfolio, you will rank concentrated funds higher than diverse funds. The reverse is also true. Some elements have rankings set in line with NAIC

guidelines. This includes the sales and earnings growth rates in the portfolio. Some ranking boxes are shaded out because these particular categories are meant to be ranked as a group.

Deciding on the top-ranking fund is a judgement call. It is up to each individual investor to determine what is most important. Criteria differ in importance from investor to investor.

If the rankings aren't helpful to you in your comparison, don't use them. The rankings are a tool to use as you see fit. This comparison shows rankings, which we'll explain as we walk you through the form.

## Portfolio

The Portfolio Section of the Comparison Guide contains seven elements. As with the

Stock Fund Check List, an analysis of the portfolio elements helps you become familiar with a fund's holdings, and how they are spread out in terms of market capitalization, sectors, sales, earnings and P/E ratios.

## Market Capitalization

One way to determine if a fund stays true to its objective is to examine its portfolio by market capitalization. A fund's market capitalization refers to the size of the companies in the portfolio.

Since the funds in our analysis are all large blend funds, giant and large companies should dominate the portfolio. Funds #1 and #2 have 90 percent or more of their stock portfolios invested in large or giant companies. Fund #3 has 15 percent of its portfolio in giant-sized companies and 58 percent in large-sized companies, for a total of 73 percent in the largest categories.

In this comparison, we are seeking a pure large-cap fund (or as close as we can get to a pure large-cap fund). An investor who seeks a pure large-cap blend fund may feel

| Fund Name | | Fund #1 | RANK | Fund #2 | RANK | Fund #3 | RANK |
|---|---|---|---|---|---|---|---|
| Market Capitalization | Giant % | 38 | | 54.0 | | 15.0 | |
| | Large % | 52 | | 42.3 | | 58.0 | |
| | Medium % | 7.8 | | 3.7 | | 20.6 | |
| | Small % | 2.2 | | 0 | | 6.1 | |
| | Micro % | 0 | 1 | 0 | 1 | 0 | 2 |

| Fund Name | | | Fund #1 | RANK | Fund #2 | RANK | Fund #3 | RANK |
|-----------|--|--|---------|------|---------|------|---------|------|
| Sector Analysis | INFORMATION | Software % | 3.2 | | 4.0 | | 9.2 | |
| | | Hardware % | 10.0 | | 8.6 | | 6.0 | |
| | | Media % | 11.2 | | 2.9 | | 20.0 | |
| | | Telecom % | 3.0 | | 6.4 | | 18.1 | |
| | SERVICE | Health % | 11.9 | | 16.3 | | 0 | |
| | | Consumer % | 12.0 | | 6.7 | | 17.4 | |
| | | Business % | 6.1 | | 1.3 | | 3.2 | |
| | | Financial % | 17.9 | | 20.7 | | 14.6 | |
| | MANUFACTURING | Goods % | 9.0 | | 10.0 | | 0 | |
| | | Ind. Materials % | 7.9 | | 11.1 | | 11.5 | |
| | | Energy % | 5.0 | | 7.9 | | 0 | |
| | | Utilities % | 2.8 | 1 | 4.1 | 2 | 0 | 3 |

| Super Sector | Fund #1 | Fund #2 | Fund #3 |
|--------------|---------|---------|---------|
| Information | 27.4 | 21.9 | 53.3 |
| Services | 47.9 | 45.0 | 35.2 |
| Manufacturing | 24.7 | 33.1 | 11.5 |

*Figure 12.1: Super Sector Make-up*

more comfortable with Fund #1 and #2 than Fund #3, which holds more of its portfolio in mid- and small-cap companies. Funds #1 and 2 receive the first place ranking, while Fund #3 gets the second place.

### Sector Analysis

In the sector analysis section of the Comparison Guide, you compare the sector breakdowns of the three funds. If you are ranking the funds, decide whether you prefer a fund that concentrates its portfolio on a few sectors or one that spreads the portfolio across more sectors. As noted in Chapter 9, Morningstar's sector ranking system has three super sectors, with four sectors under each super sector.

These super sectors, and the specific industry sectors under them, are Information Economy (software, hardware, media and telecommunications), Services Economy (health, consumer services, business services and financial services) and Manufacturing Economy (consumer goods, industrial materials, energy and utilities).

*In terms of super sectors, the three funds aren't that different, although the individual sector makeup varies considerably. The super sector makeup can be found in Figure 12.1.*

Looking at the industry sectors on the form, we see that Fund #1 is the most diversified fund, with 10 percent or more of the fund's assets spread over the hardware, media, health, consumer services and financial services. Fund #2 is a little less diversified, with the most assets in the financial

services sector. Fund #3 has the most concentrated portfolio, with more than a half of its assets in technology companies as seen in the software, hardware, media and telecom sectors.

Consider your overall investing needs when analyzing a particular fund's sector allocation. Think about how a fund will fit into your overall portfolio.

In this comparison, we're looking for a fund with the most diversified portfolio, so we'll award the first place ranking to Fund #1, followed by Fund #2 and then Fund #3. If you were looking for a more concentrated portfolio, the rankings would be reversed.

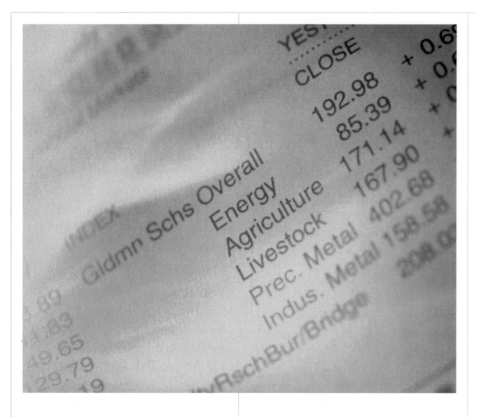

## Number of Stocks in the Portfolio

The total number of stocks in a fund portfolio is another measurement of a fund's diversification. Portfolios with a smaller number of stocks and/or a smaller number of sectors are more likely to be volatile than a more diversified portfolio. In this comparison we are looking for a more diversified fund. Fund #2 has the most stocks in the portfolio, followed by Fund #1 and then Fund #3 with the smallest number of stocks.

## Total Assets

The funds in this comparison exhibit quite a range in terms of total assets. The smallest fund, Fund #2, has $552 million in assets, while the largest, Fund #3, has more than $25 billion in assets. While large funds in general are harder for a fund manager to maneuver than smaller funds, funds that invest in large and giant-sized companies can more easily invest large amounts of money in these types of companies than they could in small and mid-sized companies.

Consequently, we'll leave this variable unranked in this comparison. If we were comparing two small cap funds, the fund with the lowest asset size would get a ranking higher than funds with more assets.

## Sales Growth

Since companies must sell products or services to generate earnings, a fund's average sales growth rate is an important measurement of how the companies in the portfolio are growing their businesses. Sales growth is an historical measurement that examines a company's growth during a four-year period.

Since sales growth is a driver of earnings growth and stock price appreciation, we rank the

| Fund Name | Fund #1 | RANK | Fund #2 | RANK | Fund #3 | RANK |
|---|---|---|---|---|---|---|
| Number of Stocks in Portfolio | 98 | 2 | 122 | 1 | 37 | 3 |
| Total Assets $ | 2,815m | -- | 552m | -- | 25,176m | -- |
| Sales Growth % | 8.0 | 3 | 16 | 1 | 12.5 | 2 |
| Trailing Earnings % | 8.0 | 3 | 14.5 | 1 | 11.0 | 2 |
| P/E Ratio | 25.0 | 1 | 31.0 | 3 | 28.0 | 2 |

| Number of Stocks in Portfolio | 98 | 2 | 122 | 1 | 37 | 3 |
|---|---|---|---|---|---|---|
| Total Assets $ | 2,815m | -- | 552m | -- | 25,176m | -- |
| Sales Growth % | 8.0 | 3 | 16 | 1 | 12.5 | 2 |
| Trailing Earnings % | 8.0 | 3 | 14.5 | 1 | 11.0 | 2 |
| P/E Ratio | 25.0 | 1 | 31.0 | 3 | 28.0 | 2 |

| Number of Stocks in Portfolio | 98 | 2 | 122 | 1 | 37 | 3 |
|---|---|---|---|---|---|---|
| Total Assets $ | 2,815m | -- | 552m | -- | 25,176m | -- |
| Sales Growth % | 8.0 | 3 | 16 | 1 | 12.5 | 2 |
| Trailing Earnings % | 8.0 | 3 | 14.5 | 1 | 11.0 | 2 |
| P/E Ratio | 25.0 | 1 | 31.0 | 3 | 28.0 | 2 |

| Fund Name | Fund #1 | RANK | Fund #2 | RANK | Fund #3 | RANK |
|---|---|---|---|---|---|---|
| Number of Stocks in Portfolio | 98 | 2 | 122 | 1 | 37 | 3 |
| Total Assets $ | 2,815m | -- | 552m | -- | 25,176m | -- |
| Sales Growth % | 8.0 | 3 | 16 | 1 | 12.5 | 2 |
| Trailing Earnings % | 8.0 | 3 | 14.5 | 1 | 11.0 | 2 |
| P/E Ratio | 25.0 | 1 | 31.0 | 3 | 28.0 | 2 |

| Number of Stocks in Portfolio | 98 | 2 | 122 | 1 | 37 | 3 |
|---|---|---|---|---|---|---|
| Total Assets $ | 2,815m | -- | 552m | -- | 25,176m | -- |
| Sales Growth % | 8.0 | 3 | 16 | 1 | 12.5 | 2 |
| Trailing Earnings % | 8.0 | 3 | 14.5 | 1 | 11.0 | 2 |
| P/E Ratio | 25.0 | 1 | 31.0 | 3 | 28.0 | 2 |

fund with the highest sales growth rate first. Fund #2 has the highest sales growth rate, followed by Fund #3 and then Fund #1.

## Trailing Earnings

A fund's trailing earnings growth rate is the weighted average of earnings growth rates for the companies in a fund's portfolio during the past four years.

In this comparison, we favor the fund that invests in companies with the highest average portfolio earnings growth rate. Company earnings growth generally leads to higher stock prices—in the long term—which in turn leads to growth in a fund's net asset value.

Fund #2 with an average trailing portfolio earnings growth rate of 14.5 percent ranks first, followed by Fund #3 with 11 percent and Fund #1 with 8 percent.

## Price/Earnings

The price/earnings ratio is the weighted average of the P/E ratios of the individual stocks in a fund. The P/E is the price-to-earnings ratio, which you obtain by dividing a stock's price by its projected long-term earnings.

Selecting the number one ranking fund in this category is another judgment call. Some fund investors prefer funds

with lower average P/E ratios in the belief that fund managers aren't paying too much for the companies in the portfolio.

Others prefer funds with high P/E ratios in the belief that fast- growing companies will propel stock prices and fund net asset values higher. We'll rank the fund with the lowest average P/E ratio highest: Fund #1 at 25, Fund #3 at 28 and Fund #2 at 31.

## Conclusion

A comparison of funds shows how the companies in a particular portfolio can differ. Whether a manager deliberately plans to feature companies in a particular market capitalization or sector, or whether he picks the best companies he can find, the results can make a big difference in how a portfolio looks.

In the next Chapter we'll examine the remaining elements of the Comparison Guide, focusing on management, management's track record and the funds' costs.

# Stock Fund Comparison Guide —Management and Costs

## Contrast Fund Variables

In the Comparison Guide's second and third sections, you examine the funds' management and costs. Superior funds boast some of the best long-term performance records. Make sure your fund at least bests a comparable market index over a long period of time, such as 10 years.

Check out which fund is the top performer in terms of tax efficiency and cost. These are bottom-line numbers that can mean the difference between success and failure in a mutual fund investment.

**Management**

**Costs**

**Final Rankings**

## Management

The Management Section draws a number of components from the Stock Fund Check List so that you can evaluate the management characteristics of up to three funds. Included in this section are the funds' management tenure, total return, tax efficiency measurements and five-year average turnover rate.

## Management Tenure

Because NAIC investors buy fund shares for the long term, we seek fund managers with a demonstrated commitment to a particular fund. Since the managers of Funds #1 and #3 have more than five years of experience, they are both awarded the number one ranking. Fund #2's manager has been with that fund for three-and-one-half years, a year-and-one-half shy of the five-year goal. To see if this manager has other relevant experience in managing a large blend fund, you can ask the

fund company for a résumé or background information.

A manager with experience successfully managing a very similar fund is likely to do well with this fund. If not, you can

look for another fund with more experienced management.

As a rule of thumb, a fund with a manager having less than the requisite five years of experience wouldn't even be included in an NAIC stock fund comparison. However, in some 401(k)-type plans investors have few choices, and must consider funds with less experienced management.

| | Fund Name | Fund #1 | RANK | Fund #2 | RANK | Fund #3 | RANK |
|---|---|---|---|---|---|---|---|
| | Management Tenure | 10 | 1 | 3.5 | 2 | 7.5 | 1 |
| | Total Return % 10-Year Avg. | 12.7 | 1 | -- | -- | -- | -- |
| MANAGEMENT | 5-Year Avg. | 11.2 | 2 | -- | -- | 13.0 | 1 |
| | 3-Year Avg. | 4.5 | 3 | 7.0 | 1 | 5.8 | 2 |
| | Taxes % 10-Year Avg. | 0.73 | 1 | -- | -- | -- | -- |
| | 5-Year Avg. | 0.84 | 1 | -- | -- | 2.0 | 2 |
| | 3-Year Avg. | 0.29 | 1 | 0.90 | 3 | 0.69 | 2 |
| | 5-Yr Average Turnover Rate % | 18 | 1 | 35 | 2 | 61 | 3 |

| Fund Name | Fund #1 | RANK | Fund #2 | RANK | Fund #3 | RANK |
|---|---|---|---|---|---|---|
| **MANAGEMENT** Management Tenure | 10 | 1 | 3.5 | 2 | 7.5 | 1 |
| Total Return % 10-Year Avg. | 12.7 | 1 | -- | -- | -- | -- |
| 5-Year Avg. | 11.2 | 2 | -- | -- | 13.0 | 1 |
| 3-Year Avg. | 4.5 | 3 | 7.0 | 1 | 5.8 | 2 |
| Taxes % 10-Year Avg. | 0.73 | 1 | -- | -- | -- | -- |
| 5-Year Avg. | 0.84 | 1 | -- | -- | 2.0 | 2 |
| 3-Year Avg. | 0.29 | 1 | 0.90 | 3 | 0.69 | 2 |
| 5-Yr Average Turnover Rate % | 18 | 1 | 35 | 2 | 61 | 3 |

## Total Return

A fund's total return is a measure of a fund's gains during a period of time. The higher the total return for a particular period the better.

Fund #1 earns the first place ranking in total return for the 10-year period; the other funds are not ranked because their managers have less than 10 years of service. For the five-year period, Fund #3 gets the first place ranking, followed by Fund #1. Fund #2 is unranked because its manager hasn't been with the fund for the full five-year period.

As far as the three-year total return goes, Fund #2 is ranked first, Fund #3 is second and Fund #1 is third. Because the manager of Fund #2 doesn't have a five-year track record, this fund's management performance is very difficult to assess. In the short term, it has outperformed the other two funds in the comparison. We can't yet assess how this manager will perform during a long period of time.

You'll notice that total returns for Funds #1 and #3 dropped

substantially between the five- and three-year periods. There is a simple explanation: a bear market began in Spring 2000, two years into the three-year total return period. All the

major market indexes dropped significantly from their bull market highs, including the S&P 500.

## Percentage of Taxes

The percentage of taxes measures a fund's tax efficiency. To get this percentage for all three funds, you draw directly from Section 2C of the Check List.

For investors who hold fund shares in taxable accounts, the more tax efficient a fund is, the less they will pay of their total return in taxes. If you are investing in a tax-deferred account, you can skip this step in the Comparison Guide.

In this comparison, we are seeking a tax-efficient fund. Fund #1 is the most tax-efficient fund for 10-, five- and three-years, so it is awarded the number one ranking. Fund #3 gets the second place ranking for five years and three years, while Fund #2, the most tax-inefficient fund, gets the number three ranking for the three-year period.

| Fund Name | Fund #1 | RANK | Fund #2 | RANK | Fund #3 | RANK |
|---|---|---|---|---|---|---|
| **MANAGEMENT** Management Tenure | 10 | 1 | 3.5 | 2 | 7.5 | 1 |
| Total Return % 10-Year Avg. | 12.7 | 1 | -- | -- | -- | -- |
| 5-Year Avg. | 11.2 | 2 | -- | -- | 13.0 | 1 |
| 3-Year Avg. | 4.5 | 3 | 7.0 | 1 | 5.8 | 2 |
| Taxes % 10-Year Avg. | 0.73 | 1 | -- | -- | -- | -- |
| 5-Year Avg. | 0.84 | 1 | -- | -- | 2.0 | 2 |
| 3-Year Avg. | 0.29 | 1 | 0.90 | 3 | 0.69 | 2 |
| 5-Yr Average Turnover Rate % | 18 | 1 | 35 | 2 | 61 | 3 |

| | Fund Name | Fund #1 | RANK | Fund #2 | RANK | Fund #3 | RANK |
|---|---|---|---|---|---|---|---|
| MANAGEMENT | Management Tenure | 10 | 1 | 3.5 | 2 | 7.5 | 1 |
| | Total Return % 10-Year Avg. | 12.7 | 1 | -- | -- | -- | -- |
| | 5-Year Avg. | 11.2 | 2 | -- | -- | 13.0 | 1 |
| | 3-Year Avg. | 4.5 | 3 | 7.0 | 1 | 5.8 | 2 |
| | Taxes % 10-Year Avg. | 0.73 | 1 | -- | -- | -- | -- |
| | 5-Year Avg. | 0.84 | 1 | -- | -- | 2.0 | 2 |
| | 3-Year Avg. | 0.29 | 1 | 0.90 | 3 | 0.69 | 2 |
| | 5-Yr Average Turnover Rate % | 18 | 1 | 35 | 2 | 61 | 3 |

### 5-Year Average Turnover Rate

In any comparison, we award the fund with the lowest turnover the highest ranking. Of the funds in this comparison, Fund #1 is ranked first. Fund #2 exceeds the 20 percent target by 15 percentage points, but is still significantly below the category five-year average return of 85.8 percent, derived from the data on the large blend overview sheet. Fund #2 ranks second.

Fund #3 is ranked last because it has the highest turnover rate in the comparison. If none of the funds in your comparison meets the 20 percent standard, award first place to the fund with the lowest turnover. Using this comparison as an example, clearly 35 percent turnover is superior to 61 percent turnover. Both are lower than the category average.

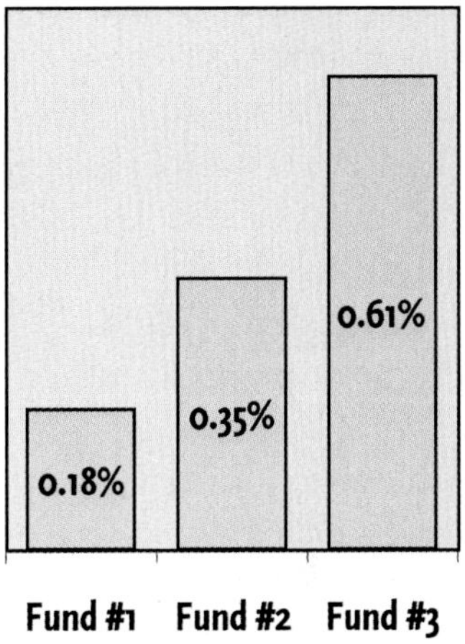


*Figure 13.1: Turnover Rate Comparison*

## Investor Profile: Christine Curtis

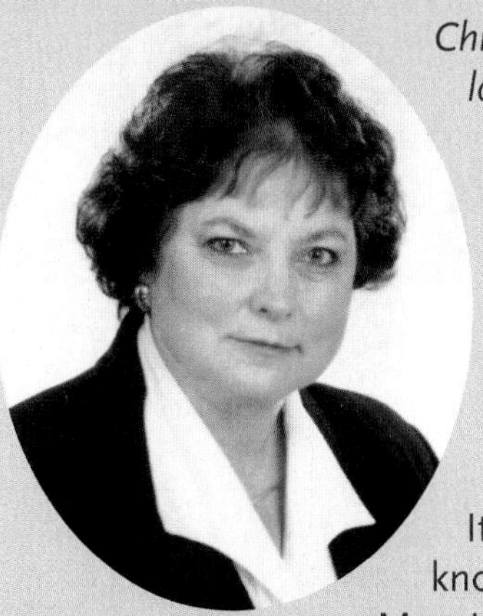

*Christine Curtis, chairman of the National Investor's Association Advisory Board, is a long-time NAIC member. She's invested in funds since 1985.*

**Q. What common mistakes should fund investors try to avoid?**

Realize what the real cost is of holding a particular fund—not only the expense ratio, but any sales charges as well as brokerage commissions, fund family fees and other costs. Don't go for funds that do a lot of trading—turnover has high costs in and of itself. Make sure you are really diversified.

**Q: How has the NAIC Mutual Fund Program helped you?**

It has made me more astute in selecting funds—I've gained a lot of personal knowledge. Through self-study, I've found out how to read and interpret the Morningstar report. The Handbook really led me through the tools so I knew how to complete the forms. The tools in this program are valuable because they help you line things up and categorize them in a consistent fashion from fund to fund. It makes it much easier to find good funds when you can use the same form to evaluate them. In that way, this program is extraordinarily valuable to investors to help them make decisions and to chose from thousands of funds.

**Q: What, in your opinion, is the major difference between NAIC's investing philosophy and other investing practices?**

NAIC's philosophy is common sense—that aspect jumped out at me when I first was exposed to NAIC. It's a reasonable, conservative approach that is easily understandable. There is no hocus-pocus. I liked the fact that there were volunteers there to help me—people were motivated and willing to give their time to help others and to answer questions.

## Costs

While you can't control a fund's costs, you can control how much you pay in fund fees by investing your money in low-cost funds. As discussed in Chapter 11, fund companies assess a number of different fees, and it pays to find the highest quality fund you can at the lowest possible price. When ranking any expenses in this section, the lowest number always gets the highest ranking.

## Expense Ratio

In this comparison, Fund #2 wins first place with an expense ratio of .42. Fund #1, with an expense ratio of .65 comes in second and Fund #3 comes in third place with an expense ratio of 1.03 percent. While Fund #3 is much higher than Funds #2 and #1, it is lower than the large blend category average, which is 1.23 percent according to Morningstar.

Only one of the three funds in our comparison has a 12b-1 fee and that fund is ranked last. We omit mention of the management fee in the Comparison Guide, as it is a cost that is already included in the expense ratio.

## Loads

In any comparison, you would award the fund with the lowest load the highest ranking. Only one of the funds in this comparison carries a load, which is Fund #2 with a front-end load. Funds #1 and #3 are no-load funds and will get the first place ranking.

## Redemption Fees

Redemption fees are short-term fees designed to discourage market timers from trading in and out of fund shares. Because NAIC investors purchase fund shares for the long term, a time-limited redemption fee that is in place for a short period of time, such as three months, six months or even one year, is not a major disincentive to investing. Still, it's better not to have a redemption fee than to have one in case something major changes with the fund and you want to sell your shares. We rank Fund #1 and 2 first, followed by #3, which has a 1 percent redemption fee.

## Other Category

The Comparison Guide leaves several blank spaces at the

| Fund Name | Fund #1 | RANK | Fund #2 | RANK | Fund #3 | RANK |
|---|---|---|---|---|---|---|
| Expense Ratio % | 0.65 | 2 | 0.42 | 1 | 1.03 | 3 |
| 12b-1 Fee % | 0 | 1 | 0 | 1 | 0.25 | 2 |
| Load: Front / Back / Level % | 0 | 1 | 3 (front) | 2 | -- | 1 |
| Redemption Fee % | 0 | 1 | 0 | 1 | 1.0 | 2 |
| | | | | | | |
| | | | | | | |
| | 1st 12 2nd 3 3rd 3 | | 1st 8 2nd 4 3rd 2 | | 1st 3 2nd 9 3rd 4 | |

| | | | | | | |
|---|---|---|---|---|---|---|
| Expense Ratio % | 0.65 | 2 | 0.42 | 1 | 1.03 | 3 |
| 12b-1 Fee % | 0 | 1 | 0 | 1 | 0.25 | 2 |
| Load: Front / Back / Level % | 0 | 1 | 3 (front) | 2 | -- | 1 |
| Redemption Fee % | 0 | 1 | 0 | 1 | 1.0 | 2 |
| | | | | | | |
| | | | | | | |
| | 1st 12 2nd 3 3rd 3 | | 1st 8 2nd 4 3rd 2 | | 1st 3 2nd 9 3rd 4 | |

| Fund Name | Fund #1 | RANK | Fund #2 | RANK | Fund #3 | RANK |
|---|---|---|---|---|---|---|
| **COST** Expense Ratio % | 0.65 | 2 | 0.42 | 1 | 1.03 | 3 |
| 12b-1 Fee % | 0 | 1 | 0 | 1 | 0.25 | 2 |
| Load: Front / Back / Level % | 0 | 1 | 3 (front) | 2 | -- | 1 |
| Redemption Fee % | 0 | 1 | 0 | 1 | 1.0 | 2 |
| **OTHER** | | | | | | |
| | 1st 12 2nd 3 3rd 3 | | 1st 8 2nd 4 3rd 2 | | 1st 3 2nd 9 3rd 4 | |

bottom of the form for you to add any elements that you would like to compare between funds. There are a number of elements either on the Check List or on the Morningstar report that you might want to use in these spaces.

You could include the minimum purchase amount of the funds or the fund's median market capitalization or low minimum balance fees. It's totally up to you how to use the Other category. If you are satisfied that the elements in the Comparison Guide tell you what you need to know about the fund, you can leave this area blank.

## Final Rankings

We've finished our comparison, and have ranked each fund according to certain criteria. Remember that the particular rankings of different items vary from investor to investor. If the ranking system helps you in your fund

selection process, use it. If it doesn't, don't. It is totally optional.

We did use the ranking in this comparison as a guide, not as a straightjacket. In terms of the pure numbers, Fund #1 scored 12 first-place rankings, three second-place rankings and three third-place ranking. Fund #2 scored eight first-place rankings, four second-place rankings and two third-place rankings. Fund #3 scored three first-place rankings, nine second-place rankings and four last-place rankings.

You need to decide which elements in the comparison analysis are most important to you. For some investors, total return reigns, and they will select the fund with the best

returns, regardless of other considerations. For other investors, tax efficiency is the top criteria, and they will weigh the tax elements of the analysis more heavily than other items such as market capitalization or total return. A third investor might go for the fund with the lowest cost.

This particular analysis is somewhat complicated, as the lowest cost fund is one in which the manager hasn't been around for the prerequisite five years and which also carries a 3 percent front-end load. The fund with the highest five-year total return is the most tax inefficient.

Fund #1 comes out on top by the numbers, but the evaluation of funds goes beyond adding up the numbers and figuring out the more important rankings. Weigh the criteria in your analysis; crunch the numbers decide on your priorities and then pick the fund that best meets your investing goals.

| Fund Name | Fund #1 | RANK | Fund #2 | RANK | Fund #3 | RANK |
|---|---|---|---|---|---|---|
| **COST** Expense Ratio % | 0.65 | 2 | 0.42 | 1 | 1.03 | 3 |
| 12b-1 Fee % | 0 | 1 | 0 | 1 | 0.25 | 2 |
| Load: Front / Back / Level % | 0 | 1 | 3 (front) | 2 | -- | 1 |
| Redemption Fee % | 0 | 1 | 0 | 1 | 1.0 | 2 |
| **OTHER** | | | | | | |
| | 1st 12 2nd 3 3rd 3 | | 1st 8 2nd 4 3rd 2 | | 1st 3 2nd 9 3rd 4 | |

# Stock Fund Trend Report

## Follow Vital Trends

Once you've bought shares in a fund that meets your investing goals, one task remains: monitoring the fund's trends. By keeping your finger on a fund's pulse, you'll know if something changes.

Even the best funds suffer setbacks from time to time. Your job is to investigate and see if a setback is a one-time event outside the manager's control—

such as a bear market—or due to a fundamental change in fund policies.

A fundamental change, such as a manager resignation or institution of new fees, may cause you to re-evaluate your commitment to the fund. One-time setbacks are part of the investing landscape, and aren't usually a reason to sell your fund shares.

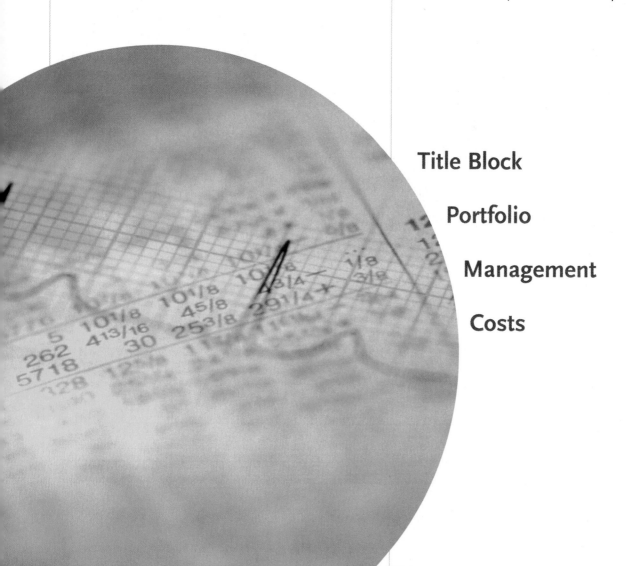

**Title Block**

**Portfolio**

**Management**

**Costs**

## Overview

The Stock Fund Trend Report, the third of NAIC's stock fund analysis tools, is one-page. It's designed to help you assess a fund's key characteristics on an ongoing basis.

Funds aren't static entities. Managers come and go; investment policies change and investing styles go in and out of favor. Any or all of these events is a call for you to re-evaluate your fund. You can do this quickly and easily using the Trend Report and a fund's latest Morningstar report.

Morningstar follows a five-month cycle in issuing fund reports. You can expect a new report approximately twice a year. Notice the top bar in the Trend Report main data section, which is entitled "Portfolio Analysis Date." This is where you insert the portfolio analysis date of the Morningstar report that you are using to update your Trend Report.

Morningstar's reporting cycle can change if Morningstar reclassifies your fund into another part of the style box, since Morningstar issues fund reports based on their categorization of a fund.

If Morningstar reclassifies your mid-cap blend fund as a large-cap blend fund, its report will move from the mid-cap blend section to the large-cap blend section. The new report will be issued on a different cycle. As with the Comparison Guide, the fund in this analysis is not an actual fund but a fund designed for teaching purposes.

The Trend Report covers the same ground as the Comparison Guide. The portfolio composition element in the old Equity Mutual Fund Trend Report was removed to make room for other elements such as sector analysis.

The Trend Report's function is to prompt you to track a fund's key elements throughout your entire ownership of a fund's

## Stock Fund Trend Report™

Fund Category: _Large Blend_

Fund Name: _Sample_

Taxable Acct.: _X_  Tax-Deferred Acct.: ___

| | | | 6/00 | 12/00 | 5/01 | 11/01 | 4/02 | |
|---|---|---|---|---|---|---|---|---|
| **PORTFOLIO** | Portfolio Analysis Date | | 6/00 | 12/00 | 5/01 | 11/01 | 4/02 | |
| | Market Capitalization | Giant % | 59.0 | 50.9 | 43.4 | 32.6 | 38.0 | |
| | | Large % | 37.2 | 43.8 | 50.1 | 59.6 | 52.0 | |
| | | Medium % | 3.8 | 4.5 | 4.9 | 5.7 | 7.8 | |
| | | Small % | 0 | 0.8 | 1.5 | 2.0 | 2.2 | |
| | | Micro % | 0 | 0 | 0.1 | 0.1 | 0 | |
| | Sector Analysis / INFORMATION | Software % | 10.3 | 10.3 | 8.2 | 7.5 | 6.2 | |
| | | Hardware % | 7.5 | 7.0 | 7.1 | 7.1 | 7.4 | |
| | | Media % | 9.4 | 8.7 | 8.4 | 8.0 | 7.5 | |
| | | Telecom % | 3.5 | 3.7 | 3.0 | 2.7 | 2.0 | |
| | SERVICE | Health % | 21.9 | 20.7 | 22.7 | 22.7 | 23.8 | |
| | | Consumer % | 5.8 | 5.8 | 5.8 | 6.2 | 6.2 | |
| | | Business % | 10.0 | 10.7 | 11.4 | 11.8 | 11.8 | |
| | | Financial % | 10.8 | 12.5 | 14.6 | 16.2 | 18.1 | |
| | MANUFACTURING | Goods % | 13.6 | 13.6 | 11.8 | 10.9 | 9.8 | |
| | | Ind. Materials % | 2.7 | 0.4 | 0.4 | 0.3 | 0.3 | |
| | | Energy % | 4.5 | 5.0 | 5.0 | 5.1 | 5.5 | |
| | | Utilities % | 0 | 1.6 | 1.6 | 1.5 | 1.4 | |
| | Number of Stocks in Portfolio | | 92 | 94 | 94 | 96 | 98 | |
| | Total Assets $ | | 4,867m | 4,952m | 4,211m | 3,724m | 3,988m | |
| | Sales Growth % | | 16.0 | 18.0 | 16.0 | 14.0 | 13.0 | |
| | Trailing Earnings % | | 18.9 | 18.3 | 16.7 | 15.8 | 15.6 | |
| | P/E Ratio | | 32.0 | 31.4 | 26.7 | 27.1 | 28.0 | |
| **MANAGEMENT** | Management Change ? | | No | No | No | No | No | |
| | Total Return %  10-Year Avg. | | 18.7 | 16.2 | 12.5 | 11.8 | 12.7 | |
| | 5-Year Avg. | | 16.9 | 15.1 | 10.8 | 9.9 | 11.2 | |
| | 3-Year Avg. | | 15.7 | 13.8 | 7.9 | 2.4 | 4.5 | |
| | Taxes %  10-Year Avg. | | 0.92 | 0.90 | 0.94 | 0.93 | 0.83 | |
| | 5-Year Avg. | | 0.98 | 0.95 | 1.01 | 1.00 | 0.94 | |
| | 3-Year Avg. | | 0.88 | 0.90 | 1.27 | 0.36 | 0.43 | |
| | 5-Yr. Average Turnover Rate % | | 15.0 | 19.5 | 31.0 | 25.0 | 22.0 | |
| **COST** | Expense Ratio % | | 0.57 | 0.57 | 0.60 | 0.65 | 0.65 | |
| | 12b-1 Charges % | | -- | -- | -- | -- | -- | |
| | Load - Front / Back / Level % | | -- | -- | -- | -- | -- | |
| | Redemption Fee % | | -- | -- | -- | -- | -- | |
| **OTHER** | Next Issue Date | | 12/00 | 5/01 | 11/01 | 4/02 | 9/02 | |
| | | | | | | | | |
| | | | | | | | | |
| | | | | | | | | |

© 2000 National Association of Investors Corporation, 711 West Thirteen Mile Road, Madison Hgts., Michigan 48071

shares. NAIC's philosophy of buy-and-hold doesn't mean you should buy-and-ignore. Internal changes in a fund, or changes in your investing plan and needs, may dictate a sale of your funds shares.

## Problems vs. Blips

While some changes in a fund are cause for alarm and a reason to sell, others are just blips on the investing landscape. We'll go over the difference between the two and provide a list of red flags or circumstances under which you should consider selling your fund shares. Appearance of a red flag in your fund doesn't mean you should call the fund company and sell your shares on the spot, but are a sign that you should do more research and decide whether to sell or hold.

In considering red flags and reasons to sell, investors in a taxable account should consider their tax situation before selling. If you've owned your fund shares for many years and have a sizeable gain, selling your shares will involve paying taxes on that gain. If your fund has performed poorly, you could have a taxable loss. While tax considerations shouldn't totally drive your portfolio management decisions, they are a consideration.

Short of selling your shares, if you participate in an automatic investment plan and have serious concerns about your fund, you can stop your investment plan while you resolve those concerns.

For many investors, a change in the management of an actively managed fund is a red flag. Some investors sell their funds shares immediately and seek a replacement fund, while others hold off, investigating the manager's successor. Regardless of who takes over the operation of the fund, portfolio and management strategies are likely to change.

Management is key to the success of an actively managed fund. If the new manager isn't on par in terms of experience and expertise with the old manager, why hang onto your fund shares?

---

### Figure 14.1: Red Flags

**The following is a list of Trend Report red flags:**

- Change in management at an actively-managed fund
- Merger into another fund
- Change in investment objective or strategy
- New or higher fees
- Sustained rise in the turnover rate
- Continual poor performance vs. a comparable index fund

If you receive a proposal from your fund company to merge your fund into another fund, watch out. Fund companies don't always merge funds into those of a similar objective and style, so if you go along with the merger, you could be investing in a substantially different fund.

At the very least, you'll be investing in a new fund that you need to investigate. If the new fund doesn't meet your requirements, sell your fund shares and look for a new fund.

A change in the fund's investment objective is equally serious, and bears watching. Many investors purchase fund shares to fill a specific niche in their portfolio, and if a fund radically alters its objectives and strategies, you could find it overlapping with other funds in your portfolio.

*If your fund expenses rise to an unacceptable level, seriously consider selling your fund shares and finding a less expensive fund. Check the Morningstar category average to see what the average no-load fund charges. You don't want to pay more than that, and should try to pay less. Also compare to a low-cost index fund. In Figure 14.2 is an example of how a fund's expense ratio can increase.*

While one year's increase in the turnover rate isn't a red flag in and of itself, this is a trend that bears close

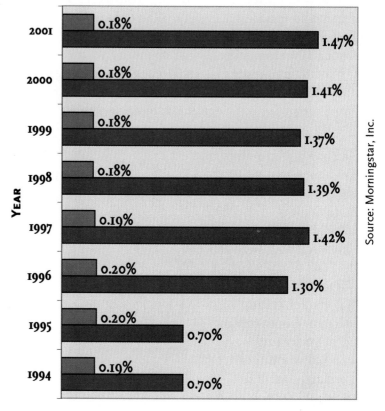

**Rising Expense Ratio: Hancock vs. Large Blend Index Fund**

| Year | Hancock Core Equity A | Large Blend Index Fund |
|------|----------------------|------------------------|
| 2001 | 0.18% | 1.47% |
| 2000 | 0.18% | 1.41% |
| 1999 | 0.18% | 1.37% |
| 1998 | 0.18% | 1.39% |
| 1997 | 0.19% | 1.42% |
| 1996 | 0.20% | 1.30% |
| 1995 | 0.20% | 0.70% |
| 1994 | 0.19% | 0.70% |

Source: Morningstar, Inc.

■ **Hancock Core Equity A** ■ **Large Blend Index Fund**

*Figure 14.2: Going Up, Up and Up...*

watching, especially if the increase is significant. If the turnover rate continues to rise, expect your costs to increase and the tax efficiency of your fund to decrease.

A serious drop in fund performance is a red flag or a blip, depending on the circumstances. Before selling your shares on a performance drop alone, look into its causes. Is the entire market down, or is the section of the market that your fund invests in down, or is the drop particular to your fund alone?

Value funds were out of favor in the late 1990s, as many had lagging performance and sagging asset bases. Much of this poor performance was common to all value funds, based on the fact that high-tech growth stocks were in favor with the market, and high-dividend value stocks were out of favor. Turn the clock ahead a year or two and you find that value funds are showing strong performance and growth funds are declining.

If your fund's performance is superior to its peer group and a comparable market index during a time when the market is down or a particular sector is out of favor, this is one sign that your fund continues to do well, despite the short-term downturn. However, if your fund's performance trails peer group and comparable index measures quarter after quarter, consider selling your shares. There is no reason to hang on indefinitely to a poor-performing fund with so many others available.

If your regular update of the Trend Report shows no problems or concerns, you may want to invest more money in the fund, if you aren't already regularly investing with an automatic investment plan.

## Title Block

When you start a Trend Report on a fund that you own, begin by filling in the Title Block. Indicate the fund's category, its name and whether it is in

**Stock Fund**
**Trend Report**

Investment Education Since 1951

Fund Category: _Large Blend_
Fund Name: _Sample_
Taxable Acct.: _X_ Tax-Deferred Acct.: ___

| Portfolio Analysis Date | | 6/00 | 12/00 | 5/01 | 11/01 | 4/02 | |
|---|---|---|---|---|---|---|---|
| Market Capitalization | Giant % | 59.0 | 50.9 | 43.4 | 32.6 | 38.0 | |
| | Large % | 37.2 | 43.8 | 50.1 | 59.6 | 52.0 | |
| | Medium % | 3.8 | 4.5 | 4.9 | 5.7 | 7.8 | |
| | Small % | 0 | 0.8 | 1.5 | 2.0 | 2.2 | |
| | Micro % | 0 | 0 | 0.1 | 0.1 | 0 | |

a taxable account or a tax deferred account. In this Trend Report we're examining a fund in a taxable account, so that box is checked.

## Portfolio

The Trend Report's Portfolio Section covers familiar ground: the fund's market capitalization, sector analysis, total stocks in the portfolio, total assets, sales growth, trailing earnings growth rate and price/earnings.

## Market Capitalization

By keeping track of a fund's market capitalization, you can see if it remains true to its investment objective.

*This fund keeps 90 percent or more of its assets in the giant and large categories. This shows it is staying true to its large blend objective and categorization. Figure 14.3 is a breakdown of the market capitalization in a pie chart for the first, third and last reporting periods.*

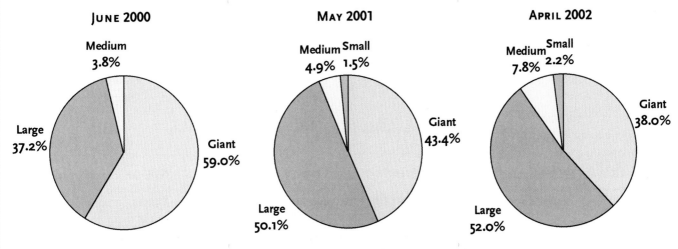

Figure 14.3: Trend Report Market Cap Pie Chart

| Portfolio Analysis Date | | | 6/00 | 12/00 | 5/01 | 11/01 | 4/02 | |
|---|---|---|---|---|---|---|---|---|
| Sector Analysis | INFORMATION | Software % | 10.3 | 10.3 | 8.2 | 7.5 | 6.2 | |
| | | Hardware % | 7.5 | 7.0 | 7.1 | 7.1 | 7.4 | |
| | | Media % | 9.4 | 8.7 | 8.4 | 8.0 | 7.5 | |
| | | Telecom % | 3.5 | 3.7 | 3.0 | 2.7 | 2.0 | |
| | SERVICE | Health % | 21.9 | 20.7 | 22.7 | 22.7 | 23.8 | |
| | | Consumer % | 5.8 | 5.8 | 5.8 | 6.2 | 6.2 | |
| | | Business % | 10.0 | 10.7 | 11.4 | 11.8 | 11.8 | |
| | | Financial % | 10.8 | 12.5 | 14.6 | 16.2 | 18.1 | |
| | MANUFACTURING | Goods % | 13.6 | 13.6 | 11.8 | 10.9 | 9.8 | |
| | | Ind. Materials % | 2.7 | 0.4 | 0.4 | 0.3 | 0.3 | |
| | | Energy % | 4.5 | 5.0 | 5.0 | 5.1 | 5.5 | |
| | | Utilities % | 0 | 1.6 | 1.6 | 1.5 | 1.4 | |

## Sector Analysis

The Trend Report reveals which sectors a fund is invested in, and how those percentages have changed over five reporting periods. Throughout the five reporting periods, the manager has been gradually reducing the percentage of assets invested in the Information Economy super sector (software, hardware, media and telecom).

The manager gradually increased the percentage of assets invested in the Service Economy super sector (health care, consumer services, business services and financial services) and reduced the Manufacturing Economy super sector (consumer goods, industrial materials, energy and utilities).

The time period covered by this Trend Report includes the burst of the technology stock speculation bubble, when many formerly highly favored stocks in all Information Economy sectors swooned. Under these circumstances,

many fund managers reduced their holdings in this area as future sales and earnings growth expectations were substantially eroded.

## Number of Stocks in the Portfolio & Total Assets

This fund is consistent in regard to the number of stocks in the portfolio, holding between 92 to 98 stocks in the

five periods. Numbers indicate that the portfolio is expanding a bit, but this isn't something that is likely to dramatically affect the fund's performance.

In our example fund, assets drop significantly from the second reporting period to the fourth reporting period, then rebound slightly in the last reporting period.

Investor redemptions can have a significant impact on a fund. When investors want their money back, managers must frequently sell stock. These sales must take place whether the manager really wants to sell stock or not. Such sales may also leave investors in taxable accounts with capital gains taxes on the sale of

| Number of Stocks in Portfolio | 92 | 94 | 94 | 96 | 98 | |
|---|---|---|---|---|---|---|
| Total Assets $ | 4,867m | 4,952m | 4,211m | 3,724m | 3,988m | |

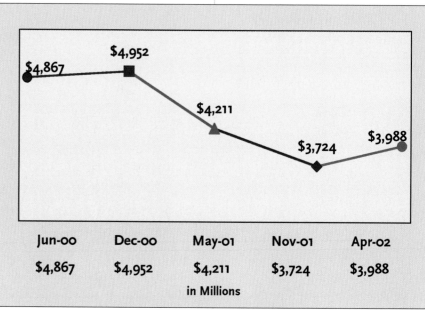

| Jun-00 | Dec-00 | May-01 | Nov-01 | Apr-02 |
|---|---|---|---|---|
| $4,867 | $4,952 | $4,211 | $3,724 | $3,988 |

in Millions

*14.4 Trends In Asset Growth*

| Portfolio Analysis Date | 6/00 | 12/00 | 5/01 | 11/01 | 4/02 | |
|---|---|---|---|---|---|---|
| Sales Growth % | 16.0 | 18.0 | 16.0 | 14.0 | 13.0 | |
| Trailing Earnings % | 18.9 | 18.3 | 16.7 | 15.8 | 15.6 | |
| P/E Ratio | 32.0 | 31.4 | 26.7 | 27.1 | 28.0 | |

profitable stock positions in the fund.

A decline in the number of shareholders can mean higher costs to remaining shareholders. This is because the fund's expenses are spread over a smaller number of assets or shareholders.

## Sales Growth, Trailing Earnings & Price/Earnings

From this Trend Report, it is evident that the fund's sales and trailing portfolio earnings growth rates are slowing during the five reporting periods. There are many reasons why the portfolio sales and earnings growth rates have fallen. Company sales and earnings rates fell significantly during the 2000-2002 recession. Also, companies in the portfolio could individually be faltering, experiencing problems with their businesses.

In a similar fashion to the trailing portfolio earnings growth rate, the average P/E ratio for this fund is falling, though not in a straight descent. Along with earnings growth, P/E ratios decreased during the most recent recession. With profits taking a big hit, investors were

unwilling to pay such high prices for many companies, resulting in a lowering of many company's P/E ratios.

## Management

As fund investors, we pay portfolio managers to invest our money. An essential part of any checkup on the welfare of our fund involves an examination of management and management trends.

### Management Change?

The bottom line in regard to fund management once you purchase funds shares is, "Has there been a management change?" This is the question you answer on the Trend Report with a simple yes or no.

If management changes, watch out. Many new managers sell

some, or all, of the previous manager's holdings in an effort to put their mark on the fund. This usually causes turnover to skyrocket and impairs a fund's tax efficiency. Gather information about the new manager's background. If the incoming manager's record doesn't reflect superior performance managing a similar fund, think seriously about selling your shares and finding a new fund.

## Total Return

To get a feeling for a fund's performance in different types of markets, we examine its 10-, five- and three-year total return figures. For our sample fund, total return numbers for the 10-, five- and three-year time periods decline in the first four reporting periods of the trend report.

This decline was due to a bear market that began in the spring of 2000 and was especially severe for technology

| | Portfolio Analysis Date | 6/00 | 12/00 | 5/01 | 11/01 | 4/02 | |
|---|---|---|---|---|---|---|---|
| **MANAGEMENT** | Management Change ? | No | No | No | No | No | |
| | Total Return %    10-Year Avg. | 18.7 | 16.2 | 12.5 | 11.8 | 12.7 | |
| | 5-Year Avg. | 16.9 | 15.1 | 10.8 | 9.9 | 11.2 | |
| | 3-Year Avg. | 15.7 | 13.8 | 7.9 | 2.4 | 4.5 | |
| | Taxes %    10-Year Avg. | 0.92 | 0.90 | 0.94 | 0.93 | 0.83 | |
| | 5-Year Avg. | 0.98 | 0.95 | 1.01 | 1.00 | 0.94 | |
| | 3-Year Avg. | 0.88 | 0.90 | 1.27 | 0.36 | 0.43 | |
| | 5-Yr. Average Turnover Rate % | 15.0 | 19.5 | 31.0 | 25.0 | 22.0 | |

| | Management Change ? | No | No | No | No | No | |
|---|---|---|---|---|---|---|---|
| **MANAGEMENT** | Total Return %    10-Year Avg. | 18.7 | 16.2 | 12.5 | 11.8 | 12.7 | |
| | 5-Year Avg. | 16.9 | 15.1 | 10.8 | 9.9 | 11.2 | |
| | 3-Year Avg. | 15.7 | 13.8 | 7.9 | 2.4 | 4.5 | |
| | Taxes %    10-Year Avg. | 0.92 | 0.90 | 0.94 | 0.93 | 0.83 | |
| | 5-Year Avg. | 0.98 | 0.95 | 1.01 | 1.00 | 0.94 | |
| | 3-Year Avg. | 0.88 | 0.90 | 1.27 | 0.36 | 0.43 | |
| | 5-Yr. Average Turnover Rate % | 15.0 | 19.5 | 31.0 | 25.0 | 22.0 | |

companies. Funds in virtually every category were affected to one degree or another, and many large blend funds experienced declines in total return. Since this is an overall market condition, and not a fundamental change in the fund, this should not prompt you to sell fund shares.

## % Taxes

This section examines the percentage of the funds total return paid out to taxes in three time periods: 10, five and three years. For the 10-year period, the tax-efficiency figures are

consistent, and actually decline a bit in the last period to .83. For the five-year period, the figures are higher than the three-year period, but still fairly consistent. The three-year period is the most volatile, with numbers ranging from a low of .36 in November 2001 to a high of 1.27 in May 2001.

The three-year average figures for the November 2001 period drops so far because total return for this period hits a low of 2.4 percent for the three-year period in November 2001. Tax-adjusted return was quite low as well, leaving a very low number for tax efficiency.

Tax efficiency decreased the most in the May 2001 and this change can be traced to the jump in the turnover rate in the same time period. Increasing turnover generally leads to poor tax efficiency.

### 5-Year Average Turnover Rate

This fund's average five-year turnover varies from a low of 15 percent in mid-2000 to a high of 31 percent in mid-2001. Any rise in the turnover rate is cause for concern. In this case, the turnover rate falls from the high of 31 percent back down to 22 percent in April 2002.

We saw earlier in this report that fund assets were indeed falling during this time period, which could account for the spike in turnover. Fund managers may also sell stock if they believe some of their holdings are overvalued.

Despite the rise in turnover, this figure is quite low to begin with, especially when

| Portfolio Analysis Date | | 6/00 | 12/00 | 5/01 | 11/01 | 4/02 | |
|---|---|---|---|---|---|---|---|
| Management Change ? | | No | No | No | No | No | |
| Total Return %   10-Year Avg. | | 18.7 | 16.2 | 12.5 | 11.8 | 12.7 | |
| 5-Year Avg. | | 16.9 | 15.1 | 10.8 | 9.9 | 11.2 | |
| 3-Year Avg. | | 15.7 | 13.8 | 7.9 | 2.4 | 4.5 | |
| Taxes %   10-Year Avg. | | 0.92 | 0.90 | 0.94 | 0.93 | 0.83 | |
| 5-Year Avg. | | 0.98 | 0.95 | 1.01 | 1.00 | 0.94 | |
| 3-Year Avg. | | 0.88 | 0.90 | 1.27 | 0.36 | 0.43 | |
| 5-Yr. Average Turnover Rate % | | 15.0 | 19.5 | 31.0 | 25.0 | 22.0 | |

| Management Change ? | | No | No | No | No | No | |
|---|---|---|---|---|---|---|---|
| Total Return %   10-Year Avg. | | 18.7 | 16.2 | 12.5 | 11.8 | 12.7 | |
| 5-Year Avg. | | 16.9 | 15.1 | 10.8 | 9.9 | 11.2 | |
| 3-Year Avg. | | 15.7 | 13.8 | 7.9 | 2.4 | 4.5 | |
| Taxes %   10-Year Avg. | | 0.92 | 0.90 | 0.94 | 0.93 | 0.83 | |
| 5-Year Avg. | | 0.98 | 0.95 | 1.01 | 1.00 | 0.94 | |
| 3-Year Avg. | | 0.88 | 0.90 | 1.27 | 0.36 | 0.43 | |
| 5-Yr. Average Turnover Rate % | | 15.0 | 19.5 | 31.0 | 25.0 | 22.0 | |

| | Portfolio Analysis Date | 6/00 | 12/00 | 5/01 | 11/01 | 4/02 | |
|---|---|---|---|---|---|---|---|
| COST | Expense Ratio % | 0.57 | 0.57 | 0.60 | 0.65 | 0.65 | |
| | 12b-1 Charges % | -- | -- | -- | -- | -- | |
| | Load - Front / Back / Level % | -- | -- | -- | -- | -- | |
| | Redemption Fee % | -- | -- | -- | -- | -- | |

| | Next Issue Date | 12/00 | 5/01 | 11/01 | 4/02 | 9/02 | |
|---|---|---|---|---|---|---|---|
| OTHER | | | | | | | |
| | | | | | | | |

compared to other large blend funds, which have turnover rates in excess of 80 percent. Although the most recent five-year average turnover rate is slightly above the NAIC benchmark of 20 percent, there isn't a cause for concern in this slight increase.

## Costs

Looking at expense ratio trends, you want to see this ratio staying level or declining, especially if fund assets are rising substantially. Between June 2000 and April 2002, the expense ratio increased by 8.8 percent. The increase in expense ratio could be linked to the decline in fund assets, which fell from $4.9 billion in June of 2000 to a low of 3.7 billion in November of 2001. Assets rebounded slightly at the end of the last reporting period.

As investors sell their shares, there are fewer accounts to share expenses, so the management company or adviser may increase the expense ratio to cover the fund's costs.

This is a trend you should watch carefully. An 8.8 percent increase in your cost is no minor matter, and costs could rise further, impacting your total return. Still, this fund's costs are much less than the average large blend fund, which stood at 1.23 percent in 2000 according to Morningstar.

The fund carries no loads, sales charges or redemption fees to date. Keep your eye on the fund as this can change.

## Other

The Other Section allows you to include elements important to you in your trend analysis. You may want to include elements from the Morningstar report or the Check List. You can also leave it blank if the elements already included tell you what you need to know about the fund.

The Next Issue Update is a unique item to the Trend Report. This is where you can note when Morningstar will put out another update on your fund. You can find this information on the front page of each section of the

*Morningstar Mutual Funds* publication that also lists an index of the funds covered. The next update date is located on the lower right-hand corner of the page.

What can we conclude about the sample fund after subjecting it to the Trend Report? Have there been any red flags? If you owned the fund, would it be worth keeping?

Overall, the fund is solid. Management is experienced, expenses are low, and total return is consistent. If you owned shares in the fund, it would be a good idea to keep an eye on the expenses to see if they keep increasing. However, they are still very low compared to other funds of the same type. There aren't any red flags, and the fund is in general superior to other large blend funds.

# Exploring Other Fund Types

## Analyze Other Funds

Our sample analyses in Chapters 8 to 14 focused on large-cap blend funds. Other types of funds—including small-cap, mid-cap and international funds—pose some different challenges. This chapter provides a brief overview of the unique qualities of these types of funds.

But despite some differences, the Check List, Comparison Guide and Trend Report analyze virtually any type of stock mutual fund. All stock funds share many common characteristics which make them suitable for NAIC analysis.

By using NAIC's evaluation tools on any type of stock mutual fund, you'll have a better chance to find funds that meet your investing needs.

Mid-Cap Funds

Small-Cap Funds

Foreign Stock Funds

## Overview

The NAIC Stock Fund Check List, Comparison Guide and Trend Report were designed to help investors evaluate all types of stock mutual funds. However, different types of funds have different characteristics, so this chapter will lay out some of the issues you should consider when analyzing mid-cap, small-cap and foreign funds.

Evaluating such funds isn't substantially different than evaluating a large-cap blend fund like Dreyfus Appreciation. The information that follows offers you some caveats to consider when looking at different types of funds.

## Mid-Cap Funds

Mid-cap stock funds generally invest in mid-cap companies, according to Morningstar's capitalization definitions. As of

this writing, the average mid-cap blend fund's market capitalization is $6.47 billion, compared with the average large-cap blend fund's market cap, which is $48.5 billion.

*Figure 15.1 shows the differences in the market capitalization of the average mid-cap blend and large-cap blend portfolios. According to Morningstar, the average mid-cap blend fund held at least 50 percent of their portfolio in mid-cap stocks, at least 15 percent of their portfolio in large-cap stocks, and at least 10 percent of their portfolio in small-cap stocks as of the closing months of 2001.*

Mid-cap funds offer attractive return potential with less volatility than small-cap funds.

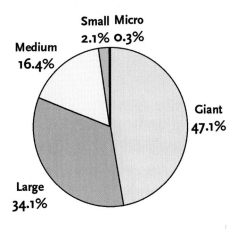

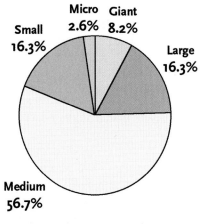

*Figure 15.1: Comparison of Market Capitalization of Holdings in Large-cap Blend and Mid-cap Blend Funds*

123

Mid-cap blend and growth funds usually hold companies with higher average trailing portfolio earnings growth rates, sales growth rates and average P/E ratios than do large-cap blend and growth funds.

Companies in the mid-cap range tend to fall into two categories: grown-up small-cap companies, and fallen large-cap companies. The former is found frequently in the portfolios of mid-cap growth funds, while the latter reside in the mid-cap value category.

As far as expenses go, mid-cap funds generally sport higher expense ratios than large-cap funds, but lower expense ratios than small-cap funds. Of course, specific funds vary widely in terms of their expense ratios and other key characteristics.

For example, the funds with the lowest expense ratio of all the mid-cap funds covered by Morningstar are the Vanguard Extended Market Index Fund and the Vanguard Mid-Cap Index Fund with expense ratios of .25 percent. The fund with the highest expense ratio is the IPO Aftermarket Fund, with an expense ratio of 2.5 percent, 10 times higher than the Vanguard index funds.

*Figure 15.2 shows a comparison of the average expense ratios for no-load, front-end load, back-end load and level load funds in the mid- and large-cap blend categories.*

As far as turnover rates go, mid-cap funds generally have higher five-year average turnover rates than large-cap funds. Growth funds in both categories have the highest turnover rates, followed by blend and value funds.

## MEET THE INVESTOR: BILL BIEDENSTEIN

*Bill Biedenstein, an NAIC Chapter Director in St. Louis, Mo., teaching fund classes using the NAIC Mutual Fund Programs*

**Q. What is the major difference between NAIC's investing practices and other investing practices?**

There are quite a few differences, but what runs through them all is the fact that NAIC is a community of investors, a learning community that recognizes people as capable of understanding the financial markets and making their own investment decisions after doing their own homework. Investment clubs and informed individuals come together to learn through classes and forums, either online or in actual gatherings. To my knowledge, there are few other groups that bring people together in a regular and concerted way to become educated on the financial markets.

**Q: How has the NAIC Mutual Fund Program helped you?**

The program has organized my thinking and given me the confidence that I can spot an excellent mutual fund when I see one. The concepts are easy to understand.

**Q: What common mistakes can fund investors avoid?**

Many investors have no idea of what investing style their portfolio manager employs. Does he typically buy value stocks or growth stocks? What is the turnover rate on an annualized basis? Check the 'under the hood' performance of the fund in Morningstar to see how often the manager trades, and manager expenses.

Many investors go after the top-performing fund of the previous year. One year is not an adequate period to evaluate the performance of a fund manager. Look for funds that do well in longer periods of time.

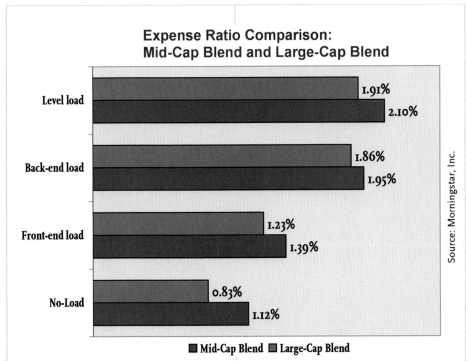

Expense Ratio Comparison:
Mid-Cap Blend and Large-Cap Blend

Level load — 1.91% / 2.10%

Back-end load — 1.86% / 1.95%

Front-end load — 1.23% / 1.39%

No-Load — 0.83% / 1.12%

Source: Morningstar, Inc.

■ Mid-Cap Blend ■ Large-Cap Blend

*Figure 15.2: Expense Ratio Comparison*

### Small-Cap Funds

The explosive growth potential of small- and micro-cap companies is a compelling argument for small-cap mutual funds. Small-cap funds generally have higher sales growth and portfolio earnings growth rates than either large or mid-cap funds. Average P/E ratios tend to be higher as well, reflecting the faster growth of smaller companies.

The returns of small- and micro-cap companies don't correlate well with those of large-cap companies, meaning that small-cap stocks perform quite differently from bigger companies. So, holding a fund concentrated in this sector provides significant

diversification from a large-cap fund of any type. However, before investing in this sector be aware that small-cap funds can be quite volatile.

Before evaluating specific small-cap funds, look for funds with managers and management objectives truly committed to the small-cap corner of the market. Some funds start out as small-cap funds, but as their holdings grow, end up holding more mid-cap than small-cap companies. Managers of small-cap companies face a cruel dilemma: they can sell their winners when they grow too large, and remain a true small-cap fund, or they can hold onto their winners and end up turning into a mid-cap fund.

Like mid-cap funds, small-cap funds tend to have higher turnover ratios than large-cap funds. One reason for this higher turnover rate is that to remain true to their investment objectives managers must sell many of their most successful companies as they grow larger and move into either mid- or large-cap territory.

Many small-cap funds hold mid-cap companies. In fact, according to Morningstar overview sheets, the average small-cap value, blend and

In terms of expense ratio, small-cap funds of all types generally have higher expense ratios than large-cap funds. In some cases, small-cap fund expenses are about equal to mid-cap funds, or slightly higher.

### Foreign Stock Funds

Chapter 5 provides a brief overview of some of the major characteristics of funds holding foreign companies. In this chapter we'll cover some specifics on how international and global funds differ from large-cap funds. International funds exclusively invest outside the United States, while global funds invest both inside and outside the United States.

Traditionally, funds with significant amounts of assets invested overseas have had higher expense ratios than U.S. funds. This is due to several

growth funds had between 26.3 percent and 30.5 percent of their assets invested in mid-cap companies. However, they also had between 60 and 80 percent of their asset invested in true small-cap

territory: small- and micro-cap companies.

*The comparison in Figure 15.3 shows the different market capitalization makeup for an average small-cap value, blend and growth fund.*

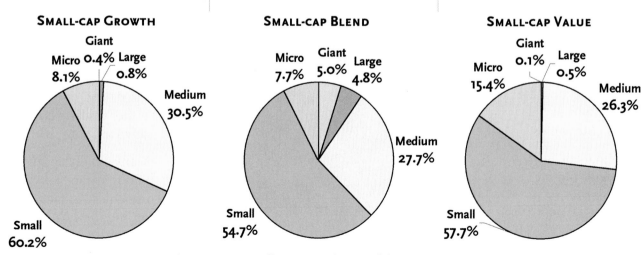

*Figure 15.3: Small Cap Funds' Portfolio Composition*
Source: Morningstar, Inc.

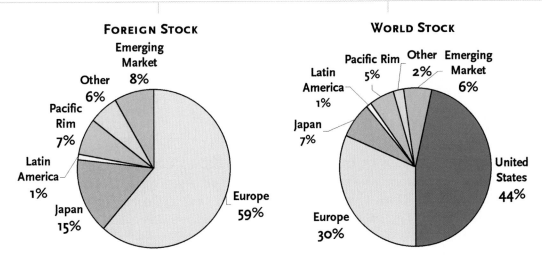

**FOREIGN STOCK**

- Emerging Market 8%
- Other 6%
- Pacific Rim 7%
- Latin America 1%
- Japan 15%
- Europe 59%

**WORLD STOCK**

- Pacific Rim 5%
- Latin America 1%
- Other 2%
- Emerging Market 6%
- Japan 7%
- United States 44%
- Europe 30%

Source: Morningstar, Inc. (due to rounding, the numbers don't add up to 100%)

*Figure 15.4: Foreign and Global Funds' Regional Exposure*

factors, including the additional expenses involved in gathering and analyzing information about foreign companies and higher overseas brokerage costs.

The average no-load international fund has had an expense ratio of 1.23 percent, .40 percentage points higher than the no-load fund average for large-blend funds. For global funds this ratio has been even higher at 1.45 percent.

*Taking a look at these funds' portfolios, their assets are spread into companies in many different countries. The graph in Figure15.4 provides an analysis of their portfolios by region, as analyzed by Morningstar. Due to rounding, the numbers don't add up to 100 percent.*

## Conclusion

Although mid-cap, small-cap and international funds do possess some different characteristics from large-cap funds, they aren't extremely significant. In fact, many domestic stock funds invest at least a portion of their holdings overseas, so you can get exposure to foreign companies by investing in those types of funds.

You can still use the Stock Fund Check List, Comparison Guide and Trend Report to identify, compare and follow these types of funds. Despite some variations, the vast majority of stock funds' chief characteristics—their portfolio, management and costs—are more similar than they are different.

# Bond Fund Tools

## *Funds of a different color*

*Years of history shows NAIC investors that true growth is found by investing in stocks and stock mutual funds for the long-term. Other types of investments don't offer the same growth potential.*

*The following section on bond fund investing is offered to educate investors wanting to explore these funds. Bonds and bond funds aren't as safe as they seem, and investors need to arm themselves with knowledge before investing.*

## Bond Fund Check List

**NAIC**
Investment Education Since 1951
www.better-investing.org
**BOND FUND**
**Check List** ™

Ⓐ Fund Name: _____
Ⓑ Ticker Symbol: _____
Ⓒ Category: _____
Ⓓ Minimum Purchase($): _____   Ⓔ Add'l($): _____
Ⓕ Min Auto Inv Plan($): _____   Ⓖ Add'l($): _____
Ⓗ IRA($): _____
Ⓘ Data Reference: _____   Ⓙ Page No _____
Ⓚ Current NAV($): _____
Ⓛ Taxable: _____   Ⓜ Tax-Deferred: _____

**1. FUND INVESTMENT CHARACTERISTICS**

A. Stated Investment Objective: _____
 • What are the fund's investment criteria & investment policies?

B. Portfolio Composition:   Cash ___%   Bonds ___%   Stocks ___%   Other ___%

C. Portfolio Analysis Date: _____   D. Average Effective Maturity: _____

E. Average Effective Duration: _____   F. Average Credit Quality: _____

G. Credit Analysis: US Govt ___%   AAA ___%   AA ___%   A ___%   BBB ___%   BB ___%   B ___%
 Below B ___%   NR/NA ___%   Special Securities ___%

**2. FUND MANAGEMENT CHARACTERISTICS**

A. 1. Fund Manager: _____   Years: _____   2. Date Fund Started: _____

B. Management Record:

| | Initial Year | | | | | |
|---|---|---|---|---|---|---|
| 1 Current Management Period: (enter all years) | | | | | | |
| 2 Total Return % | | | | | | |
| 3 Income Return % | | | | | | |
| 4 Capital Return % | | | | | | |
| 5 +/- Total Return % - Lehman Agg. Bond | | | | | | |
| 6 +/- Total Return % - Other Index | | | | | | |

C. Long-Term Total Return (%):   3 Yr. Avg. _____   5 Yr. Avg. _____   10 Yr. Avg. _____

D. 5 Yr. Avg. Turnover Rate (%): Years: _____   Total ___ Average ___
 Turnover Rate: _____

**3. COST CONSIDERATIONS**

A. Expense Ratio _____%
 The expense ratio includes a number of separate expenses, including:
 1. Management Fee _____%   2. 12b-1 Marketing & Distribution Fee _____%
B. Fund Peer Group Average Expense Ratio _____%
C. Loads:   Front-end _____%   Back-end _____%   Level _____%
D. Redemption Fee _____%
 Note: Investors also pay fund brokerage commissions

© 2003 National Association of Investors Corporation, 711 West Thirteen Mile Road, Madison Hgts., Michigan 48071

---

## Bond Fund Comparison Guide

**NAIC**
Investment Education Since 1951
**Bond Fund Comparison Guide** ™

Fund Category: _____
Date: _____
Taxable Acct.: _____   Tax-Deferred Acct.: _____

| | | FUND #1 | FUND #2 | FUND #3 |
|---|---|---|---|---|
| Fund Name | | | | |
| Portfolio Composition (%) | Cash | | | |
| | Bonds | | | |
| | Stocks | | | |
| | Other | | | |
| Average Effective Duration | | | | |
| Average Credit Quality | | | | |
| Credit Analysis (%) | US Govt | | | |
| | AAA | | | |
| | AA | | | |
| | A | | | |
| | BBB | | | |
| | BB | | | |
| | B | | | |
| | Below B | | | |
| | NR/NA | | | |
| | Special Securities | | | |
| Manager Tenure | | | | |
| Total Return % | 10-Year Avg. | | | |
| | 5-Year Avg. | | | |
| | 3-Year Avg. | | | |
| 5-Year Average Turnover Rate % | | | | |
| Expense Ratio % | | | | |
| 12b-1 Charges % | | | | |
| Load: Front / Back / Level % | | | | |
| Redemption Fee % | | | | |

1st   2nd   3rd      1st   2nd   3rd      1st   2nd   3rd

© 2003 National Association of Investors Corporation, 711 West Thirteen Mile Road, Madison Hgts., Michigan 48071

---

## Bond Fund Trend Report

**NAIC**
Investment Education Since 1951
**Bond Fund Trend Report** ™

Fund Category: _____
Fund Name: _____
Taxable Acct.: _____   Tax-Deferred Acct.: _____

| | | | | | |
|---|---|---|---|---|---|
| Portfolio Analysis Date | | | | | |
| Portfolio Composition | Cash % | | | | |
| | Bonds % | | | | |
| | Stocks % | | | | |
| | Other % | | | | |
| Average Effective Duration | | | | | |
| Average Credit Quality | | | | | |
| Credit Analysis | US Govt | | | | |
| | AAA | | | | |
| | AA | | | | |
| | A | | | | |
| | BBB | | | | |
| | BB | | | | |
| | B | | | | |
| | Below B | | | | |
| | NR/NA | | | | |
| | Special Securities | | | | |
| Management Change? | | | | | |
| Total Return % | 10-Year Avg. | | | | |
| | 5-Year Avg. | | | | |
| | 3-Year Avg. | | | | |
| 5-Year Average Turnover Rate % | | | | | |
| Expense Ratio % | | | | | |
| 12b-1 Charges % | | | | | |
| Load: Front / Back / Level % | | | | | |
| Redemption Fee % | | | | | |
| Next Issue Date | | | | | |

© 2003 National Association of Investors Corporation, 711 West Thirteen Mile Road, Madison Hgts., Michigan 48071

---

The **Bond Fund Check List** is based on the Stock Fund Check List. While stock and bond funds are in many ways very different, many of the key elements are similar. Bond fund investors look for long-term management and low cost as do stock fund investors. Bond fund investors must also consider elements and risks unique to bond funds.

The **Bond Fund Comparison Guide,** like its sister stock fund tool, allows you to compare bond funds to each other. Bond funds vary widely in terms of the types of bonds they hold, so its useful to compare a few funds to others before settling on a particular fund that will help you meet your investing needs.

The **Bond Fund Trend Report** allows you to follow up on a fund after you purchase shares. It's important to keep tabs on the funds that you own to make sure that management is in place, costs are low and that above all the fund is staying true to its investment objective.

# Bond Funds— Income Alternatives

## Investing for Income

Investors seeking diversification—and who are in need of income—look to bonds and bond funds as a viable source. Bond funds are a large and growing section of the mutual fund market and are one option for income-oriented investors.

Bond funds may seem like a safe haven during times of market turmoil, but they have risks of their own.

Before investing, make sure you understand the risks specific to bond funds.

This chapter introduces you to bonds, money market funds and bond funds, and their risks. It details the types of bond funds that are available in the marketplace.

**Money Market Funds**

**Bond Fund Risks**

**Types of Bond Funds**

## Overview

When you buy a bond, you loan money to a company or governmental entity. For the privilege of borrowing your money, the company or governmental entity pays you interest during the lifetime of the loan, and returns your initial investment at the end of the loan's term. Bonds are issued with varying terms, ranging from months to decades. When you buy shares in a bond fund, you're loaning money to many different companies or governmental entities. Shareholders in bond funds receive income in the form of interest payments. The fund receives this income and distributes it to shareholders on a regular basis. For most bond funds, this occurs monthly.

Owning shares in a bond fund is different from owning an individual bond. A bond matures at a specific point in time. In contrast, the many bonds in a fund mature at different times. The value of those individual bonds in a bond fund changes according to different variables that we'll discuss later.

Many individual and institutional investors prefer individual bonds to bond funds. Owning a number of

| | Equity Funds | Hybrid Funds | Bond Funds | Money Market Funds | Total |
|---|---|---|---|---|---|
| 1990 | $0.239 | $0.036 | $0.291 | $0.498 | $1.065 |
| 1991 | $0.405 | $0.052 | $0.394 | $0.542 | $1.393 |
| 1992 | $0.514 | $0.078 | $0.504 | $0.546 | $1.643 |
| 1993 | $0.741 | $0.145 | $0.619 | $0.565 | $2.070 |
| 1994 | $0.853 | $0.164 | $0.527 | $0.611 | $2.155 |
| 1995 | $1.249 | $0.210 | $0.599 | $0.753 | $2.811 |
| 1996 | $1.726 | $0.253 | $0.645 | $0.902 | $3.526 |
| 1997 | $2.368 | $0.317 | $0.724 | $1.059 | $4.468 |
| 1998 | $2.978 | $0.365 | $0.831 | $1.352 | $5.525 |
| 1999 | $4.042 | $0.379 | $0.812 | $1.613 | $6.846 |
| 2000 | $3.962 | $0.346 | $0.811 | $1.845 | $6.965 |
| 2001 | $3.418 | $0.346 | $0.925 | $2.285 | $6.975 |

Page 23— Assets of Mutual Funds, 1990–2001 (trillions of dollars)

*Figure 16.1 Money Market Funds Grow*
Source: 2002 Mutual Fund Fact Book, Copyright ©2002 Investment Company Institute (www.ici.org). Reprinted with permission.

different individual bonds offers portfolio diversification without some of the risks particular to bond funds.

Bond funds are popular investment vehicles. Like stock funds, they offer instant diversification. Purchasing bonds or bond funds will help you diversify your portfolio. Bonds and bond funds can certainly be volatile, but when placed in a portfolio along with stocks or stock funds they can help insulate that portfolio from the sharp swings of a stock-only portfolio.

### Money Market Funds

Money market funds, a type of very short-term bond fund, are an alternative to bank saving accounts for investors who want to earn a higher rate of return while preserving their principal. These funds are sponsored by many institutions, including banks, brokerages and mutual fund companies.

Money market funds invest in short-term instruments with maturities of 90 days or less. A share in a money market fund represents ownership in a pool of short-term securities that pay interest. Money market fund managers must comply with government regulations restricting the percentage of a fund's total assets that can be invested in a single issue.

While money market funds are low risk, the U.S. Government does not insure money market funds offered outside of banks, savings and loans, and credit unions. Insured money market funds generally offer a slightly lower interest rate than uninsured funds.

Although many are not insured, uninsured money market funds haven't lost any investor principal through the summer of 2003. Money market funds strive to maintain a stable share price of $1, although interest rates vary among funds. Because of their stable net asset value, they don't distribute capital gains.

The bottom line is that money market accounts are very low risk. Because money market funds invest in short-term securities, they are extremely sensitive to interest rates. Their yields fluctuate with changing interest rates, and will decline when interest rates go down, and rise when interest rates climb.

Investors poured assets into money market funds in the 1990s, quadrupling money market fund assets from $498.3 billion in 1990 to 2,285 billion in 2001.

Like other types of funds, money market funds carry expense ratios that cover their operating expenses. Before investing in a money market fund, research its expense ratio and compare it with other funds. With such a wide variety of funds available, its important to compare costs and chose a fund with low expenses.

## Bond Fund Risks

Investors in bonds and bond funds face certain rewards and risks. Should a company you buy stock in either directly or through a fund go bankrupt, that stock will most likely become worthless. However, if you own a bond in a bankrupt company either directly or through a bond fund, it is likely that you will get some of your money back. Also, if you purchase a bond in a financially stable company you will get your interest payments and principal back whether the company's stock price increases or not.

Some risks involved in bond ownership are common to both bonds and bond funds, while other types of risk are particular to bond funds. Major risks are interest rate risk and credit quality risk.

## Interest Rate Risk

The rise and fall of interest rates impacts the value of bonds and bond funds. The Federal Reserve Board controls short-term interest rates, and makes changes in those rates based on evidence and predictions about current and future economic growth and the threat of inflation.

If the Federal Reserve Board believes that the economy is slipping into a recession, it may decide to lower or "ease" interest rates in an effort to stimulate the economy. Lower interest rates encourage businesses and individuals to purchase capital goods and big-ticket items, such as a house or car, because borrowing costs are lower.

On the other hand, if the Federal Reserve Board believes that the economy is growing too quickly, it may raise interest rates in an effort to curb inflation. Higher inflation means price increases in goods and services. Higher interest rates slow the economy down, as it becomes more expensive for businesses and individuals to purchase capital goods and big-ticket items.

Interest rate cycles are very different than stock market cycles. While the stock market does have up and down cycles, the general market bias is upward. Interest rates don't keep going up, but vary according to the economy and economic policy.

Changes in Federal Reserve Board interest rate policies profoundly affect bonds and bond funds. This is because bonds are issued with a certain percentage yield and changes in interest rates render that yield either more or less valuable to current investors. Yield is a measurement of the percentage in interest paid to the bondholder by the bond issuer, based on the current price or face value of the bond.

Just like stocks, bonds are traded in an active market. While interest rate changes don't affect a bond's interest payments or its ultimate redemption value, they do affect the resale value of a bond in the bond market.

Here's how it works: when interest rates rise, the value of a bond falls. Rising interest rates render existing bonds with lower interest rates less valuable. Investors would rather purchase newly issued bonds with higher interest rates than older bonds with lower interest rates.

If you own an older bond with a lower interest rate than current prevailing rates and you sell that bond, it will most likely sell for less than you paid for it because it pays less in interest than newly issued bonds. If you hold the bond until maturity you will get your principal back and will continue to receive the interest payments associated with that bond.

This scenario works in reverse when interest rates fall. Interest rate declines render existing bonds more valuable than newly issued bonds because existing bonds carry higher

interest rates. If you wanted to sell an older bond with a higher interest rate you would most likely be able to sell it for more than it is worth because it carries a higher yield.

Interest rate increases or decreases often affect longer maturity bonds more than bonds with shorter maturities. Maturity refers to the point in time when the issuer pays off a bond. For example a 10-year bond issued in 1997 would mature in 2007.

### The Yield Curve

*A comparison between the interest rates of bonds of varying maturities is captured in the yield curve. The yield curve is a plot of various bond maturities that shows the bond's current yields versus their maturity dates. An example of the yield curve is seen in the illustration in Figure 16.2.*

The most well-known yield curve is that of U.S. Treasury bills and bonds of maturities of three months to 30 years. The line of the yield curve begins with the three-month Treasury bill and ends with the 30-year Treasury bond.

Since there is more chance that interest rates will vary in the long term than in the short term, investors in longer-term bonds take on more risk than investors in shorter-term bonds. To compensate investors for this additional risk, bonds with longer maturities normally offer higher yields than bonds with shorter maturities. This is reflected in the normal yield curve, where as bond maturities lengthen, yields increase, and the slope of the yield curve goes upward.

The short-term end of the yield curve is set by Federal Reserve

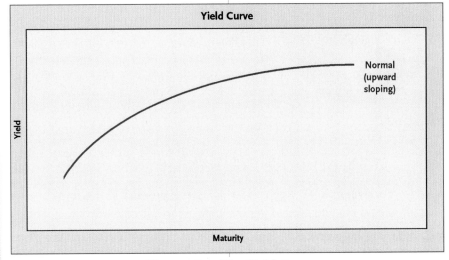

*Figure 16.2: The Yield Curve*
Source: Fabozzi, Frank, editor, *The Handbook of Fixed Income Securities,* sixth edition (2001), McGraw-Hill. Reprinted with permission

policy, while the long-term end of the yield curve is reflective of what bond investors expect in terms of economic growth and inflation in the future. The yield curve isn't always "normal" and can take on other forms based on Federal Reserve policies and market expectations.

Many newspapers and financial publications include the U.S. Treasury yield curve. A look at the yield curve tells you where interest rates are at that particular moment in time.

### Bond Fund Maturities

Bond funds hold many bonds with different maturity dates.

As the bonds in the portfolio mature, the manager replaces them with newly issued bonds or existing bonds purchased in the bond markets.

Managers of bond funds trade bonds in and out of their portfolio in an effort to increase the fund's income and capital gains potential. The nature of a bond fund dictates that the fund doesn't have a particular maturity date, just an average maturity date that reflects the maturity of all of the bonds in the portfolio.

This is a crucial difference between bonds and bond funds. If you own an individual

bond, you can hold that bond to maturity and get your initial investment amount back from the issuing company or government, regardless of what has happened to interest rates during the time that you owned the bond. One important caveat: the issuing company or governmental body must still be in a solid financial condition. We'll cover these issues related to bond and bond fund credit quality later in this chapter.

This isn't the case with bond funds. Because the individual bonds in the portfolio have varying maturity dates that are affected by interest rates, you

---

## EXPERT PROFILE: ROY WEITZ

*Roy Weitz is the proprietor of Fund Alarm (www.fundalarm.com), an investor advocacy Web site.*

**Q: What advice would you give new fund investors?**

First, take a deep breath. Mutual fund investing can seem complex and overwhelming, but there are actually just a few basic principles that almost anyone can master. Next, read two or three good introductory books on fund investing, beginning with this one. Third, based on your reading, come up with an asset allocation, which is the percentage of your total portfolio that you wish to invest in stock and bond funds. Then, and only then, are you ready to even think about selecting specific funds.

**Q: What common mistakes should fund investors try to avoid?**

- Don't get too fancy: four or five plain-vanilla funds are probably the most anyone needs.

- Don't trade too much, but don't ignore your funds, either. For example, if you own four funds, you might need to change one of those funds every three to five years, at most.

- Keep your eye on fund expenses, which are expressed in the form of an expense ratio. If several funds fit your asset allocation, you should generally invest in the one with the lowest expense ratio.

- Don't try to hit homeruns. Slow and steady almost always wins the investment race. This advice is especially important if you are coming to fund investing later in life, say in your 40s or 50s. You will never be able to completely make up for lost time, so relax, do the best you can, and don't do anything foolish. At least you've gotten started.

## FIGURE 16.3: MORNINGSTAR CREDIT ANALYSIS RATINGS AND DEFINITIONS

| Rating | Definition | Grade |
|---|---|---|
| U.S. Government | Bonds issued and backed by the government; highest quality and safety | Investment |
| AAA | Bonds issued by government-linked agencies and corporations; very high quality | Investment |
| AA | Corporate bonds; upper medium grade | Investment |
| A | Corporate bonds; upper medium grade | Investment |
| BBB | Corporate bonds; lowest investment grade | Investment |
| BB | Corporate bonds; low grade, speculative | "Junk" |
| B | Corporate bonds; very speculative | "Junk" |
| Below B | Corporate bonds; substantial risk; may be in default | "Junk" |
| NR/NA | Corporate bonds; not rated by major rating agencies | |

Source: Morningstar Data

can lose money by investing in a bond fund. The net asset value of a bond fund is computed daily based on the current value of the bonds in the portfolio, and the value of these bonds constantly fluctuates.

When interest rates are rising, bond fund investors may not get all of their principal back and may not see a recovery in the fund's net asset value until interest rates stabilize or fall again. If the fund is poorly managed or is paying investors higher yields at the expense of its principal value, investors may never recover their initial investment.

The opposite is true when interest rates are falling. Investors will see an increase in the net asset value of their funds when interest rates fall. So the risk of an erosion in bond fund values when interest rates rise is somewhat offset by the potential for an increase in bond fund values when interest rates fall.

If you buy shares in bond funds for the income potential, be aware of how interest rate movements can affect the value of your bond fund. You'll be better off if you invest in a high-quality fund with the expectation of holding your shares for the long term. You can get in just as much trouble trying to time the bond market as you could trying to time the stock market.

### Credit Risk

When you invest in a bond fund, you lend money to a corporation, governmental body or other entity. You need to assess the combined ability of the issuers of the bonds in a bond fund portfolio to pay the stated interest and repay your money when the bonds mature.

This is a difficult task for fund managers to undertake, and is even more difficult for individual investors. Fortunately, a number of credit rating agencies are in the business of examining a

corporation or governmental body's finances in an effort to assess their ability to make continued interest payments and repay investors' principal.

These companies assess credit quality, which in the simplest terms is a measurement of a bond issuer's ability to remain solvent. Bond rating companies issue credit ratings on thousands of corporations and governmental agencies. Different firms use different ranking systems which are all letter-based systems with rankings ranging from the highest (AAA or Aaa) to the lowest (D).

*Within this ranking system, there are two overall categories: investment grade bonds and non-investment grade (or junk) bonds. Figure 16.3 shows a table giving an overview of the major credit rating companies' grades and what they mean.*

Investment grade rankings are those believed by the credit

rating agencies to be safe investments, while non-investment grades are quite risky. Within those broad categories there are different grades, which reflect the soundness of the governmental bodies or companies issuing the bond.

Credit rating companies constantly review the financial statements and condition of governmental bodies and corporations. As the economy and the individual circumstances of these issuers change, credit rating firms lower or raise ratings. They may indicate at times that they are reviewing a particular company with a view to either raising or lowering its rating in the future.

Keep in mind that credit rating agencies aren't perfect. Their assessment of a company's financial condition may be inaccurate, or a company may not be upfront with its financial statements. A company that seemed in good financial condition with solid credit ratings can fail, while others in seemingly poor condition with low credit ratings may remain in business, improving their finances.

The U.S. Government backs its treasury bonds, bills and notes with its full faith and credit. These government-backed

bonds are considered the safest, highest quality bond investment. Just below these bonds in safety are the bonds of federal government agencies, followed by those of financially stable corporations.

Lower on the scale are companies in weaker financial condition. The weakest companies' debt is below investment grade, meaning there is a higher risk for investors that the bond's interest rate payments will not be made and that principal will not be repaid.

Bond funds carry an average credit quality rating which reflects the quality of the bonds in the portfolio. When you invest in a high-grade bond or bond fund, it is very likely that you or the bond fund will

receive interest payments in full and on time and that the principal will be repaid.

Therefore, interest rates on high-quality bonds and bond funds tend to be lower, reflecting this certainty.

On the other hand, if you invest in low-quality bonds or bond funds, there is much less certainty that you will get your interest payments on time or have your principal returned to you or the fund. Because of the higher amount of risk involved in investing in low quality bonds or bond funds, investors are compensated with higher interest rates.

Below-investment grade bond funds are also known as high-yield or "junk" bond funds. While the yields of these funds are enticing, there is a high risk that the issuers of the bonds in the bond fund may experience credit downgrades or may actually default. When an issuer defaults on a bond obligation, interest payments to investors cease and principal may or may not be repaid.

Credit downgrades and issuer defaults can have a very negative effect on the net asset value of a high-yield bond fund. Unwary investors have lost significant amounts of money by investing in these bond funds. Many conservative investors who want to preserve their capital avoid all types of junk bonds and junk bond funds.

## Types of Bond Funds

Morningstar breaks bond funds into two categories: taxable and tax-exempt. Taxable bond funds purchase bonds issued by the federal government and corporations. The interest and any capital gain generated by these bonds are subject to federal, state and local taxes, unless they are held in a tax-deferred account such as an IRA or 401(k) plan.

There are many different types of bond funds that can be categorized as general taxable bond funds. These include bond funds that hold federal government bonds and bills, bonds issued by federal government agencies, bonds issued by corporations, and bonds issued by foreign governments and corporations.

Tax-exempt bonds, also known as municipal bonds, are those issued by state and local governments or state and local governmental agencies. The interest generated by these bonds is not subject to federal tax.

Investors can also escape payment of federal, state and, in some cases, local tax; if they invest in municipal bond funds that purchase bonds issued by the state they live in. For example, a resident of

California could invest in a California state bond fund. This strategy is only beneficial for residents of states with high tax rates, according to tax experts.

Municipal bonds and bond funds are subject to the same risks and rewards as taxable bond funds. Interest rates and credit ratings can affect both municipal bonds and bond funds negatively or positively.

Tax-free bonds are also rated by credit rating agencies, and some are high-grade issues, while others are not. In fact, there are junk municipal bonds, and default on the part of municipal bond issuers, while uncommon, is not unheard of. Carefully investigate the credit quality of any bond or bond fund before you invest.

Morningstar divides funds into three categories based on the bonds in the funds' portfolio. Short-term funds generally invest in bonds with a maturity between one and four years; intermediate-term funds invest in bonds with a maturity of four to 10 years; long-term bond funds invest in bonds with maturities of 10 years or more.

Bond index funds fall into Morningstar's broad bond fund categories. There are a number of different types of bond index funds, which attempt to replicate the performance of a

certain part of the bond market. There are bond index funds based on many bond market indexes, ranging from those focused on short-term bonds to those focused on long-term bonds. This category includes municipal and taxable bonds.

While not all index funds are created equal—there are actually some loaded index funds—low-cost bond index funds are a worthy option for those considering investing in a bond fund. Many low-cost bond index funds outperform their actively managed counterparts. When comparing bond funds, seriously consider including a bond index fund of like quality and duration in your comparison to get a better feeling for all of your options.

# Bond Fund Check List— Title Block & Portfolio

## Evaluating Bond Funds

Like their stock counterparts, NAIC's bond fund tools help you evaluate individual bond funds, compare them to other bond funds and track a fund's performance over time. The bond fund tools take elements common to all funds from the stock fund forms, and add characteristics unique to bond funds.

When investing for income, examine a bond fund's credit quality and measurements of maturity. Look for a fund with the elements that fit your investing horizon and overall financial plan.

Title Block

Investment Objective

Portfolio Composition

Average Effective Maturity

Average Effective Duration

Average Credit Quality

Credit Analysis

## Overview

Use the Bond Fund Check List to evaluate virtually any type of bond fund, as well as the bond portion of a balanced fund. This one-page, one-sided form examines the key elements in a bond fund. The example fund for the Bond Fund Check List is the Dodge & Cox Income Fund. This fund is used as an example; no investment recommendation is intended.

The Morningstar report for the Dodge & Cox Income Fund is on page 140 in this chapter. The report is keyed so you can locate where each item on the Check List is located on the Morningstar report. The Check List is on page 141, filled in with data from the Morningstar report. The Morningstar Overview sheet for the intermediate-term bond fund category is on page 142.

In earlier chapters we have covered in depth many of the key items on the Check List. Therefore, we will focus here almost exclusively on the elements unique to bond fund analysis. We'll refer you to the appropriate chapters for a full explanation of certain elements such as fund costs, which are similar for a bond fund or a stock fund.

## Title Block

The Title Block Section of the Bond Fund Check List differs significantly from the Stock Fund Check List's Title Block in one area: bond fund categories. See Chapter 8 for a detailed explanation of the other terms in the Title Block.

Dodge & Cox Income is classified as an intermediate-term bond fund by Morningstar. Morningstar divides the bond fund universe into two basic categories: taxable bond funds and municipal bond funds. Dodge & Cox Income is a taxable bond fund.

Within the taxable bond fund category, Morningstar further classifies funds by their portfolio holdings into 11 sub-categories. Funds are categorized by their average maturity—the length of time before a bond comes due for repayment—or the type of bond held by the fund. According to Morningstar, intermediate-term bond funds have an average effective maturity of more than four but less than 10 years.

## Fund Portfolio Characteristics

A fund's investment characteristics include key elements related to the fund's portfolio.

## Stated Investment Objective

The fund's stated investment objective in Section 1A tells you a fund's investing strategies and what types of bonds the manager purchases to reach that objective. Because Morningstar doesn't list the prospectus objective on the fund's report, get a prospectus from Dodge & Cox or check the

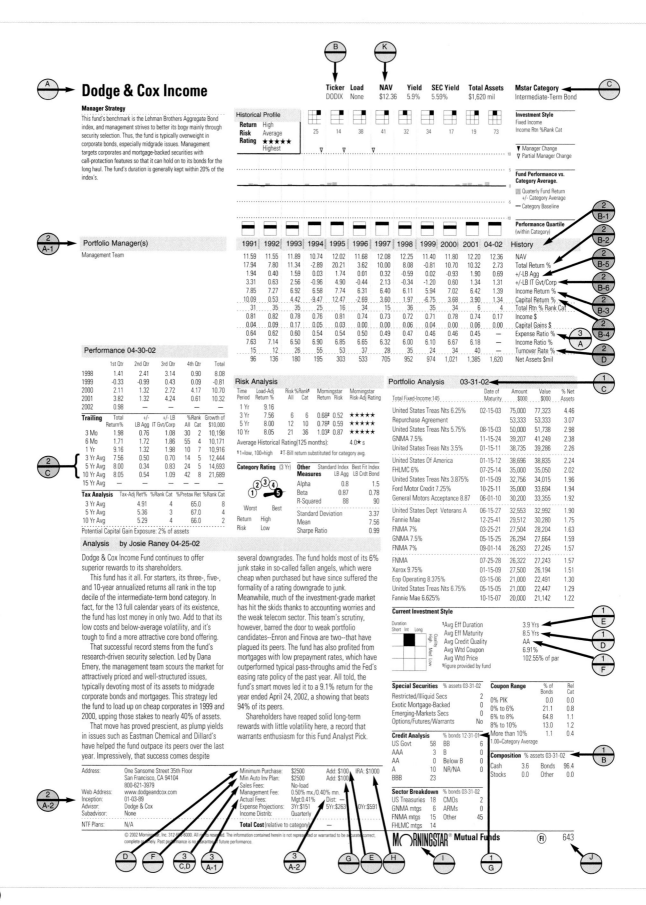

# NAIC®

Investment Education Since 1951

www.better-investing.org

## BOND FUND
# Check List™

(A) Fund Name: _Dodge & Cox Income_
(B) Ticker Symbol: _DODIX_
(C) Category: _Intermediate-Term Bond_
(D) Minimum Purchase($): _2500.00_   (E) Addt'l($): _100.00_
(F) Min Auto Inv Plan($): _2500.00_   (G) Addt'l($): _100.00_
(H) IRA($): _1000.00_
(I) Data Reference: _Morningstar_      (J) Page No. _643_
(K) Current NAV($): _12.36_
L. Taxable: _____   M. Tax-Deferred: _____

## 1. FUND INVESTMENT CHARACTERISTICS

(A) **Stated Investment Objective:** _High & Stable Rate of Income, Capital Preservation_
· What are the fund s investment criteria & investment policies?

(B) **Portfolio Composition:**

| Cash | Bonds | Stocks | Other |
|------|-------|--------|-------|
| 3.6 % | 96.4 % | 0 % | 0 % |

(C) **Portfolio Analysis Date:** _3/31/02_      (D) **Average Effective Maturity:** _8.5_

(E) **Average Effective Duration:** _3.9_      (F) **Average Credit Quality:** _AA_

(G) **Credit Analysis:** US Govt _58_% AAA _3_% AA _0_% A _10_% BBB _23_% BB _6_% B _0_%
Below B _0_% NR/NA _0_% Special Securities _2_%

## 2. FUND MANAGEMENT CHARACTERISTICS

(A) (1) **Fund Manager:** _Team_   **Years:** _13_      (2) **Date Fund Started:** _1/89_

(B) **Management Record:**

| | Initial Year | | | | | | | | | |
|---|---|---|---|---|---|---|---|---|---|---|
| (1) Current Management Period: enter all years | 1992 | 1993 | 1994 | 1995 | 1996 | 1997 | 1998 | 1999 | 2000 | 2001 |
| (2) Total Return % | 7.8 | 11.34 | -2.89 | 20.21 | 3.62 | 10.0 | 8.08 | -0.81 | 10.70 | 10.32 |
| (3) Income Return % | 7.27 | 6.92 | 6.58 | 7.74 | 6.31 | 6.40 | 6.11 | 5.94 | 7.02 | 6.42 |
| (4) Capital Return % | 0.53 | 4.42 | -9.47 | 12.47 | -2.69 | 3.60 | 1.97 | -6.75 | 3.68 | 3.90 |
| (5) +/- Total Return % - Lehman Agg. Bond | 0.40 | 1.59 | 0.03 | 1.74 | 0.01 | 0.32 | -0.59 | 0.02 | -0.93 | 1.90 |
| (6) +/- Total Return % - Other Index | 0.63 | 2.56 | -0.96 | 4.90 | -0.44 | 2.13 | -0.34 | -1.20 | 0.60 | 1.34 |

(C) **Long-Term Total Return (%):**   3 Yr. Avg. _7.56_   5 Yr. Avg. _8.00_   10 Yr. Avg. _8.05_

(D) **5 Yr. Avg. Turnover Rate (%):**

| | Initial Year | | | | | | |
|---|---|---|---|---|---|---|---|
| Years: | 1997 | 1998 | 1999 | 2000 | 2001 | Total | Average |
| Turnover Rate: | 28 | 35 | 24 | 34 | 40 | 161 | 32.2 |

## 3. COST CONSIDERATIONS

(A) Expense Ratio _0.45_ %
The expense ratio includes a number of separate expenses, including:
(1) Management Fee _.41_ %   (2) 12b-1 Marketing & Distribution Fee _—_ %
(B) Fund Peer Group Average Expense Ratio _1.02_ %
(C) Loads:   Front-end _—_ %   Back-end _—_ %   Level _—_ %
(D) Redemption Fee _—_ %

Note: Investors also pay fund brokerage commissions

## ◎ Overview: Intermediate-Term Bond

Funds in this category have durations that have stayed between 3.5 and six years, on average, over the past 36 months. They generally invest in some combination of high-quality corporate bonds, mortgages, and Treasuries, though many hold large stakes in a single sector and can own some junk bonds.

### Fund Analyst Picks    04-25-02

Metropolitan West Total Return Bond p.628: No worries.

Dodge & Cox Income p.612: It shouldn't come as a surprise that this fund is chalking up another exceptional year.

FPA New Income p.620: Traveling outside the herd hasn't been detrimental for this fund.

Fremont Bond p.621: This hidden gem is a bit less hidden.

Vanguard Total Bond Market Index p.644: A cheap, easy way to own the investment-grade, U.S. bond market.

### Update   Eric Jacobson 04-25-02

Who would have thought that the staid old telecom sector could do so much damage?

As has been the pattern, interest rates have been all over the map over the past several months, both zigging and zagging since the middle of last year. What's made an even bigger impact, however, have been investment-grade telecom issuers such as Qwest and WorldCom, which have had a very rough go of it lately, bringing down funds with exposure to them, and helping to sully the market in general. The Lehman Brothers U.S. Credit index, which covers the high-grade corporate market, was down about 0.3% during the first quarter of 2002, while returns for other sectors were generally positive. As if to add insult to injury, the beaten-down high-yield sector has come back with a vengeance, returning 1.7% during the same period.

The average fund in this category, meanwhile, was either too heavily exposed to the telecom sector, or simply couldn't overcome its expense burden. Through April 23, 2002, the group's average entrant returned 1.2% for the year to date, while the Lehman Brothers Aggregate Bond index logged a 1.65% gain.

Most of our favorite funds have actually performed quite well against that backdrop, with FPA New Income blasting to the top of the category, and Dodge & Cox Income and Fremont Bond both turning in impressive showings. Perennial favorite Metropolitan West Total Return Bond hasn't been as stellar, though, thanks in part to its own Qwest exposure and holdings in Calpine, which was thrown out with the Enron bath water.

Despite the trials and tribulations experienced here, we still view this category as core territory. Some of the best managers in the business invest money in styles that fall into this group, and over the long term, many of them have been able to cut an excellent risk/reward profile.

| | Total Return % vs. Morningstar Risk (5 Years) | | | | | |
|---|---|---|---|---|---|---|

● Funds in Category

+/- LB IT Gvt/Corp

| Top Funds | Best 5 Yr Return% | | Lowest 5 Yr Morningstar Risk | | Highest 5 Yr Morningstar Rating |
|---|---|---|---|---|---|
| ○ | Dreyfus Interm-Term Inc | 9.09 | □ FPA New Income | 0.38 | Dodge & Cox Income |
| | Fremont Bond | 8.56 | Metro West Total Ret | 0.55 | Dreyfus Interm-Term Inc |
| | Metro West Total Ret | 8.48 | Stein Roe Interm Bond | 0.58 | FPA New Income |
| | PIMCO Total Return Instl | 8.43 | Dodge & Cox Income | 0.59 | Fremont Bond |
| | Western Asset Core | 8.29 | Vanguard Total Bd Idx | 0.62 | Harbor Bond |

| 1991 | 1992 | 1993 | 1994 | 1995 | 1996 | 1997 | 1998 | 1999 | 2000 | 2001 | 03-02 | History |
|---|---|---|---|---|---|---|---|---|---|---|---|---|
| 24.31 | 10.72 | 15.06 | -1.32 | 22.60 | 6.23 | 11.51 | 9.82 | 2.19 | 12.76 | 11.03 | 0.84 | Top Decile Average |
| 16.95 | 7.38 | 10.64 | -4.08 | 17.79 | 3.30 | 8.91 | 7.50 | -1.29 | 9.65 | 7.49 | -0.23 | Total Return % |
| 11.87 | 4.60 | 6.65 | -8.44 | 13.63 | 1.13 | 6.53 | 4.28 | -3.98 | 4.99 | 3.91 | -1.43 | Bottom Decile Average |
| 0.95 | -0.02 | 0.89 | -1.16 | -0.68 | -0.31 | -0.77 | -1.17 | -0.46 | -1.98 | -0.93 | -0.33 | +/-LB Agg |
| 2.32 | 0.21 | 1.86 | -2.15 | 2.48 | -0.76 | 1.04 | -0.92 | -1.68 | -0.45 | -1.49 | 0.00 | +/-LB IT Gvt/Corp |
| 0.81 | 0.79 | 0.88 | 0.91 | 0.95 | 0.96 | 0.97 | 1.00 | 0.99 | 1.00 | 1.00 | — | Expense Ratio % |
| 8.06 | 7.03 | 6.14 | 6.02 | 6.48 | 6.11 | 6.08 | 5.77 | 5.66 | 6.13 | 5.68 | — | Income Ratio % |
| 95 | 106 | 110 | 126 | 137 | 147 | 143 | 141 | 149 | 162 | 191 | — | Turnover Rate % |
| 28.99 | 38.08 | 52.05 | 52.73 | 71.91 | 81.69 | 102.07 | 134.41 | 147.02 | 158.38 | 201.75 | 219.46 | Net Assets $bil |
| 87 | 105 | 135 | 166 | 189 | 201 | 230 | 253 | 269 | 282 | 306 | 313 | # Funds, excluding multiple share classes |

### Performance

| | 1st Qtr | 2nd Qtr | 3rd Qtr | 4th Qtr | Total |
|---|---|---|---|---|---|
| 1999 | -0.53 | -1.11 | 0.42 | -0.06 | -1.29 |
| 2000 | 1.84 | 1.12 | 2.73 | 3.72 | 9.65 |
| 2001 | 3.02 | 0.41 | 3.91 | 0.02 | 7.49 |
| 2002 | -0.23 | — | — | | |

### Trailing

| | Total Return % | +/- LB Agg | +/- LB IT Gvt/Corp | %Rank All Funds |
|---|---|---|---|---|
| 3 Mo | -0.23 | -0.33 | 0.00 | 63 |
| 6 Mo | -0.20 | -0.34 | -0.06 | 85 |
| 1 Yr | 4.11 | -1.23 | -1.05 | 33 |
| 3 Yr Avg | 5.31 | -1.18 | -1.08 | 30 |
| 5 Yr Avg | 6.40 | -1.17 | -0.67 | 46 |
| 10 Yr Avg | 6.83 | -0.55 | -0.05 | 55 |
| 15 Yr Avg | 7.39 | -0.62 | -0.14 | 56 |

### Tax Analysis

| | Tax-Adj Ret% | % Pretax Ret |
|---|---|---|
| 3 Yr Avg | 2.39 | 97.7 |
| 5 Yr Avg | 3.61 | 97.6 |
| 10 Yr Avg | 3.91 | 97.4 |

### Risk Analysis

| | Morningstar Return | Score Risk | Morningstar Risk-Adj Rating |
|---|---|---|---|
| 3 Yr | 0.03 | 0.71 | ★★★ |
| 5 Yr | 0.31 | 0.75 | ★★★ |
| 10 Yr | 0.57 | 0.92 | ★★★ |
| Wtd Avg | 0.21 | 0.75 | ★★★ |

### Other Measures

| | | | Standard Index LB Agg |
|---|---|---|---|
| Standard Deviation | 3.70 | Alpha | -1.0 |
| Mean | 5.31 | Beta | 0.96 |
| Sharpe Ratio | 0.19 | R-Squared | 85 |

### Morningstar Category Correlation

| | Highest | | Lowest |
|---|---|---|---|
| Long-Term Bond | 0.97 | Utilities | -0.20 |
| Interm Govt | 0.96 | Japan Stock | -0.17 |
| Short-Term Bond | 0.95 | Div Pac/Asia | -0.15 |

### Average Expense Ratios

| Front-End Load | 1.00 | Level Load | 1.66 |
|---|---|---|---|
| Deferred Load | 1.64 | No-Load | 0.67 |

### Portfolio Analysis    Top 20 Holdings

| Average Fixed-Income: 214 | Date of Maturity | % Net Assets |
|---|---|---|
| GNMA 6.5% | — | 4.77 |
| GNMA 7% | — | 1.44 |
| FNMA 6% | — | 0.94 |
| GNMA 7.5% | — | 0.62 |
| GNMA 8% | — | 0.54 |
| US Treasury Note 4.625% | 05-15-06 | 0.52 |
| GNMA 6% | — | 0.44 |
| FNMA TBA 6% | — | 0.42 |
| US Treasury Note 3.625% | 01-15-08 | 0.41 |
| US Treasury Note 3.375% | 01-15-07 | 0.39 |
| FNMA TBA 7% | — | 0.36 |
| GNMA TBA 7% | — | 0.36 |
| US Treasury Note 5.625% | 05-15-08 | 0.36 |
| FNMA TBA 6.5% | — | 0.33 |
| FNMA 6.5% | — | 0.32 |
| US Treasury Note 3.875% | 01-15-09 | 0.32 |
| US Treasury Bond 5.25% | 11-15-28 | 0.29 |
| US Treasury Note 6.5% | 02-15-10 | 0.27 |
| US Treasury Note 5% | 08-15-11 | 0.26 |
| FNMA 6.5% | 11-01-25 | 0.25 |

### Coupon Range % of assets

| 0% | 1.2 |
|---|---|
| 0% to 6% | 26.3 |
| 6% to 8% | 59.4 |
| 8% to 10% | 10.6 |
| more than 10% | 2.5 |

### Special Securities   % of assets

| Restricted/Illiquid Securities | 3 |
|---|---|
| Exotic Mortgage-Backed | 0 |

### Credit Analysis  % of bonds 03-31-02

| US Govt | 33 | BB | 3 |
|---|---|---|---|
| AAA | 26 | B | 1 |
| AA | 6 | Below B | 0 |
| A | 16 | NR/NA | 2 |
| BBB | 15 | | |

### Cash Inflows

| | Cash Flow % | % Total Assets Tax Bond | All |
|---|---|---|---|
| 2002 | -1.7 | 36.68 | 5.44 |
| 2001 | -8.0 | 36.14 | 5.06 |
| 2000 | -9.8 | 34.22 | 3.78 |
| 1999 | 0.7 | 30.09 | 3.29 |
| 1998 | -7.2 | 28.50 | 3.80 |

### Investment Style

| Avg Effective Duration | 4.7 Yrs |
|---|---|
| Avg Effective Maturity | 8.0 Yrs |
| Avg Credit Quality | AA |
| Avg Wtd Coupon | 6.73% |
| Avg Wtd Price | 102.08% of par |

### Composition  % of assets 03-31-02

| Cash | 7.9 |
|---|---|
| Stocks | 0.9 |
| Bonds | 89.0 |
| Other | 2.3 |

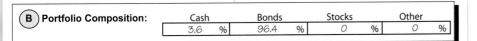

| B Portfolio Composition: | Cash | Bonds | Stocks | Other |
|---|---|---|---|---|
| | 3.6 % | 96.4 % | 0 % | 0 % |

fund's Web site. The prospectus is easily downloaded from the fund family's Web site (www.dodgeandcox.com) or you can call the 1-800 number that is listed on the bottom left-hand side of the Morningstar report and request a copy.

According to the prospectus for Dodge & Cox Income, "the fund seeks a high and stable rate of current income, consistent with long-term preservation of capital. A secondary objective is to take advantage of opportunities to realize capital appreciation." Next, the fund reveals that management pursues this objective by investing in a diversified group of high-quality bonds, including governmental bonds, government agency bonds and corporate bonds with high credit ratings.

## Portfolio Composition

A bond fund's assets should be concentrated in bonds. Dodge & Cox Income has 96.4 percent of its assets in bonds, as seen in Section 1B of the Bond Fund Check List.

## Portfolio Analysis Date

| C Portfolio Analysis Date: | 3/31/02 |
|---|---|

The portfolio analysis date in Section IC is the date that the fund's holdings were reported to Morningstar. Because of the reporting schedules of funds, this data can be somewhat outdated. However, because the management of Dodge & Cox Income practices a buy-and-hold philosophy, holdings tend to stay fairly stable.

## Average Effective Maturity

| D Average Effective Maturity: | 8.5 |
|---|---|

A bond fund's average effective maturity in Section 1D is a measurement of the average point at which the bonds in the portfolio will mature. To obtain this figure, Morningstar weighs the maturities of all the bonds in the portfolio by the market value of each particular bond.

A bond fund's average effective maturity is an indication of how sensitive a fund is to interest rate changes. As noted in Chapter 16, when interest rates rise, bond prices fall, and when interest rates decline, bond prices rise.

Because bond funds are a collection of bonds, funds with longer average effective maturities will be more affected by interest rate changes than those with shorter average effective maturities.

Dodge & Cox Income's average effective maturity of 8.5 years

places it in the intermediate taxable bond fund category.

## Average Effective Duration

| E Average Effective Duration: | 3.9 |
|---|---|

While maturity is a crude measurement of a bond's current interest rate sensitivity, duration is a precise measurement of how a bond will react to future interest rate movements.

For individual bonds, the duration calculation takes into consideration the flow and timing of interest payments, the bond's maturity and its value. By using duration, you can get a handle on how long it will take for a bond to repay your investment in today's dollars.

For bond funds, duration is a measure of how much a bond fund's share price will change in response to rising or falling interest rates. As a predictive tool, duration is an essential concept for bond fund investors to grasp because it tells you how your fund will respond to future short- and long-term interest rate changes. This indicates how volatile a fund's net asset value will be in times of interest rate increases or declines. This is why the Bond Fund Check List examines a fund's average effective duration in Section 1E.

To calculate duration, fund companies take into

# CHAPTER SEVENTEEN

## FIGURE 17.1: DURATION IN ACTION

Bond prices move in the opposite direction of interest rates. Therefore, an interest rate increase results in a decline in the price of a bond, while an interest rate decrease results in a gain in the price of a bond.

If interest rates increased by 1 percent, Dodge & Cox Income's net asset value would fall by **3.9 percent** because the fund's current duration is 3.9 years.

At the fund's current net asset value of $12.42, a decline of 3.9 percent translates into a loss of 48 cents per share in net asset value. The fund's NAV would fall from $12.42 to $11.96.

If interest rates fell by that same 1 percent, Dodge & Cox Income's net asset value would rise by **3.9 percent** because the duration is 3.9 years.

At the fund's current net asset value of $12.42, a rise of 3.9 percent translates into a gain of 48 cents per share. The fund's NAV would increase from $12.42 to $12.90.

consideration all the interest and prepayments as well as any return of principal for all of the bonds in the fund's portfolio. Morningstar's reports present duration information supplied by the fund companies.

Funds with shorter durations are less sensitive to interest rate changes than funds with longer durations. For example, a fund with a duration of eight years will be twice as sensitive to interest rate changes as a fund with a duration of four years.

*There is a direct relationship between a fund's duration and how its net asset value will change in response to interest rate shifts. In Figure 17.1 we examine what the effect of a*

*change in interest rates would be on our example fund, the Dodge & Cox Income Fund. Dodge & Cox Income has an average effective duration of 3.9 years.*

The fund's duration is lower than average in the intermediate-term bond fund category, which is 4.7 years, according to Morningstar. According to Dodge & Cox, the fund generally maintains a duration within 10 percent of its benchmark.

**Average Credit Quality**

Credit quality is a measurement of a bond issuer's ability to

make timely interest payments and to repay a shareholder's principal when a bond is redeemed. A bond fund's average credit quality in Section 1F is a snapshot of the portfolio's overall credit quality. To calculate this figure, Morningstar averages each bond's credit rating and adjusts it based on its relative ranking within the portfolio, meaning this is a weighted average.

As noted in Chapter 16, federal government bonds receive the highest credit ratings from credit rating agencies. Next are government agency bonds and corporations in sterling financial condition. Companies with high credit worthiness are assigned a variety of investment grade ratings. Those companies in very weak financial condition receive credit ratings that are non-investment grade or "junk".

*Morningstar's rating of Dodge & Cox Income's average credit quality is AA. In general, this means that the bonds in the fund's portfolio are high quality. The highest investment grade rating is AAA; the lowest is BBB—with eight grades in between. The illustration in Figure 17.2 shows how Dodge & Cox Income Fund's average credit quality of AA fits into the credit quality spectrum.*

**Credit Analysis**

Section 1G, credit analysis, shows how the bond portfolio

144

G Credit Analysis: US Govt 58 %    AAA 3 %    AA 0 %    A 10 %    BBB 23 %    BB 6 %    B 0 %
Below B 0 %    NR/NA 0 %    Special Securities 2 %

breaks down by credit quality. We already know the average credit quality of the entire portfolio from Section 1F. Now we see how the bonds in the portfolio fall into the various credit-rating categories.

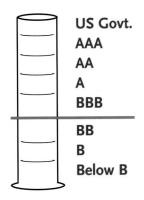

*Figure 17.2: The Credit Quality Spectrum*

According to Morningstar, "Like the style box, the credit analysis can help investors determine whether a fund's portfolio meets a desired standard of quality. It can also shed light on the management strategy of the fund. If the fund holds a large percentage of assets in lower-quality issues, the fund follows a more aggressive style and is probably more concerned with yield than credit quality."

Morningstar generally follows the credit rating systems of Moody's and Standard & Poor's as seen in Chapter 16, but it does vary somewhat. While

Standard & Poor's and Moody's classify federal government bonds, bills and notes as grade AAA, Morningstar classifies them under a separate "government bonds" heading. This category also includes bonds issued by government-backed agencies.

Dodge & Cox Income's bond portfolio consists of 94 percent investment-grade bonds. In addition, more than half of the bond portfolio is concentrated in the government bond category, meaning that this portion of the portfolio is of the highest possible quality.

While the individual portfolio makeup of the Dodge & Cox Income Fund and the average intermediate-term bond fund differ, they are virtually identical in terms of the amount of investment grade bonds held in the bond portfolios.

When analyzing a fund's portfolio, pay special attention to the percentage of special securities in the fund portfolio. This is listed on the Morningstar report under Special Securities.

This includes a number of categories, the most important of which is restricted and illiquid securities. These securities are issues that are difficult to fairly price and may not be easily sold. Funds with a significant portion of their portfolios in restricted and illiquid securities have a special degree of risk because it is difficult for fund management and outside analysts to assess the true value of such issues.

*Dodge & Cox Income has 2 percent of its portfolio invested in restricted and illiquid securities, which is the average for the intermediate-term bond fund category. This isn't a significant percentage of the entire portfolio. The pie chart in Figure 17.3 shows the credit analysis breakdown of the fund's portfolio and the credit analysis breakdown of the bond portfolio of the average intermediate-term bond fund.*

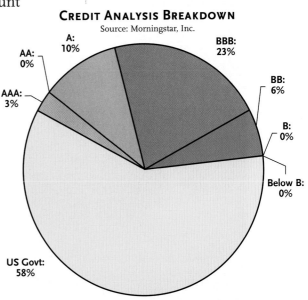

**CREDIT ANALYSIS BREAKDOWN**
Source: Morningstar, Inc.

*Figure 17.3: Credit Analysis Breakdown*

# *Bond Fund Check List—Management & Costs*

## *Bond Fund Check-up*

*When evaluating bond funds, be sure to examine a fund's management and costs. For actively managed funds, look for experienced management. Since many bond fund investors seek income, assess a fund's historical income return to see if it will meet your needs.*

*Compare the fund's performance to market indexes as well. Low-cost index funds are a viable choice for*

*many conservative bond fund investors. While turnover is higher for bond funds than stock funds, it has the same effects.*

*Consider low-cost index funds, as bonds can offer less opportunity for managers to add value than stocks. Costs matter more for bond funds because historical total return is less than stock funds.*

**Fund Manager**

**Management Record**

**Total Return**

**Turnover**

**Costs**

## Fund Management Characteristics

Section 2 of the Bond Fund Check List includes many items we saw previously on the Stock Fund Check List, including entries for fund management tenure, management record, turnover rate and the tax analysis.

### Fund Manager

It isn't easy to find out much about Dodge & Cox Income Fund's management from the Morningstar report. Section 2A1 is where we list the fund manager's name and tenure. Under the Portfolio Manager section, a management committee is listed. While a team management approach is a legitimate approach to fund portfolio management, it makes it difficult to discern who is running a fund and how experienced they are.

By checking the Dodge & Cox Web site, you see that the company's Fixed Income Strategy Committee manages the fund. This committee is composed of 11 members and has an average of 13 years of experience with Dodge and Cox. We're always looking for management with at least five years of experience or more.

Section 2A2 covers the date the fund started, which was in January 1989. So the fund has been in existence for 14 years.

### Management Record

To assess the management record of bond funds, examine annual total return, income return, capital return and the fund's record in contrast to a well-established market benchmark in Sections 2B 1, 2,

3, 4, 5 and 6. As in the case of the Stock Fund Check List, we're logging in data for all 10 years since the current management team has been in charge for that entire period.

Generally speaking, a bond fund's total return is less than stock funds over a long period of time, so don't expect stock fund returns from a bond fund. Also, keep in mind that because bond funds are primarily

| 2. FUND MANAGEMENT CHARACTERISTICS | | | | | | | | | | |
|---|---|---|---|---|---|---|---|---|---|---|
| (A) ① Fund Manager: _____ Team _____ Years: 13 ② Date Fund Started: 1/89 | | | | | | | | | | |

| (B) Management Record: | Initial Year | | | | | | | | | |
|---|---|---|---|---|---|---|---|---|---|---|
| ① Current Management Period: enter all years | 1992 | 1993 | 1994 | 1995 | 1996 | 1997 | 1998 | 1999 | 2000 | 2001 |
| ② Total Return % | 7.8 | 11.34 | -2.89 | 20.21 | 3.62 | 10.0 | 8.08 | -0.81 | 10.70 | 10.32 |
| ③ Income Return % | 7.27 | 6.92 | 6.58 | 7.74 | 6.31 | 6.40 | 6.11 | 5.94 | 7.02 | 6.42 |
| ④ Capital Return % | 0.53 | 4.42 | -9.47 | 12.47 | -2.69 | 3.60 | 1.97 | -6.75 | 3.68 | 3.90 |
| ⑤ +/- Total Return % - Lehman Agg. Bond | 0.40 | 1.59 | 0.03 | 1.74 | 0.01 | 0.32 | -0.59 | 0.02 | -0.93 | 1.90 |
| ⑥ +/- Total Return % - Other Index | 0.63 | 2.56 | -0.96 | 4.90 | -0.44 | 2.13 | -0.34 | -1.20 | 0.60 | 1.34 |

components as "Income Return" and "Capital Return" and provides annual percentage returns listed on their reports underneath the second index comparison. Add the income return to the capital return and you'll get the total return figure listed on the Morningstar report.

For stock funds, the capital return is the key component, as investors expect the companies owned by the fund to appreciate and raise the fund's net asset value over a long period of time. For bond funds, income return is the key component as bond fund investors count on these funds for income.

The income return is the more stable component of the total return picture for bond funds than capital return. A bond fund's capital return is strongly influenced by interest rates and will increase when interest rates fall, and decline when interest rates rise.

income vehicles, the net asset value for these funds stays fairly stable during a long period of time. This is why we don't examine net asset value on a year-to-year basis like we do in the Stock Fund Check List.

A fund's total return has two components: capital appreciation and income. Morningstar describes these

Income return reflects the portion of the fund's total return that was gained from the income distributions of the bonds in the fund's portfolios. By examining a bond fund's income return, you can get a better feeling for the stream of income you are likely to receive if you purchase shares in a particular fund.

For Dodge & Cox Income, total returns have fluctuated from –2.89 percent in 1994 to 20.21 percent the next year. Income returns are much more stable, ranging from 5.94 to 7.74 percent with an average of 6.67 percent over the 10-year period.

Taking a look at Dodge & Cox Income's capital return, you can see wide swings. In 1994, the capital return was –9.47 percent, and in 1995 it rose more than 20 points to 12.47 percent. Many bond fund investors seek not only a steady stream of income but also preservation of their capital. Not many investors realize how volatile bond funds can be, and that you need a long-term perspective, just as you do when investing in stock funds, to ride out the ups and downs.

This also illustrates the effect that interest rate movements have on bond fund total return. Dodge & Cox Income's total return was depressed in 1994 due to rising interest rates and falling bond prices, and then spiked in 1995 as rates dropped and bond prices rose.

In addition, we look at a fund's income return rather than it's yield for several reasons. Morningstar provides yearly income return figures, while the yield figure is only listed currently for the entire portfolio. You can track income return, while yield is a snapshot of one particular moment in time. Also, fund managers can prop up yield through various maneuvers that can endanger investor's principal.

Investors who over-focus on a fund's yield ignore other important criteria in selecting a bond fund, and may be badly burned. High-yield, or junk bond funds, tend to have the highest yields. These are also the most risky bond funds from an investor's perspective.

While it's important to pay attention to income return, capital return is also important as it fluctuates more than income return. In fact, changes in interest rates, credit issues with the bonds in the portfolio and other factors can affect a fund's capital returns to such an extent that they can offset any income return causing the fund to actually lose some of your investment principal.

Bond funds are not immune to principal loss or gain. While many investors perceive them as safer than stock funds and less volatile, they can be just as unsafe and volatile, but for different reasons.

As with a stock fund, when you invest in a bond fund you want to invest in a low-cost fund with superior management that can outperform market indexes or benchmarks. Morningstar uses the Lehman Brothers Aggregate Bond Index as a benchmark for all bond funds. This index is a proxy for the total investment-grade bond market.

Morningstar provides a second, more targeted, index comparison, directly underneath the Aggregate Bond Comparison on the Morningstar bond fund report. The particular index used depends on the portfolio composition of the subject bond fund. For the Dodge & Cox Income Fund, Morningstar uses a combination of the

## MEET THE INVESTOR: SHEILA WYSS

*Sheila Wyss, a Chapter Director with NAIC's Kansas City Chapter, has invested in mutual funds for 15 year. She teaches classes based on the NAIC fund tools.*

**Q. What advice would you give to a new fund investor?**

Do your own research—look for no-load funds. Evaluate fund management's experience and track record. Look for funds that have had the same manager for five to 10 years. Look for low expenses compared to other funds in a similar category.

**Q: What common mistakes should fund investors avoid?**

Jumping in and out of a fund. Paying loads and high expenses.

**Q: How has the NAIC Mutual Fund Program helped you?**

By giving me the tools to avoid the above mistakes.

**Q: What, in your opinion, is the major difference between NAIC's investing philosophy and other investing practices?**

Same for funds as for stocks—pick well-managed companies and/or the funds that invest in them and hold for the long-term. Be disciplined about adding more money on a regular basis.

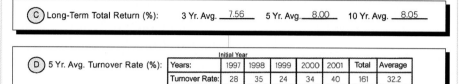

| C | Long-Term Total Return (%): | 3 Yr. Avg. | 7.56 | 5 Yr. Avg. | 8.00 | 10 Yr. Avg. | 8.05 |

| D | 5 Yr. Avg. Turnover Rate (%): | Years: | Initial Year | | | | | Total | Average |
|---|---|---|---|---|---|---|---|---|---|
| | | | 1997 | 1998 | 1999 | 2000 | 2001 | | |
| | | Turnover Rate: | 28 | 35 | 24 | 34 | 40 | 161 | 32.2 |

Lehman Brothers Government Bond Index and the Lehman Brothers Corporate Bond Index. These indexes track the returns of government bonds and investment-grade corporate debt.

Dodge & Cox Income has outperformed the Lehman Brothers Aggregate Bond Index eight out of the past 10 years and the other index six times out of the past 10 years.

Dodge & Cox's returns also hold up against the indexes in longer-term comparisons. In the Performance section of the fund's Morningstar report, it shows that the fund has outperformed both indexes for the three, five and 10-year annual total return periods. The strongest performance is the 10-year number versus the Lehman Brothers Intermediate Term Government/Corporate, where it beat the index by 1.09 percent per year.

Many investors give strong consideration to bond index funds. A number of low-cost index funds invest in different portions of the bond market. There are low cost index funds available that attempt to replicate the performance of the Lehman Brothers Aggregate Bond Index.

## Long-Term Total Return

As total return and its components fluctuate from year to year, it's important to get an overall perspective for how a fund has performed in the long-term in Section 2C. Dodge & Cox Income's total return numbers are very consistent through the three, five and 10-year periods. The three-year number is 7.56 percent, rising to 8 percent for the five-year total return and to 8.05 percent for the 10-year total return numbers.

## 5-Year Average Turnover Rate

A fund's turnover rate in Section 2D is a rough measurement of the amount of buying and selling of securities a fund manager does in a certain period of time. Bond fund turnover tends to be higher than stock fund turnover.

Several factors account for the higher turnover rate experienced by bond funds. Bonds generate much more income than stocks, which bond fund managers must reinvest by purchasing more bonds for the portfolio.

*Also, bonds mature, unlike stocks, which can theoretically be held forever. Even bond fund managers with a buy-and-hold philosophy must replace maturing bonds with either new or existing bonds. Many bond fund managers buy and sell bonds in an effort to add value to their funds, just as stock fund managers do with stock. Dodge & Cox Income's five-year average portfolio turnover rate is 32.2 percent. This is quite a bit lower than the average intermediate-term bond fund, which has a five-year portfolio turnover rate of 157 percent. The graph in Figure 18.1 shows how little the fund's turnover rate has fluctuated between 1997 and 2001.*

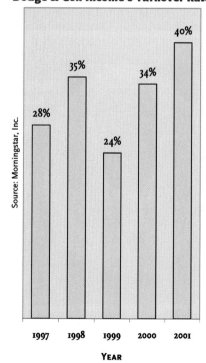

**Dodge & Cox Income's Turnover Rate**

*Figure 18.1: Turnover Rate*

High turnover rates result in the same consequences for shareholders in bond funds as they do in stock funds: increased brokerage costs and higher tax liabilities for investors in taxable accounts.

## Costs

When investing in any type of fund, your objective should be to purchase shares in the highest quality fund at the lowest possible cost. Section 3 of the Bond Fund Check List deals with the costs of owning bond funds.

Dodge & Cox Income is a low-cost, no-load bond fund. Its expense ratio of .45 percent is considerably lower than its peer group average, which is 1.02 percent. The fund has no 12b-1 fees, load or redemption fee.

## Conclusion

The Bond Fund Check List is a tool to simply evaluate virtually any type of bond fund. When analyzing a bond fund, keep some key considerations in mind, as bond funds can be very risky investments under certain circumstances.

● **What is the fund's duration?**

Bond funds with long durations are extremely sensitive to interest rate changes, and unwary investors can lose a lot of principal investing in such funds. When looking for a bond fund to serve as a core bond fund holding, you're well advised to stick with a short or intermediate term fund with a duration of five years or less.

● **Is the fund's average credit quality A or higher?**

Bond funds with low credit quality frequently offer seductively high yields, tempting investors into "junk" bond territory. The vast majority of bond fund investors are better off with high quality funds that invest in government and /or high quality corporate bonds. While even high quality bonds can experience problems, it is much less likely than with "junk" bonds. "Junk" bond funds can be quite volatile and can lose a good chunk of an investor's principal if a manager makes a wrong bet or two.

● **Has the fund manager been with the fund for five years or more?**

As with stock funds, we look for managers that make a commitment to a fund who have a long-term investing philosophy.

● **Is the fund low cost?**

Because bond funds generally return less than stock funds, costs are even more important. Low costs can make the difference between solid and so-so returns in bond fund investing.

---

| 3. COST CONSIDERATIONS |
| --- |

Ⓐ Expense Ratio __0.45_ %
   The expense ratio includes a number of separate expenses, including:
   ① Management Fee ___.41__ %   ② 12b-1 Marketing & Distribution Fee _____–____%
Ⓑ Fund Peer Group Average Expense Ratio __1.02__ %
Ⓒ Loads:   Front-end _____–___%   Back-end _____–____ %   Level _____–____%
Ⓓ Redemption Fee _____–____%
   Note: Investors also pay fund brokerage commissions

# Bond Fund Comparison Guide

## Compare Funds

After selecting several bond funds using the Bond Fund Check List, find the best of the best with the Bond Fund Comparison Guide. The Bond Fund Comparison Guide contains many of the same key elements as the Check List so you can rank characteristics according to your investment preferences.

**Title Block**

**Portfolio**

**Management**

**Costs**

## Overview

The Bond Fund Comparison Guide is a one-page, one-sided form that allows you to compare up to three bond funds. You can draw the information you need for the Comparison Guide from a filled-in Check List, or draw data directly from the Morningstar report. Like its stock fund counterpart, you can use the Bond Fund Comparison Guide in many different ways.

You can compare three funds in the same category, three funds in different categories or three funds with different asset bases. Many investors prefer to use the form to make an apples-to-apples comparison between three funds in the same category.

The Bond Fund Comparison Guide has three sections: Portfolio, Management and Cost. The Comparison Guide also features an "Other" section. Using this tool, you can rank funds according to your investment preferences, or leave the rankings blank. The example funds used in this Comparison Guide aren't real funds, but funds designed for teaching purposes. Throughout this section, the example funds

| Fund Name | | Fund #1 | RANK | Fund #2 | RANK | Fund #3 | RANK |
|---|---|---|---|---|---|---|---|
| Portfolio Composition (%) | Cash | 6.5 | | 2.5 | | 12.4 | |
| | Bonds | 93.0 | | 97.5 | | 87.6 | |
| | Stocks | .5 | | 0 | | 0 | |
| | Other | 0 | 2 | 0 | 1 | 0 | 3 |
| Average Effective Duration | | 4.8 | 1 | 4.6 | 1 | 5.8 | 2 |
| Average Credit Quality | | AA | 1 | AA | 1 | A | 2 |

are referred to as Fund #1, Fund #2 and Fund #3.

In this specific comparison, we're looking for a high-quality, low-cost and low duration fund. This kind of fund is a conservative choice that will meet the needs of many bond fund investors.

### Title Block

The first step in filling out the Bond Fund Comparison Guide is to complete the Title Block. Note the fund category, date of the comparison and whether the fund is in a taxable or tax-deferred account.

### Portfolio

### Portfolio Composition

All three funds hold a large majority of their assets in bonds, which is appropriate for a bond fund. When a fund

holds a large percentage of its assets in cash, the fund's total return can suffer, as cash placed in a short-term investment vehicle earns less interest.

Fund #2 receives the #1 ranking as it has the highest percentage of its assets invested in bonds, followed by Fund #1. Fund #3 has the last-place ranking as it has a large cash stake (12.4 percent) and a smaller amount of total assets invested in bonds.

### Average Effective Duration

A fund's duration measures its sensitivity to interest rate changes. The lower a fund's duration is, the less sensitive the fund's portfolio will be to changes in interest rates.

Because many bond fund investors seek to preserve their capital—and funds with lower duration tend to preserve capital more than funds with

Investment Education Since 1951

**Bond Fund
Comparison
Guide ™**

Fund Category: <u>Intermediate-Term Bond</u>

Date: <u>1/1/03</u>

Taxable Acct.: ____ Tax-Deferred Acct.: ____

|  |  |  | FUND #1 | RANK | FUND #2 | RANK | FUND #3 | RANK |
|---|---|---|---|---|---|---|---|---|
|  | Fund Name |  | Fund #1 |  | Fund #2 |  | Fund #3 |  |
| **PORTFOLIO** | Portfolio Composition (%) | Cash | 6.5 |  | 2.5 |  | 12.4 |  |
|  |  | Bonds | 93.0 |  | 97.5 |  | 87.6 |  |
|  |  | Stocks | .5 |  | 0 |  | 0 |  |
|  |  | Other | 0 | 2 | 0 | 1 | 0 | 3 |
|  | Average Effective Duration |  | 4.8 | 1 | 4.6 | 1 | 5.8 | 2 |
|  | Average Credit Quality |  | AA | 1 | AA | 1 | A | 2 |
|  | Credit Analysis (%) | US Govt | 34 | 2 | 58 | 1 | 0 | 3 |
|  |  | AAA | 26 |  | 6 |  | 34 |  |
|  |  | AA | 6 |  | 3 |  | 0 |  |
|  |  | A | 12 |  | 15 |  | 11 |  |
|  |  | BBB | 17 |  | 16 |  | 37 |  |
|  |  | BB | 5 |  | 3 |  | 12 |  |
|  |  | B | 0 |  | 0 |  | 8 |  |
|  |  | Below B | 0 |  | 0 |  | 0 |  |
|  |  | NR/NA | 0 |  | 0 |  | 0 |  |
|  |  | Special Securities | 3 | 3 | 2 | 2 | 0 | 1 |
| **MANAGEMENT** | Manager Tenure |  | 4 | 2 | 10 | 1 | 8 | 1 |
|  | Total Return % 10-Year Avg. |  | -- | -- | 6.7 | 1 | -- | -- |
|  | 5-Year Avg. |  | -- | -- | 7.65 | 1 | 6.5 | 2 |
|  | 3-Year Avg. |  | 7.2 | 2 | 7.5 | 1 | 7.0 | 3 |
|  | 5-Year Average Turnover Rate % |  | 191 | 3 | 56 | 1 | 112 | 2 |
| **COST** | Expense Ratio % |  | .90 | 3 | .37 | 1 | .48 | 2 |
|  | 12b-1 Charges % |  | .25 | 2 | 0 | 1 | 0 | 1 |
|  | Load: Front / Back / Level % |  | 0 | -- | 0 | -- | 0 | -- |
|  | Redemption Fee % |  | 0 | -- | 0 | -- | 0 | -- |
| **OTHER** |  |  |  |  |  |  |  |  |
|  |  |  |  |  |  |  |  |  |
|  |  |  |  |  |  |  |  |  |

| 1st | 2 | 2nd | 5 | 3rd | 3 | | 1st | 11 | 2nd | 1 | 3rd | -- | | 1st | 3 | 2nd | 5 | 3rd | 3 |

| Fund Name | Fund #1 | RANK | Fund #2 | RANK | Fund #3 | RANK |
|---|---|---|---|---|---|---|
| Average Effective Duration | 4.8 | 1 | 4.6 | 1 | 5.8 | 2 |
| Average Credit Quality | AA | 1 | AA | 1 | A | 2 |

| Credit Analysis (%) | | Fund #1 | RANK | Fund #2 | RANK | Fund #3 | RANK |
|---|---|---|---|---|---|---|---|
| | US Govt | 34 | 2 | 58 | 1 | 0 | 3 |
| | AAA | 26 | | 6 | | 34 | |
| | AA | 6 | | 3 | | 0 | |
| | A | 12 | | 15 | | 11 | |
| | BBB | 17 | | 16 | | 37 | |
| | BB | 5 | | 3 | | 12 | |
| | B | 0 | | 0 | | 8 | |
| | Below B | 0 | | 0 | | 0 | |
| | NR/NA | 0 | | 0 | | 0 | |
| | Special Securities | 3 | 3 | 2 | 2 | 0 | 1 |

a higher duration—we will award the first place ranking in this comparison to the fund with the lowest duration. Fund #1 and Fund #2 are so close in duration they tie for first place in this comparison, followed by Fund #3.

## Average Credit Quality

A fund's average credit quality is a measurement of the credit worthiness of the bonds in the portfolio. A portfolio composed of high-credit quality bonds is less risky than one made up of lower-quality bonds. In this comparison, we rank the fund with the best credit quality first.

According to Morningstar's credit ranking system, the highest credit quality bond rating is U.S. Government, followed by AAA, AA and A rated bonds. Fund #1 and #2 receive the first place ranking with an average credit quality of AA, followed by Fund #3 with an average credit quality of A.

Keep in mind that while higher quality bonds are less risky, they typically yield less than lower-quality bonds. Some

fund managers are quite skilled at blending a portfolio of high and lower quality bonds to enhance yield and total return. The difference between a portfolio with an average credit quality of AA and A isn't huge.

## Credit Analysis

When evaluating the credit analysis section in this comparison, look for the fund with the highest-quality portfolio. One way to assess a fund's portfolio is to divide the portfolio between investment-grade and non-investment-grade bonds, and award the top ranking to the fund with the highest percentage of its portfolio invested in investment-grade bonds. Non-investment-grade bonds are those with a rating of BB or below.

*You can also divide the portfolio in terms of U.S. government securities and non-government securities, and award the top ranking to the fund with the highest percentage of bond assets in government securities. Using this evaluation method, Fund #2*

*achieves the highest ranking followed by Fund #1 and Fund #3. Fund #3 clearly has the lowest-grade portfolio, with 20 percent of its bonds in the below-investment grade category. The graphic in Figure 19.1 shows the portion of each fund's portfolio in investment-grade and non-investment-grade bonds.*

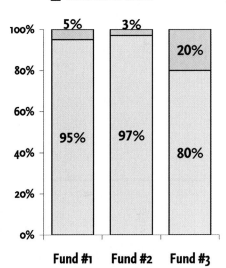

Figure 19.1: Credit Evaluation

## Special Securities

Special securities include restricted and illiquid securities and other types of unusual securities. For bond funds, a high percentage of assets invested in restricted and illiquid and other special securities can be risky for investors. These securities are more difficult for fund managers to value and sell.

Investors purchasing bond funds for income potential and

| Fund Name | | Fund #1 | RANK | Fund #2 | RANK | Fund #3 | RANK |
|---|---|---|---|---|---|---|---|
| Credit Analysis (%) | US Govt | 34 | 2 | 58 | 1 | 0 | 3 |
| | AAA | 26 | | 6 | | 34 | |
| | AA | 6 | | 3 | | 0 | |
| | A | 12 | | 15 | | 11 | |
| | BBB | 17 | | 16 | | 37 | |
| | BB | 5 | | 3 | | 12 | |
| | B | 0 | | 0 | | 8 | |
| | Below B | 0 | | 0 | | 0 | |
| | NR/NA | 0 | | 0 | | 0 | |
| | Special Securities | 3 | 3 | 2 | 2 | 0 | 1 |

| | | Fund #1 | RANK | Fund #2 | RANK | Fund #3 | RANK |
|---|---|---|---|---|---|---|---|
| Manager Tenure | | 4 | 2 | 10 | 1 | 8 | 1 |
| Total Return % | 10-Year Avg. | -- | -- | 6.7 | 1 | -- | -- |
| | 5-Year Avg. | -- | -- | 7.65 | 1 | 6.5 | 2 |
| | 3-Year Avg. | 7.2 | 2 | 7.5 | 1 | 7.0 | 3 |
| 5-Year Average Turnover Rate % | | 191 | 3 | 56 | 1 | 112 | 2 |

capital preservation won't want to see more than 10 percent of a bond fund's assets invested in special securities. The fund with the smallest percentage in special securities wins the first place ranking. Fund #3 ranks first, followed by Fund #2 in second place and Fund #1 in third place.

## Management

### Fund Manager Tenure

In comparing fund manager tenure, you should look for managers who have been with a fund for a minimum of five years. In this comparison, Fund #2 with 10 years of

management experience and Fund #3 with eight years of experience gain the first place ranking. Fund #1 has a manager with less than five years experience and receives the last place ranking.

## Total Return

Total return is a fund's average return to investors after deducting costs, but not including sales charges (loads) and other non-asset based expenses. Investors in any type of fund seek the highest possible total return over a given period of time.

For the 10-year time period, Fund #2 is the only fund ranked because it is the only fund with a manager with 10

---

### MEET THE EXPERT: MERCER BULLARD

*Mercer Bullard, a law professor at the University of Mississippi, is the chief executive officer of Fund Democracy, a non-profit shareholder advocacy group. Formerly employed with the SEC, Bullard teaches and writes on mutual fund topics.*

**Q. What advice would you give to a new fund investor?**

Develop an investment plan, spending a good amount of time on your asset allocation, and then choose funds based on the factors that are the most powerful predictors of future performance: expenses and long-term investment performance (minimum 10 years).

**Q: What steps could funds take to be more shareholder-friendly?**

They could provide investors with individualized data that shows their actual investment performance and expenses in dollars, and make accounting for sales of specific fund shares – which can substantially reduce shareholders' taxes – easier for shareholders to track and report to the IRS.

**Q: What is the most important area that you'd like to see the SEC focus on in terms of mutual fund regulation?**

Promoting competition, such as by requiring more transparent and easily understood disclosure of expenses, resisting industry efforts to water-down rules preventing self-dealing between funds and their sponsors, and providing greater incentives for funds to be internally managed (as is Vanguard).

| Fund Name | Fund #1 | RANK | Fund #2 | RANK | Fund #3 | RANK |
|---|---|---|---|---|---|---|
| Manager Tenure | 4 | 2 | 10 | 1 | 8 | 1 |
| Total Return % 10-Year Avg. | -- | -- | 6.7 | 1 | -- | -- |
| 5-Year Avg. | -- | -- | 7.65 | 1 | 6.5 | 2 |
| 3-Year Avg. | 7.2 | 2 | 7.5 | 1 | 7.0 | 3 |
| 5-Year Average Turnover Rate % | 191 | 3 | 56 | 1 | 112 | 2 |
| Manager Tenure | 4 | 2 | 10 | 1 | 8 | 1 |
| Total Return % 10-Year Avg. | -- | -- | 6.7 | 1 | -- | -- |
| 5-Year Avg. | -- | -- | 7.65 | 1 | 6.5 | 2 |
| 3-Year Avg. | 7.2 | 2 | 7.5 | 1 | 7.0 | 3 |
| 5-Year Average Turnover Rate % | 191 | 3 | 56 | 1 | 112 | 2 |
| COST — Expense Ratio % | .90 | 3 | .37 | 1 | .48 | 2 |
| 12b-1 Charges % | .25 | 2 | 0 | 1 | 0 | 1 |
| Load: Front / Back / Level % | 0 | -- | 0 | -- | 0 | -- |
| Redemption Fee % | 0 | -- | 0 | -- | 0 | -- |

| FUND #1 | | | FUND #2 | | | FUND #3 | | |
|---|---|---|---|---|---|---|---|---|
| 1st 2 | 2nd 5 | 3rd 3 | 1st 11 | 2nd 1 | 3rd -- | 1st 3 | 2nd 5 | 3rd 3 |

years or more experience. For the five-year period, Fund #2 again comes out on top, followed by Fund #3. For the three-year period, Fund #2 is ranked first again, followed by Fund #1 and then Fund #3.

## 5-Year Average Turnover Rate

The five-year average turnover rate is a rough measure of how much buying and selling of securities a fund manager does in a particular time period. Where turnover is concerned, the lower the number the better. In this comparison, Fund #2 receives the first place ranking, followed by Fund #3 and #1.

## Costs

Costs are a key factor in what you take home from a bond fund. The higher the costs, the more difficult it is for a fund manager to outperform a bond market index. A number of

costs and fees are associated with ownership of funds.

*A fund's expense ratio expresses the percentage of your assets deducted each fiscal year for day-to-day operating costs. As with any type of fund-related expense, the lower the cost, the better. Figure 19.2 compares the expense ratio of these three funds.*

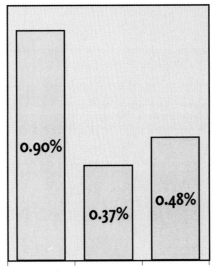

Figure 19.2: Expense Ratio Comparison

Fund #2 gets the top ranking for the expense ratio, followed by Fund #3 and then Fund #1. Funds #2 and #3 tie for the number one ranking for 12b-1 marketing and distribution fee as they have no fee, while Fund #1 has a .25 percent 12b-1 fee. None of the funds have loads.

## Comparison Guide Rankings & Wrap-Up

In examining the rankings for each of the funds, Fund #2 clearly comes out on top. By most general fund and bond fund measurements, it is the superior fund. Credit quality is high and duration is low. The manager has been at the helm for a full 10 years and the total return is impressive. Costs are low.

Fund #3 has a longer duration, which means it is more sensitive to interest rate changes, and the turnover is high too. Fund #1 has the highest expenses and the manager with the least amount of experience.

While your criteria may vary, we began this comparison seeking a high-quality, low-duration and low-cost fund, and Fund #2 clearly best meets that criterion of the funds in this comparison.

# Bond Fund Trend Report

## Review Trends

Once you purchase bond fund shares, use the Bond Fund Trend Report to follow your funds on an ongoing basis. Review the fund's key elements when a new Morningstar report is issued.

Make sure that fund management is following the same strategy that brought success in the past. If the fund deviates significantly from its chosen path, review it carefully and decide whether it continues to meet your investing goals and needs.

**Title Block**

**Portfolio**

**Management**

**Costs**

## Overview

The Bond Fund Trend Report is the third in the series of bond fund tools. It is a one-page, one-sided form designed to help you evaluate a fund's key elements on an ongoing basis.

Once you purchase fund shares, use the Trend Report to periodically update your assessment of the fund to make sure the fund still meets your investing goals. Notice the top bar in the Trend Report main data section, which is entitled "Portfolio Analysis Date." This is where you insert the portfolio analysis date of the Morningstar report that you are using to update your Trend Report.

The Trend Report, located on Page 160, is filled in with information from an example fund designed for educational purposes.

## Title Block

The first step in filling out the Bond Fund Trend Report is to complete the Title Block, which asks for the fund category, fund name and whether the fund is in a taxable or tax-deferred account.

Bond Fund
**Trend Report™**

Fund Category: _Intermediate-Term Bond_

Fund Name: _Bond Fund XYZ_

Taxable Acct.: _____ Tax-Deferred Acct.: _____

**Bond Fund**
# Trend Report™

Investment Education Since 1951

Fund Category: _Intermediate-Term Bond_

Fund Name: _Bond Fund XYZ_

Taxable Acct.: _____ Tax-Deferred Acct.: _____

| | | | 10/00 | 4/01 | 9/01 | 2/02 | 7/02 | |
|---|---|---|---|---|---|---|---|---|
| **PORTFOLIO** | Portfolio Analysis Date | | 10/00 | 4/01 | 9/01 | 2/02 | 7/02 | |
| | Portfolio Composition | Cash % | 2.5 | 2.3 | 2.0 | 2.6 | 3.2 | |
| | | Bonds % | 97.5 | 97.7 | 98.0 | 97.4 | 96.8 | |
| | | Stocks % | 0 | 0 | 0 | 0 | 0 | |
| | | Other % | 0 | 0 | 0 | 0 | 0 | |
| | Average Effective Duration | | 4.6 | 4.6 | 4.7 | 4.7 | 4.6 | |
| | Average Credit Quality | | AA | AA | AA | A | A | |
| | Credit Analysis | US Govt | 58 | 56 | 54 | 48 | 44 | |
| | | AAA | 6 | 4 | 3 | 3 | 3 | |
| | | AA | 3 | 3 | 6 | 3 | 3 | |
| | | A | 15 | 14 | 12 | 9 | 10 | |
| | | BBB | 16 | 18 | 18 | 24 | 25 | |
| | | BB | 3 | 4 | 7 | 8 | 9 | |
| | | B | 0 | 1 | 1 | 2 | 7 | |
| | | Below B | 0 | 0 | 0 | 0 | 0 | |
| | | NR/NA | 0 | 0 | 0 | 0 | 0 | |
| | | Special Securities | 2 | 2 | 3 | 3 | 2 | |
| **MANAGEMENT** | Management Change? | | No | No | No | No | No | |
| | Total Return % | 10-Year Avg. | 7.50 | 7.43 | 7.71 | 7.66 | 7.56 | |
| | | 5-Year Avg. | 7.65 | 7.52 | 7.60 | 7.50 | 7.71 | |
| | | 3-Year Avg. | 6.70 | 6.60 | 6.85 | 6.73 | 6.80 | |
| | 5-Year Average Turnover Rate % | | 56.0 | 56.0 | 62.0 | 62.0 | 68.0 | |
| **COST** | Expense Ratio % | | .34 | .34 | .35 | .35 | .36 | |
| | 12b-1 Charges % | | – | – | – | – | – | |
| | Load: Front / Back / Level % | | – | – | – | – | – | |
| | Redemption Fee % | | – | – | – | – | – | |
| **OTHER** | Next Issue Date | | 7/01 | 12/01 | 5/02 | 10/02 | 3/03 | |
| | | | | | | | | |
| | | | | | | | | |
| | | | | | | | | |

## Portfolio

The portfolio section of the Trend Report covers the fund's portfolio composition, average effective duration, average credit quality and the credit analysis.

## Portfolio Composition

Analyze the portfolio composition section to assure yourself that your bond fund still invests most of its assets in bonds. A significant percentage of fund assets invested in cash, stock or other can impede total return. Throughout the five reporting periods on this form, the fund invests 95 percent or more of its assets in bonds.

## Average Effective Duration

Duration is a measurement of a fund's sensitivity to interest rate movements. Investors seeking income and capital preservation from their bond funds should look for a fund with a low duration compared to its peer group. In the context of the Trend Report, the average effective duration should be stable.

The duration is remarkably stable for the example fund in the Trend Report for all five reporting periods.

## Average Credit Quality

When tracking a fund's average credit quality, watch out for significant changes. A downward revision of its average credit quality— say for an investment grade fund from AA to A or even A to BBB—means that the manager is investing in lower-quality bonds.

While this has the potential to increase your income and your total return, it is also more risky. Lower quality bonds have a higher risk of default and defaults reduce the value of a fund's portfolio and net asset value.

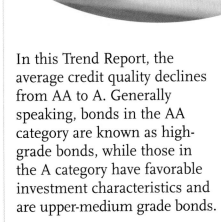

In this Trend Report, the average credit quality declines from AA to A. Generally speaking, bonds in the AA category are known as high-grade bonds, while those in the A category have favorable investment characteristics and are upper-medium grade bonds.

If you are an investor who wants to invest in a bond fund with less risk, be sure to watch

| Portfolio Analysis Date | | 10/00 | 4/01 | 9/01 | 2/02 | 7/02 | |
|---|---|---|---|---|---|---|---|
| Portfolio Composition | Cash % | 2.5 | 2.3 | 2.0 | 2.6 | 3.2 | |
| | Bonds % | 97.5 | 97.7 | 98.0 | 97.4 | 96.8 | |
| | Stocks % | 0 | 0 | 0 | 0 | 0 | |
| | Other % | 0 | 0 | 0 | 0 | 0 | |
| Average Effective Duration | | 4.6 | 4.6 | 4.7 | 4.7 | 4.6 | |
| Average Credit Quality | | AA | AA | AA | A | A | |
| Average Effective Duration | | 4.6 | 4.6 | 4.7 | 4.7 | 4.6 | |
| Average Credit Quality | | AA | AA | AA | A | A | |

| Portfolio Analysis Date | | 10/00 | 4/01 | 9/01 | 2/02 | 7/02 | |
|---|---|---|---|---|---|---|---|
| Credit Analysis | US Govt | 58 | 56 | 54 | 48 | 44 | |
| | AAA | 6 | 4 | 3 | 3 | 3 | |
| | AA | 3 | 3 | 6 | 3 | 3 | |
| | A | 15 | 14 | 12 | 9 | 10 | |
| | BBB | 16 | 18 | 18 | 24 | 25 | |
| | BB | 3 | 4 | 7 | 8 | 9 | |
| | B | 0 | 1 | 1 | 2 | 7 | |
| | Below B | 0 | 0 | 0 | 0 | 0 | |
| | NR/NA | 0 | 0 | 0 | 0 | 0 | |
| | Special Securities | 2 | 2 | 3 | 3 | 2 | |

| | | | | | | | |
|---|---|---|---|---|---|---|---|
| Credit Analysis | US Govt | 58 | 56 | 54 | 48 | 44 | |
| | AAA | 6 | 4 | 3 | 3 | 3 | |
| | AA | 3 | 3 | 6 | 3 | 3 | |
| | A | 15 | 14 | 12 | 9 | 10 | |
| | BBB | 16 | 18 | 18 | 24 | 25 | |
| | BB | 3 | 4 | 7 | 8 | 9 | |
| | B | 0 | 1 | 1 | 2 | 7 | |
| | Below B | 0 | 0 | 0 | 0 | 0 | |
| | NR/NA | 0 | 0 | 0 | 0 | 0 | |
| | Special Securities | 2 | 2 | 3 | 3 | 2 | |

this trend carefully. If the credit quality of the fund continues to decline or even stays in the A range, you may want to consider selling your fund shares and investing in a higher-quality fund.

## Credit Analysis

The Credit Analysis Section of the Trend Report allows you to spot more subtle changes in a fund's investment strategy. While a slow shift to lower-quality bonds might not immediately be reflected in the average credit quality, you will see it in the credit analysis.

If you are investing for income and want to preserve your principle, you'll want a fund with a fairly stable credit analysis section or one that is improving the credit quality of the overall portfolio by moving into higher-grade bonds.

In this case, the shift to lower-quality bonds is apparent in both the average credit quality section and the credit analysis. More of the portfolio is concentrated in lower-quality BBB bonds, and less in higher quality governmental bonds.

## Special Securities

In terms of special securities, be aware that an increase in the percentage of assets invested in special securities may increase the fund's risk profile. A small percentage of the fund's assets, such as is shown in this Trend Report, doesn't significantly affect the fund or its investors.

## Management

In the management section, we examine the stability of management, its track record and whether it adheres to a buy-and-hold investing philosophy.

## Management Change?

When evaluating a fund that you own, all you need to know is whether the same manager is at the helm of the fund that was there when you initially purchased shares. You want to see consistent management. If management changes, be on guard.

## Total Return

In terms of total return, investors look for the highest possible total return rates. With bond funds, expect more stability in total return than stock funds, as bond funds are primarily an income-producing vehicle.

| Portfolio Analysis Date | | 10/00 | 4/01 | 9/01 | 2/02 | 7/02 | |
|---|---|---|---|---|---|---|---|
| Management Change? | | No | No | No | No | No | |
| Total Return % | 10-Year Avg. | 7.50 | 7.43 | 7.71 | 7.66 | 7.56 | |
| | 5-Year Avg. | 7.65 | 7.52 | 7.60 | 7.50 | 7.71 | |
| | 3-Year Avg. | 6.70 | 6.60 | 6.85 | 6.73 | 6.80 | |
| 5-Year Average Turnover Rate % | | 56.0 | 56.0 | 62.0 | 62.0 | 68.0 | |

| Management Change? | | No | No | No | No | No | |
|---|---|---|---|---|---|---|---|
| Total Return % | 10-Year Avg. | 7.50 | 7.43 | 7.71 | 7.66 | 7.56 | |
| | 5-Year Avg. | 7.65 | 7.52 | 7.60 | 7.50 | 7.71 | |
| | 3-Year Avg. | 6.70 | 6.60 | 6.85 | 6.73 | 6.80 | |
| 5-Year Average Turnover Rate % | | 56.0 | 56.0 | 62.0 | 62.0 | 68.0 | |

| Portfolio Analysis Date | 10/00 | 4/01 | 9/01 | 2/02 | 7/02 | |
|---|---|---|---|---|---|---|
| Management Change? | No | No | No | No | No | |
| Total Return % 10-Year Avg. | 7.50 | 7.43 | 7.71 | 7.66 | 7.56 | |
| 5-Year Avg. | 7.65 | 7.52 | 7.60 | 7.50 | 7.71 | |
| 3-Year Avg. | 6.70 | 6.60 | 6.85 | 6.73 | 6.80 | |
| 5-Year Average Turnover Rate % | 56.0 | 56.0 | 62.0 | 62.0 | 68.0 | |

| COST | | | | | | | |
|---|---|---|---|---|---|---|---|
| | Expense Ratio % | .34 | .34 | .35 | .35 | .36 | |
| | 12b-1 Charges % | 0 | 0 | 0 | 0 | 0 | |
| | Load: Front / Back / Level % | 0 | 0 | 0 | 0 | 0 | |
| | Redemption Fee % | 0 | 0 | 0 | 0 | 0 | |

| OTHER | | | | | | | |
|---|---|---|---|---|---|---|---|
| | Next Issue Date | 7/01 | 12/01 | 5/02 | 10/02 | 3/03 | |
| | | | | | | | |
| | | | | | | | |

Our example fund demonstrates strong stability in the three-, five- and 10-year total return rates during the last five Morningstar reporting periods. Management is obviously consistent and keeps the fund on track.

### 5-Year Average Turnover Rate

As a fund investor, you are not only seeking the lowest turnover rate possible, but also a stable or declining turnover rate in the funds you own. A large jump in turnover is cause for concern, just as a small but steady increase is reason to investigate further.

For our example fund, turnover is climbing slowly but steadily. Read the recent fund annual or semi-annual report to see if management gives a reason for this increase. If they do, and it seems legitimate to you, it may be worth giving them the benefit

of the doubt, especially in a case like this where turnover is still far below the five-year category average of 157 percent.

### Costs

In our example fund, the expense ratio has been inching up a bit during the five reporting periods. However, the ratio is so much below the fund's peer group expense ratio of 1.02

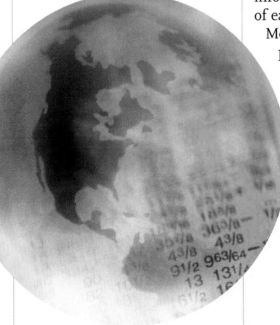

percent that a small increase isn't significant. If, however, the expense ratio continues to increase or begins to rise substantially, find out why.

The fund continues as a no load fund.

### Other

The Other section allows you to include elements important to you in your trend analysis. You may want to include elements from the Morningstar report or the Check List. You can also leave it blank if the elements already included tell you what you need to know about the fund.

The Next Issue Update is a unique item to the Trend Report. This is where you can note when Morningstar will put out another update on your fund. You can find this information on the front page of each section of the Morningstar Mutual Funds publication that also lists an index of the funds covered. The next update date is located on the lower right-hand corner of the page.

# Bringing It All Together

We hope this journey through the landscape of mutual fund investing has been productive—and will be profitable for you in the future. Our simple time-tested methodology and our fund analysis tools will help you pave the way to a secure financial future.

The world's financial markets are increasingly complex, and increasingly impact your current and future financial security. By employing sound investing principles, you'll have a better chance of securing your financial future. For the millions of Americans who lack the safety net of a pension, a sound investing strategy involving investing in mutual funds is one way to reach key financial goals.

## A Brighter Investing Future

Through these pages, we've delved into the complexities of the world of mutual fund investing, and tried to show you that it isn't as complex as it seems. The vast majority of mutual fund industry and the brokers, financial planners and insurance agents who make a living off of it would have you believe that you can't manage your own financial affairs. We're confident that you can, armed with knowledge and our simple methodology and easy-to-use tools.

While this is the end of The NAIC Mutual Fund Handbook, we hope it is the beginning of a long, productive relationship between you and NAIC.

Explore our Web site (www.better-investing.org), read other books in our *Better Investing* series, and join us at an NAIC convention or a class offered by an NAIC chapter in your area. We're here to help you learn more about investing the NAIC way.

# Resource References

A number of books, Web sites and other resources were referenced in the pages of this book. The list below is a complete run-down of all such references, provided for your information should you wish to pursue further reading outside this book. References are noted the first time they appear in the text but not in subsequent mentions.

### Chapter 1: Wealth Building the NAIC Way

Biafore, Bonnie. *The NAIC Stock Selection Handbook.* NAIC, 2003.

Gerlach, Douglas. *The NAIC Computerized Investing and the Internet Handbook,* NAIC, 2003.

Katz, Jonathan. *The NAIC Investment Club Operations Handbook,* NAIC, 2003.

*Better Investing Magazine,* the monthly magazine published by NAIC.

www.better-investing.org, NAIC's Web Site.

### Chapter 3: The Fine Print

www.sec.gov, The Securities & Exchange Commission Web site.

### Chapter 4: Building a Portfolio

www.fpanet.org, The Financial Planning Association's Web site

Tyson, Eric. *Personal Finance for Dummies,* Hungry Minds, 2000.

Tobias, Andrew. *The Only Investment Guide You'll Ever Need,* Harvest Books, 2002.

McQuade, Angele. *NAIC Official Guide,* NAIC, 2003.

www.mpower.com, a portal to mPower Consulting's Web sites

www.savingforcollege.com, the Web site of Saving For College, LLC.

www.morningstar.com, the Morningstar Web site

www.fool.com, the Motley Fool Web site

www.moneycentral.msn.com, the MSN Money Central Web site

### Chapter 7: Finding Quality Funds

*Morningstar Mutual Funds Resource Guide* (Morningstar, 2002)

www.quicken.com, the Quicken Web site

www.tiaa-cref.com, the TIAA-CREF Web site

www.standardandpoors.com, the Standard & Poor's Web site

*Money Magazine,* published monthly by AOL-Time Warner

*Kiplinger's Personal Finance Magazine,* published by Kiplinger's Washington Editors

www.businessweek.com, the Business Week Web site

www.smartmoney.com, the Smart Money Web site

www.cbsmarketwatch.com, the CBS Market Watch Web site

www.finance.yahoo.com, the Yahoo Finance Web site

www.google.com, the Google search engine Web site

### Chapter 10: Stock Fund Check List: Management

www.wilshire.com, the Wilshire Index Web site

### Chapter 17: Bond Fund Check List—Title Block & Portfolio

www.dodgeandcox.com, the Web site of Dodge & Cox Mutual Funds

# Glossary

## —A—

**Actively Managed Mutual Fund:** A mutual fund with a manager who uses strategies and data to achieve better performance than a particular market index.

**After Tax Return:** The return an investor receives on an investment after applicable taxes are paid.

**Annual Report:** A report issued on an yearly basis by a mutual fund detailing a fund's performance, expenses and holdings during a particular year.

**Asset Allocation:** The practice of dividing assets among differing investing vehicles.

**Average Credit Quality:** Assesses the overall credit quality of a bond fund's portfolio.

**Average Effective Duration:** Provides a measurement of a fund's sensitivity to interest-rate changes.

**Average Effective Maturity:** A measurement of the average maturity of the bonds in a bond fund portfolio.

**Average Price/Earnings:** As defined by Morningstar, a fund's weighted P/E average, which is calculated by using current stock prices divided by the company's projected earnings.

## —B—

**Back-end Load Fund:** A mutual fund that charges shareholders a fee (commission) to sell shares. This charge decreases the longer the investor holds the shares, eventually zeroing-out.

**Benchmark:** The performance of a group of securities used for comparison purposes.

**Blend Style of Investing:** This investing style combines elements of the growth and value styles of investing.

**Bond:** A debt instrument. When a company issues bonds, it agrees to pay bondholders a stated rate of interest until the principal is repaid on a specified date.

**Bond Fund:** A fund with a portfolio consisting primarily of corporate, municipal or U.S. Government bonds.  These funds focus on income potential rather than growth.

**Bond Ratings:** An assessment of the solvency of a particular company in terms of its ability to pay interest and repay principle to bond holders.

**Broker:** A firm or individual that arranges a transfer of securities between a buyer and a seller charging a fee for the service.

## —C—

**Capital Appreciation:** An investment gain from the price appreciation of a security.

**Capital Gain or Loss:** Profit or loss from the sale of a capital asset, such as securities.

**Capital Return:** the portion of return in a fund generated by realized and unrealized gains or losses in the value of the portfolio's securities.

**Closed-end Fund:** A company or fund that has a relatively fixed number of shares that are bought or sold on the stock exchanges. A closed-end fund's price is determined by supply and demand.

**Commission:** A sales fee charged in return for investment advice and/or the buying and selling of a security.

**Common Stock:** A representation of ownership in a corporation.

**Compounding:** Earnings that are generated from the reinvested earnings on an investment.

**Cost Basis:** The price an investor pays for a security plus any commissions, sales charges or other out-of-pocket expenses.

**Coverdell Savings Account:** Formerly known as Education IRAs, these are college savings plans established by individuals for a beneficiary's benefit.

**Current Yield:** The annual income yielded by a security, divided by its current price.

## —D—

**Diversification:** The practice of spreading investments among a range of different securities to reduce risk.

**Dividend:** A payment a company makes, in cash or stock, to its shareholders.

**Dollar Cost Averaging:** Buying a set dollar amount of a security at stated intervals.

## —E—

**Earnings Per Share (EPS):** A company's net income divided by the number of shares of common stock outstanding.

**Exchange Traded Funds:** An index-based mutual fund that trades like a stock on the stock exchanges.

**Expense Ratio:** The ratio of investor expenses to net assets of the fund.

**401(k) Plan:** An employer-sponsored retirement plan. Such plans allow employees to make tax-deferred contributions into the plan, which in some cases are matched by the employer.

**403(b) Plan:** An employer-sponsored retirement plan available to employees of educational institutions and non-profit organizations.

## —F—

**Front-end Load:** A sales charge that is assessed when a fund investment is made.

## —G—

**Government Bond:** U.S. government debt, considered to offer the lowest possible financial risk.

**Growth Style of Investing:** Managers who follow this style of investing seek companies with consistent, above average sales and earnings growth in an effort to produce long-term growth of capital.

## —H—

**Holdings:** All of the securities held by an individual, mutual fund or institution.

## —I—

**Income:** An amount of money received in return for making an investment or doing a job.

**Income Return:** The portion of a fund's total return that derives from interest distributions.

**Individual Retirement Account (IRA):** A personal, tax-deferred retirement account.

**Inflation:** An increase in the cost of consumer goods, which leads to a decline in the purchasing power of the dollar.

**Interest:** A payment to a creditor by a borrower for the use of money.

**Interest Rate:** A percentage rate at which money can be lent or borrowed.

**Intermediate-Term Bond Fund:** A bond fund that concentrates its portfolio in intermediate-term bonds. According to Morningstar, such funds focus on bonds with maturities between four and 10 years.

**Investment Adviser:** The company that manages a fund's portfolio, making the portfolio buy and sell decisions in an effort to carry out the fund's investment objective.

**Investment Grade Bond:** Bonds that are judged as likely to maintain interest and principal payments to investors.

**Investment Objective:** The financial goal pursued by an investor or mutual fund manager.

**Investment Style:** The direction a fund manager pursues to achieve a fund's investment goals.

## —J—

**Junk Bond:** A bond considered by a credit rating agency to less likely repay investors' principal or to pay interest than investment grade bonds.

## —L—

**Lehman Brothers Aggregate Bond Index:** Morningstar's benchmark for all bond funds, this index attempts to replicate the performance of the entire U.S. investment grade bond market.

**Level Load:** A sales fee charged to shareholders annually.

**Load:** A sales charge or commission assessed by some mutual funds.

**Long-Term Bond Fund:** A bond fund that concentrates its portfolio in long-term bonds. Morningstar classifies long-term bond funds as those that focus on bonds with maturities of 10 years or more.

## —M—

**Management Fee:** The amount that a mutual fund pays to the management company or investment advisor. It is expressed as a percentage of a fund's assets.

**Market Capitalization:** The value of a corporation, found by multiplying the company's stock price by its total shares outstanding. When analyzing a fund's portfolio, the average market capitalization figure is intended to show investors what size companies are held by the fund.

**Market Index:** A collection of securities constructed to replicate the performance of a certain portion of the securities markets.

**Maturities:** The point in time when a bond issuer will return the money that investors used to purchase a bond.

**Minimum Purchase Amounts:** The lowest investment a mutual fund requires for an investor to open an account.

**Municipal Bond:** A bond issued by a state, city or local government or local governmental agency. The interest payable by these bonds is not subject to federal taxes.

**Mutual Fund:** An open-end investment company that buys back or redeems its shares on command at their current net asset value.

## —N—

**Net Asset Value:** The market value of a fund's assets less any liabilities and fund expenses divided by the number of shares outstanding.

**No-load Fund:** A commission-free mutual fund.

## —O—

**Open-end Fund:** A fund that is prepared to redeem shares for cash or issue new shares.

## —P—

**Portfolio:** All of the securities held by a mutual fund.

**Portfolio Manager:** The individual or individuals responsible for the management of a mutual fund; that is, for the holding, buying, and selling of securities in a fund portfolio.

**Price/Earnings (P/E) Ratio:** The market price of a security divided by the earnings per share. Used to determine if a stock represents value at a given price.

**Prospectus:** A written document offering to sell securities, which provides information required by the Securities and Exchange Commission.

## —R—

**Redemption Fee:** A fee charged by some funds for selling fund shares before a certain period of time.

**Roth IRA:** A tax-deferred Individual Retirement Account in which an investor makes a taxable contribution and the money is not taxed when withdrawn.

## —S—

**S&P 500 index:** A measure of the performance of 400 industrial stocks, 20 transportation stocks, 40 financial stocks, and 40 public utilities in the United States, selected by a committee at Standard & Poor's. Commonly used as a performance benchmark by stock mutual funds.

**Sales:** The amount received by a company from the selling of its products and services.

**Sales Charges:** A load or commission assessed by some mutual funds.

**Sales Growth:** The rate of increase in a company's sales growth during the past four years, according to Morningstar.

**Section 529 Plans:** State-sponsored college savings plans.

**Securities:** Stocks, bonds or other instruments that investors can own and trade on financial markets.

**Securities and Exchange Commission (SEC):** The federal agency that regulates the securities business and protects the interests of the investing public.

**Short-Term Bond Fund:** A fund that invests primarily in bonds with maturity dates between one and four years, as defined by Morningstar.

**Single State Municipal Bond Funds:** Funds that have portfolios composed of municipal bonds issued by governments or governmental agencies within a single state.

**Special Securities:** Complex or illiquid securities outside of the ordinary range of investments for a mutual fund.

**Stock Fund:** A mutual fund that has a portfolio primarily composed of stock.

**Sub-advisor:** A management company hired by a fund's investment advisor to manage a fund.

## —T—

**Tax-adjusted Return:** A fund's annualized after tax total return for a certain time period.

**Tax Efficiency:** A measure of a mutual fund's history in regard to fund distributions.

**Total Return:** The performance of an investment, including dividends, interest, capital gains distributions and changes in net asset value.

**Trailing Earnings Growth Rate:** A measure of the annualized earnings growth rate of a stock fund's portfolio over the past four years, according to Morningstar.

**Turnover Rate:** A rough measure of how much buying and selling a fund manager does in a mutual fund portfolio.

**12b-1 Fee:** An annual charge deducted from a shareholder's assets to pay for a fund's distribution and marketing costs.

**Value Style of Investing:** Managers who follow this style buy companies that appear to be undervalued based on defined measurements such as the P/E ratio or price-to-book ratio.

**Yield:** The per-share cash dividend divided by the per-share market price of a stock or fund.

# *Bibliography*

Bogle, John C. *Common Sense on Mutual Funds.* John Wiley & Sons, Inc., 1999.

Fabozzi, Frank, Editor. *The Handbook of Fixed Income Securities, sixth edition.* McGraw-Hill, 2001.

Genord, Dennis, Executive Editor. *The NAIC Mutual Fund Handbook, first edition.* NAIC, 2000.

*Morningstar Mutual Funds Resource Guide.* Chicago: Morningstar, Inc. 2003.

Norton, Ralph G. *Investing for Income: A Bond Mutual Fund Approach to High-Return, Low-Risk Profits.* McGraw-Hill, 1999.

O'Hara, Thomas E. and Kenneth S. Janke, Sr. *Starting and Running a Profitable Investment Club.* New York: Times Books, 1998.

Pozen, Robert C. *The Mutual Fund Business, second edition.* Houghton Mifflin, 2002.

Thau, Annette. *The Bond Book, first edition.* McGraw-Hill, 2001.

# *Index*

# *Pass on the Gift of Lifetime Investing!*

### Send a Free NAIC Investor's Kit to a Family Member or Friend

Help a family member, friend, neighbor or co-worker become a successful long-term investor... the NAIC Way! Send us their name and we will mail them a free NAIC Investor's Kit. This kit will include information introducing them to NAIC long-term investment methods, programs and tools. The kit will also explain the benefits of lifetime investing including guidelines for starting an investment program on your own or with an investment club.

To send a free NAIC Investor's Kit to someone you know—complete the information below and mail, fax or e-mail the information to NAIC, or contact NAIC by calling toll free: 1-877-275-6242.

### Help others you know become successful long-term investors... *the NAIC way!*

*Mail to:*
**NAIC**
**P.O. Box 220**
**Royal Oak, MI 48068**

---

**___ YES, please send an NAIC Investor's Kit to the following person:**

**Name** _____

**Address**_____

**City**_____**State**_____**Zip**_____

**e-mail** _____

---

**FAX: 248-583-4880**
**e-mail: service@better-investing.org**
**NAIC Web Site: www.better-investing.org**

Investment Education Since 1951

The National Association of Investors Corporation (NAIC) is a non-profit organization of individual investors and investment clubs, based in Madison Heights, Michigan.  Founded in 1951, NAIC's mission is to increase the number of individual investors though investing in common stocks and equity mutual funds, and to provide a program of investment education and information to help its members become successful, long-term investors.  NAIC helps investors start a lifetime investment program by following
NAIC's Four Investment Principles:

*1) Invest a set sum regularly over your lifetime*

*2) Reinvest earnings and dividends*

*3) Buy growth stocks and mutual funds that concentrate on growth companies*

*4) Diversify your investments*

NAIC members who follow these investment principles have become successful investors over time.

To learn how to start a lifetime investment program using NAIC's proven methods, contact NAIC today.

**National Association of Investors Corporation**
**711 West 13 Mile Road**
**Madison Heights, MI 48071**
**1-877-ASK-NAIC (275-6242)**
**www.better-investing.org**

# About the Author

Amy B. Crane is Better Investing's mutual fund columnist. She has written extensively on a variety of fund, financial planning and investment club topics for NAIC's flagship publication since January, 2000. An NAIC member since 1997, Amy has also written for BITS, a publication of the NAIC Computer Group Advisory Board.

She is a contributing writer to the NAIC e-Learning Series, which is distributed to more than 100,000 employees in company 401(k) plans. As a content consultant for the NAIC Mutual Fund CD-ROM tutorial, Amy edited the tutorial's script. A founding member of the Better Investing Online Investor's School, she served on the school's steering committee and faculty for two years. During that time, she taught online classes on a variety of subjects including stock analysis. She has also taught mutual fund and stock investing classes to chapter audiences and investment clubs.

A graduate of Furman University in Greenville, S.C. with a B.A. in English, Amy lives in Erie, Pa. with her husband Bill and her sons, Billy and Patrick. A native of Washington, D.C., her writing background includes stints as a newspaper reporter, photographer and editor and experience in corporate communications and public relations. She is a member of the National Writer's Union. In the Erie community, Amy serves as the vice president of the Board of Directors of the Montessori Children's House of Erie and is a founding member of the Montessori Regional Charter School.

# Creative Strategies for People Who Take Fund Investing Seriously

## Receive Three Free Reports!

The Morningstar® FundInvestor Portfolios Guide, 15 Funds for the Future, and Five Principles of Profitable Fund Investing are yours free to keep even if you decide *Morningstar® FundInvestor* isn't for you.

## Get Morningstar® FundInvestor™ if you like knowing everything there is to know about:

- ▶ Weatherproofing your portfolio against wild market swings
- ▶ What mutual funds you should absolutely avoid
- ▶ Morningstar® fund portfolios for building and maintaining wealth
- ▶ Exclusive Morningstar® Fund Analyst Picks
- ▶ Undiscovered hidden gems

And you'll also benefit from the FundInvestor 500 select list. Less than 5% of all funds make this list. *Morningstar® FundInvestor* culls the 500 best and most notable funds around, then further winnows that list down to a select list of 130 Analyst Picks. We give you the returns and rankings, portfolio data, and manager information you need to make intelligent decisions.

## Call toll-free 866-608-9570

Call and start a risk-free subscription to *Morningstar® FundInvestor* for only $89. If not entirely pleased, cancel any time for a full refund of the unused portion of your subscription.

M–Fri 7am–7pm, Sat 9–4, Central time. Please mention code AFN-NAI-3H. Fax orders 312-696-6010

**NAIC**®

Investment Education Since 1951

www.better-investing.org

## STOCK FUND
# Check List™

(A) Fund Name: _Dreyfus Appreciation_
(B) Ticker Symbol: _DGAGX_
(C) Category: _Large Blend_
(D) Minimum Purchase($): _2500.00_     (E) Addt'l($): _100.00_
(F) Min Auto Inv Plan($): _100.00_     (G) Addt'l($): _100.00_
(H) IRA($): _750.00_
(I) Data Reference: _Morningstar_     (J) Page No. _____
(K) Current NAV($): _34.59_
(L) Total Assets($): _3427 (m)_
M. Taxable: _____     N. Tax-Deferred: _____

## 1. FUND INVESTMENT CHARACTERISTICS

(A) Stated Investment Objective: _Long-Term Capital Growth_
  • What are the fund s investment criteria & investment policies?

(B) Portfolio Composition:

| Cash | Stocks | Bonds | Other | Foreign |
|------|--------|-------|-------|---------|
| 3.4 % | 94.7 % | -0- % | 1.8 % | 4.7 % |

  • A cash holding of 20% or more may indicate the manager is trying to time the market...very risky!

(C) Market Capitalization:

| Giant | Large | Medium | Small | Micro |
|-------|-------|--------|-------|-------|
| 80.2 % | 18.8 % | 1.0 % | -0- % | -0- % |

  • Are the assets concentrated according to the stated objective?

(D) Total # of holdings: _50_     (E) Portfolio Analysis Date: _3/31/02_

(F) Top 10 Company Holdings:

| No. | Company Name | Sector | Assets |
|-----|--------------|--------|--------|
| 1 | Pfizer | Health | 6.77 % |
| 2 | Johnson & Johnson | Health | 5.28 % |
| 3 | Exxon Mobil | Energy | 5.11 % |
| 4 | Philip Morris | Goods | 4.58 % |
| 5 | Intel | Hardware | 4.27 % |
| 6 | Fannie Mae | Financial | 4.26 % |
| 7 | General Electric | Ind. Materials | 3.84 % |
| 8 | Citigroup | Financial | 3.47 % |
| 9 | Walgreen | Consumer | 3.30 % |
| 10 | Merck | Health | 2.98 % |
| | | | 43.86 % Total |

  • Does any one holding make up a far greater percent of assets than the others?

(G) Portfolio Sector Analysis (%):
Info _17.6_ : Software _2.4_  Hardware _6.3_  Media _3.9_  Telecom _5.1_
Service _47.9_ : Health _19.9_  Consumer _7.3_  Business _0.9_  Financial _19.7_
Manufacturing _34.5_ : Goods _17.7_  Ind Mtrls _6.9_  Energy _9.9_  Utilities _0_

  • The fewer number of holdings and sectors that the fund s assets are spread over the greater likelihood for volatility within the portfolio.